REIGATE:
Its Story Through the Ages

Plate I.

CHARLES, LORD HOWARD OF EFFINGHAM, EARL OF
NOTTINGHAM, THE LORD ADMIRAL.

REIGATE:
Its Story Through the Ages

A History of the Town and Parish

INCLUDING

REDHILL

WITH ILLUSTRATIONS AND MAPS

by

WILFRID HOOPER, LL.D., F.S.A.

(Honorary Secretary of the Surrey Archæological Society)

GUILDFORD

Surrey Archæological Society

1 9 4 5

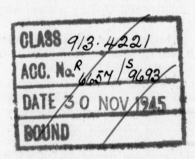

LOVE & MALCOMSON, LTD.,
REDHILL   SURREY

8888005111

INTRODUCTION

THIS volume is designed to fill what has been a long-felt want by giving for the first time a full and comprehensive factual history of Reigate, including the rise and development of the modern sister town of Redhill.

The author is a native and life-long resident who has devoted more than twenty years to studying all branches and periods of the subject from prehistoric times down to the present day. He has examined all existing local records known to him and from these and other original material both published and unpublished is able to present a mass of fresh information on many aspects and periods of local history, and in so doing to extend largely its range and interest. These records bear chiefly on the later sixteenth and following centuries and so have enabled that period to be treated on a fuller scale, though from other sources it has been possible to throw a good deal of new light on earlier ages also.

In addition to numerous illustrations there are a large-scale map of the parish, a desideratum which is too often wanting in local histories, and a map of Reigate town in the eighteenth century, based on an interesting contemporary plan.

The history of Reigate has, it is hardly necessary to remark, much that is common to the history of other English towns and parishes but with some interesting differences among which may be mentioned the abnormal size of the manorial virgate and the late survival of villeinage. Though the " debunking " of the Pilgrims' Way legend has in some eyes stripped Reigate of its medieval glamour yet against this loss can be set distinctions of a more substantial if less romantic character. It can, for instance, claim one of the earliest public libraries to be established in England, and one moreover which still retains its original building and books intact. Reigate too was chosen for one of the earliest experiments in turnpike legislation and the first to be made in Surrey. The Earlswood pitcher is one of the earliest known pieces of English medieval pot-ware, and can now with good reason be claimed as the product of a local pottery. In a later age Reigate became the chief centre of a flourishing oatmeal trade that lasted for more than a century. These are some of the topics of more outstanding interest dealt with in the following pages, and a chapter is devoted to the history of the parliamentary borough. As one of the four Surrey boroughs which preserved its representation from the thirteenth to the nineteenth century and manifested some lively stirrings after the Revolution its political history is not without interest and seemed to justify detailed treatment. A separate chapter is also given to the history of the local road system, a subject which has been generally neglected by local historians in the past and is only now beginning to receive the attention which its importance merits.

The concluding chapter brings the story of the town and parish down to modern times, and traces the rise and growth of Redhill in the nineteenth century. In this chapter and indeed throughout the volume the aim has been to give the facts as precisely as possible, for experience shows that it is often more difficult to fix the dates and other details of modern events than of those which happened in earlier times.

To the many friends and helpers who have assisted him with information or advice the author offers his most cordial thanks, and particularly to Mr. W. C. Berwick Sayers, Mr. S. C. Ratcliff, the late Mr. Alfred Smith, our former town clerk, Mr. Ernest Scears, Mr. A. W. G. Lowther, Mr. G. L. F. Grece, Messrs. Weatherby & Sons, and Mr. A. P. Hooper ; also to the following for the assistance indicated : the Surrey Archæological Society for the use of blocks of illustrations which have appeared in their volumes ; Reigate Corporation and Mr. A. Smith, for access to the manor archives ; the S.P.C.K. for access to their MS. records ; Rev. R. Talbot, vicar of Reigate, for access to the parish registers ; Miss M. M. Hooper, for designing the book cover and for use of her sketch of West Street, Reigate ; the British Publishing Co. Ltd., Gloucester, for loan of block of plan of Reigate church ; Mr. Raymond Smith, for loan of negative of the Thurland portrait ; and Mrs. M. H. Coatts, for typing and preparing the manuscript for the press.

PRINCIPAL ABBREVIATIONS

Bryant's Survey   MS. List of Reigate Burgages compiled by Wm. Bryant, 1786.

C B   Court Baron of Manor.

Ct R(s)   Court Roll(s) of Reigate Manor.

Hooper, Guide   *A Geological, Historical and Topographical Description of the Borough of Reigate and Surrounding District*, edited by T. R. Hooper, 1885.

M & B   Manning & Bray's *History of Surrey*, 3 vols., 1804-1814.

Manor Arch.   Deeds, Court Rolls and other archives of Reigate Manor.

Lambert, Banstead   Sir Hy. Lambert's *History of Banstead*, 2 vols., 1912 and 1931.

Lambert, Blechingley   Uvedale Lambert's *History of Blechingley*, 2 vols., 1921.

Palgrave   (Sir) R. F. D. Palgrave's *Hand-Book to Reigate*, 1860.

Psh. Reg(s)   Parish Register(s).

P N Surrey   *The Place Names of Surrey* (English Place Name Society, Vol. XI, 1934).

RAc. 1300   Account of reeve, 1299-1300

RAc. 1447   Account of reeve, 1446-1447.

Ridgeway   Wm. Ridgeway's MS. History of Reigate.

SAC   *Surrey Archæological Collections.*

SxAC   *Sussex Archæological Collections.*

SPDom.   *State Papers, Domestic Series.*

SRS   Publications of Surrey Record Society.

VCH   *Victoria County History of Surrey*, 4 vols., 1902-1912.

NOTE.—Until 1752 the calendar year in England commenced on the 25th March, but was then altered to commence on the 1st January. In this volume dates are given according to the new style, thus 7th February, 1622-3, appears as 7th February, 1623.

ILLUSTRATIONS

CONTENTS

APPENDICES

REIGATE:
Its Story through the Ages

CHAPTER I

PREHISTORIC REIGATE

THE parish, though not particularly rich in remains of early man, has at various times yielded considerable traces of the Stone and Bronze Ages. The Palæolithic or Old Stone Age is scantily represented by two flint implements—a broken hand-axe, possibly Mousterian, found by the writer in the disused sandpits under Redhill Common in 1927, and a late Acheulean hand-axe found at Woodhatch in 1936 and figured in the accompanying illustration (Fig. 1)[1]

The North Downs, which border the parish on that side, had not the same attraction for primitive man as the South Downs—their counterpart across the Weald. In our district the chalk escarpment, owing probably to its capping of clay-with-flints, bears no definite signs of prehistoric works apart from the old road along the crest of Colley Hill and Reigate Hill, known as the Pilgrims' Way, and the track of the old road running north which crosses it and forms a hollow way along the east side of Margery Wood. Worked flint of Neolithic type has been found on Colley Hill, and at The Clears below, but in no great abundance. It is on the parallel belt of Lower Greensand in the Holmesdale Valley beneath the Downs that the chief vestiges of early occupation have been traced.

During the years 1847 to 1860 Mr. John Shelley, of Redhill, collected several thousands of flint flakes together with some flint cores and saws and a leaf-shaped arrowhead from sandy soil near Redhill Station, the most prolific site being a field next the railway on the east side of Ladbroke Road which has since been built over. Here beneath two circular patches marked by ranker vegetation he found calcined bones and flint. Sir John Evans supposed these patches to be the remains of barrows, but more probably they marked the site of pits for storage or refuse.[2] This fine collection though classed at the time as Neolithic was, in part at least, the product of the Mesolithic culture which has since proved to be characteristic of the sandy soils of south and south-west Surrey.

Later in the nineteenth century, Mr. Sydney Webb, of Redstone Manor, Mr. Arthur Trower, of Wiggie, and other collectors gathered from the surface in the same locality as that explored by Mr. Shelley, flakes and implements of flint, including some finely worked leaf-shaped and barbed-and-tanged arrowheads which are usually associated with the Neolithic and Bronze Ages respectively. The scene of these extensive finds was the land north-east of Redhill Station in the broad valley watered by the nameless obsequent stream which flows southward through the bold gap in the Greensand ridge, now occupied by Redhill town, and joins the Mole at Sidlow Bridge. The site had obvious advantages to Stone Age man. On the light sandy soil bordering the stream, which was then of much greater volume, and the slopes of Redstone Hill on the one side and those of Red Hill on the other, he could dwell secure of an ample water supply and good hunting ground, and within sight of the North Downs where he could gain the flint for fashioning his implements and weapons.

The four flint implements from the Trower collection shown in the accompanying plate (Plate I) consist of an axe or celt found at Redstone Hill 1902 (right), a barbed-and-tanged arrowhead (centre) and knife (bottom left) found 1935 near Redstone Hill, and part of a polished flint celt from Merstham.[3] The Redstone Hill celt is a magnificent specimen of uncommon type. It is stained a light ochreous colour and is chipped over the greater part of both faces. The incurving sides are chipped to a sharp edge but the cutting end, which appears at the top of the illustration, is finely polished and polishing extends to some

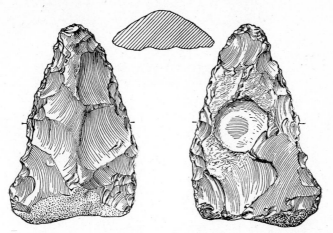

Fig. I.—PALÆOLITHIC HAND-AXE FROM REIGATE.
(Scale ½)

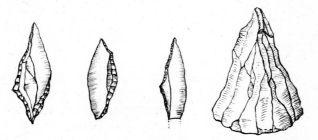

Fig. II.—PIGMY FLINTS, MEADVALE AND REIGATE.
(Scale ¼)

Plate II.

FLINT IMPLEMENTS FROM REDHILL AND MERSTHAM.

of the arêtes of the flake scars. It is unusually thin in section and may belong to the Neolithic or possibly to the succeeding Beaker period. The knife is formed out of a gray flake struck from a polished celt.

Three polished flint celts of the commoner type have been found at Reigate.[4] One of them in the writer's possession came from the sand pit in North Albert Road and is of grey flint with flattened sides. It is 6¼ inches long and tapers in width from just over 2 inches to 1¼ inch at the butt. The cutting end, however, has been reduced by coarse chipping ; the butt end also shows signs of re-chipping.

Redhill Common and Reigate Heath, which both lie on the Lower Greensand formation, have yielded, with arrow-heads and other implements of Neolithic or later forms, microlithic flints including the micro-burin, typical of the Tardenoisian phase of the Mesolithic culture which immediately preceded the Neolithic. Microliths or pigmies, so called from their diminutive size, are implements which have been delicately fashioned by secondary chipping to characteristic shapes (Fig. 2). The most prolific local sites in recent years have occurred in the Buckland sand-pits just beyond the parish boundary but the culture was very widely spread and has been traced, as already indicated, at many points along the Greensand belt.[5]

The Bronze Age lasted roughly from 1900 to 500 B.C., though there was no clear-cut division between this and the preceding Stone Age. The use of bronze spread slowly and stone continued in use long after the introduction of metal. Bronze Age folk manufactured the beautiful barbed-and-tanged arrowheads, of which some local examples have already been noticed, and buried their leading folk in round earthen barrows or tumuli, the bodies being in the Middle Bronze Age which lasted approximately from 1700 to 1000 B.C. sometimes cremated and at others inhumed unburnt though in the south of England cremation was the prevailing method and became universal in the Late Bronze Age. Barrows of this type are numerous in southern England. A series of seven such can be seen on Reigate Heath. They are marked by trees planted early in the last century, the most prominent being a group of four bowl barrows near the main road at Buckland Corner, three of which are raised on natural hillocks. This group was opened in 1809 ; two yielded nothing, the third contained a quantity of ashes and charcoal while the fourth contained an urn of coarse paste holding ashes and charcoal, the relics probably of a cremation of the Middle Bronze Age.[6]

The only objects of bronze recorded from the district are a bronze ring and loops thought to have been found near Reigate,[7] and a flat celt of the early Bronze Age found on Earlswood Common in 1817 and now in Guildford Museum. This shows incipient flanges and stop ridge.

The surface of Redhill Common is pitted and scored with holes and trenches, a legacy of the random digging for road metal that went on until comparatively recent times, though it must be admitted that some of these depressions bear a marked if accidental resemblance to Iron Age storage pits. There are however four circular enclosures on the top and northern slope of the hill which some archæologists have regarded as ring barrows, though small for this type. The fact that these earthworks are crowned by trees of old standing raises the suspicion that they may be nothing more than products of the tree-planting cult which became so fashionable on big estates in the eighteenth century. Each of the four is surrounded by a bank, in three cases there are signs of an external ditch. But they have never been opened and until they are their true character must remain doubtful. West of the topmost pair of this quartette fragments of burial urns of coarse pottery were turned up in preparing the ground for the Jubilee clump planted in 1897, the site possibly of a levelled barrow but the finds went unrecorded and were dispersed.

The remains of the Romano-British period hitherto detected have not been extensive. The discovery in the neighbourhood of Wray Common of what was supposed to be the site of a Roman tilery is the most important yet made. The site first attracted notice in 1878 when a quantity of red wall and roofing tiles was found at Doods Farm in a field that had been severed by the railway cutting between Redhill and Reigate. Box flue tiles as made for hypocausts, embossed with the same design as those used in the Roman villas at Walton Heath and Ashtead and laid lengthwise to form a drain, were traced in an adjoining field. Some nine years later in the course of building operations on part of the land further quantities of flat and hypocaust tiles came to light with what was thought to be the foundation of a kiln.[8] It seems more probable, however, that the remains were the débris not of a tilery but of a villa or associated building and that the material came from the Roman brickworks at Ashtead.

In 1817 the foundations of "an ancient building" which may have been a Roman villa were discovered on the east side of Earlswood Common while making the turnpike road from Gatton Point to Horley. According to the very meagre description furnished by Ambrose Glover, the building consisted of six apartments with a paved atrium at the west end.[9]

In 1875 traces of Roman walling were noticed in a house known as Colley Farm, Reigate, north of the Heath, while under the kitchen floor were found fragments of an amphora and a vase of pale grey ware containing clay and burnt ashes.[10].

There is no satisfactory evidence that any road in the parish is of Roman origin. Reigate lay between the Roman Stane Street on the west and the Roman road through Godstone on the east, both of which could be reached by means of the prehistoric track—the present Pilgrims' Way—along the Downs. Salmon's hypothetical road branching north-east from Stane Street through Newdigate, Reigate and Gatton though favoured by Manning and Bray has nowhere been traced and rests entirely on the supposed etymology of the place names.[11] In 1898 building operations at the northern end of Nutley Lane revealed an ancient roadway some five feet below the surface of the existing road. It was described as 12 to 15 feet wide, " composed of flints with the edges trimmed to fit, and laid very evenly." According to another version it was paved with slag stones, but no one troubled to publish an exact record. Local opinion needless to say regarded it as an authentic portion of the way trodden by the pilgrims, though the belief that it was part of a Roman road between Portslade and London or Winchester and London gained much support till Professor Haverfield pronounced against it.[12]. The discovery represented no doubt the early surface of Nutley Lane and to judge by the description may possibly have dated back to this period.

The Romans improved existing roads far oftener than they made new ones. Mr. Lowther, on the evidence of the flue tiles, suggests that one of the tracks used by them crossed Walton Heath and descended the chalk escarpment by the old road down Colley Hill and that this possibly extended northwards to join Stane Street at the same point as the branch road from the Ashtead brickworks.[13] In the historical period this track continued as Nutley Lane below Colley Hill, and though evidence is wanting of the existence of the Lane in Romano-British times it passes little more than a quarter of a mile east of the Colley Farm site.

Finds of Roman coins have not been numerous, apart from a hoard of between two and three hundred, stated to have been " chiefly Lower Empire," found about 1756 " in a field near Reigate."[14] Two gold coins of the British princes Epaticcus and Verica are said to have been found at Reigate, and a Roman " Consular " silver coin of about 44 B.C. was recovered at Redhill in 1856.[15] A sestertius of the emperor Antoninus Pius was turned up in the garden of a cottage at the corner of Sincots Road and Grove Road in 1943.

The only recorded vestige of Anglo-Saxon remains is the fragment of a cross mentioned in Chapter IV.

Camden, in his *Britannia*, quoted the " rhyming boast " of the inhabitants of Holmesdale :

> " The Vale of   Holmesdall
> Never wonne ne never shall,"

in support of the legend that they " once or twice routed the ravaging Danes," and out of this local fancy fashioned a story of how a party of Danes escaping after their defeat at the battle of Ockley, 851, was slaughtered at Battlebridge, just outside the northern edge of the parish, by the women of the neighbourhood. Unfortunately for the truth of this story it is now established that the battle was not fought at Ockley, Surrey, and the name Battlebridge has not been traced earlier than the seventeenth century.[16]

NOTES TO CHAPTER I

[1] Described in 45 *SAC* 140-1. A tooth of the mammoth (*elephas primigenius*) and bones of ox (*bos primigenius*) were found at Wiggie sandpit—now disused—in 1897.

[2] Ser. 2. I *Proc. Soc. Antiq.* 69 ; 17 *Archæological Jo.* 171 ; Evans, *Ancien Stone Implements* 2nd ed. 278 ; I *VCH* 233, where some of the flakes are figured ; Whimster, *Archæology of Surrey* 53. Some finely worked battered-back points and other material from the Shelley collection are in the Pitt-Rivers Museum, Oxford.

[3] See 37 *SAC* 90.

[4] Evans *op. cit.* 100 ; 10 *Arch. Jo.* 2. "Two stone axe-heads of uncommon forms" were recorded in 1871 from Meadvale (17 *Arch. Jo.* 171).

[5] 37 *SAC* 238, where 3 microliths from Reigate Heath are figured ; 41 *SAC* 50-78 (article by the writer, "The Pigmy Flint Industries of Surrey," with an account of the local sites at pp. 68-9).

[6] 35 *SAC* 12-13.

[7] 10 *Arch Jo.* (1853) 72-3. *Cf.* 61 *SxAC* 73-6.

[8] 6 *Arch. Jo.* 288, and information from Mr. Venner, architect of the house called "Woodthorpe" on the site of the later finds. For the Ashtead Roman site see 37 and 38 *SAC*. For flue tiles of the pattern found at Reigate see illustrations 37 *SAC* opp. 150 and 38 *SAC* opp. 7.

[9] 34 MS. Min. Soc. of Antiq. 69-71.

[10] 8 *Proc. Soc. of Antiq.* (2nd Ser.) (1879) 212-3.

[11] I *M. & B.* 271.

[12] IV *VCH.* 367 and references there given.

[13] *Croydon Regional Survey—Roman Remains Map.*

[14] 7 MS. Min. Soc. of Antiq. 287.

[15] Whimster, *Arch. of Surrey* 104 ; 13 *Arch. Jo.* 276. Several silver Roman coins of the "consular" series and early Empire are said to have been found in the neighbourhood of Furze Hill, Redhill, in the 'seventies of last century. (*The Visitors' Guide to Reigate, Redhill and their Vicinity*, 1877).

[16] *Britannia* (first published in 1586), ed. Gough, 1789, p. 168; Stenton, *Anglo-Saxon England*, 242 n. 3, *PN Surrey* 276 and 302.

CHAPTER II

MEDIEVAL REIGATE :
THE MANOR AND ITS LORDS.

THE earliest record of the manor is the entry in Domesday
Book, 1086, which translated from the Latin runs as follows :
"The King holds Cherchefelle in demesne. Edith the
Queen held it. It was then assessed for 37½ hides. Now
to the use of the King for 34 hides. The [arable] land is
[blank in MS.]. There are 3 ploughs in demesne : and
there are 67 villeins and 11 bordars with 26 ploughs.
There are two mills worth 12 shillings less 2 pence, and 12
acres of meadow. There is wood for 140 swine from the
pannage and 43 swine from the herbage. It is now worth
40 pounds, and renders so much."[1]

"The King holds in demesne" signifies that the manor
was then in his hands and had not been granted to a vassal.
At the time of the Conquest, 1066, it belonged to Edith,
widow of Edward the Confessor and daughter of earl
Godwin. The Conqueror respected her title and allowed
her to retain possession of this and her other manors during
her life. The hide was a measure of land but in Domesday
it denoted a unit of taxation. The 29 ploughs nominally
represented 3,480 acres, reckoning the plough team at 8
oxen capable of ploughing a hide of 120 acres in a year,
but in practice this maximum was not reached.[2] Part of
the land in the manor known as the demesne was reserved
for the lord's use. The arable land of the freehold and
villein tenants comprised a number of unenclosed strips of
varying size scattered in the common fields and the meadow
land was often distributed in the same way, though as will
be seen later not all the holdings were dispersed in this
manner. The demesne land consisted partly of distinct

and compact parcels but included some unenclosed strips mixed with those of the tenants in the common fields. The villeins held their lands at the will of the lord and had to perform certain services on his behalf. The bordars were the smaller tenants who occupied a cottage with a few acres of land attached and had also to perform certain labours. They subsequently disappeared from Reigate and other royal manors in Surrey and were apparently replaced by cottars, another semi-servile class of small tenants which emerged after those manors had been granted out to feudatories by the crown.[3]

The two mills were water mills on the Mole or its tributary streams. They belonged to the lord and the tenants had to carry their corn there to be ground and surrender a portion for the grinding. The tenants had the right to graze their swine in the woods and wastes of the Manor and in return the lord was entitled to a certain proportion, commonly one in seven, as rent pigs which yielded in this case 183.

Reigate gave its name to a hundred and manor as well as to the town. In Domesday the hundred and manor are called Cherchefelle—i.e., church field—the field or clearing with a church. But this was a blundered rendering of the name by the Norman scribe for in the twelfth century the name appears as Crechesfeld and like forms which point to the first element being *cruc*, the British word for a hill or barrow.[4]

In the Reeve's Account, 1447, Crouchfeld and Crouchfeldlond appear as the names of two apparently distinct tenements let to farm, the former of which may be identical with the two copyhold parcels " of pasture and alder ground called Crowchfeilds " of the 1623 Survey. These lay under Reigate Hill in the fork between Wray Lane and the present main road, and were enfranchised in 1777. They were near the Pilgrims' Way but remote from the centre of the parish and any known barrow and Reigate Hill, if the *cruc* referred to, is part of the escarpment of the North Downs without any distinguishing prominence. *Cruc* was also Old English for cross which became in Middle English *crouch*, but the 1447 forms are very late in that period and may be corrupt. The correct form of this element was

probably *cruch*.   Roger de Cruchesfeud appears as a tenant
in the Reeve's Account of 1300.   This would have been a
normal mutation of the British *cruc* which also often became
by metathesis *church* through confusion with the common
word for a place of worship.   It would be tempting by this
means to try and link Crechesfeld with the land called
Churchfeild which is described in the 1623 Survey as
adjoining the cuhrchyard, but in the absence of earlier
references this name is too late to justify the attempt.   The
probability is that it was suggested by proximity to the
parish church.[5]

Until the rise of Reigate as a separate village in the
twelfth century, the population of the thinly inhabited parish
was not centred round any one spot but lay dispersed in a
number of little settlements dotted about the parish usually
near streams and removed from the chalk and clay.[6]   These
settlements, or hamlets, if they deserved that name, formed
the nuclei of the five tithings of Santon, Colley, Linkfield,
Hooley and Woodhatch.   One that grew up round about
the church probably gained a certain importance above
the rest, owing to its central position and proximity to the
place of worship, until outstripped by the growth of Reigate
town.   The tithing, like the hundred, had a Saxon origin
and the name applied not only to a number of households,
nominally ten, whose members were bound together as
sureties for one another to preserve the king's peace, but
also to the district in which they dwelt.   Division into
tithings was common among parishes in Surrey as well as
other counties.

The name Reigate first occurs in the twelfth century, the
earliest instance so far traced being in 1170.[7]   The first
element is puzzling.   The popular rendering is ridge-gate,
signifying the way along the ridge, in reference to the old
road known as the Pilgrims' Way.   But this is unsupported
by any of the early forms and is now discredited, the latest
suggestion being that of Professor Ekwall that the compound alludes to a gap through which *reye*, i.e., roe-deer,
were hunted.   This derivation even if etymologically tenable
lacks topographical support since the nearest natural gap
in the hills is at Redhill two miles distant, irrespective of

the difficulty of understanding why so nimble an animal should require a gap for its passage.[8] Camden and Lambarde, who wrote about 1585, probably struck the right clue in associating the name with water flowing in a stream or passage. Wray Common was known in the sixteenth and seventeenth centuries as "the Wray," and in the Reeve's Account, 1447, is called "le Rie," an element which probably derives from ME (*at*) *theree* "at the stream," or alternatively from *atter ie*, "at the island or well watered land," a description well fitting this spot which lies on the Gault clay and until recently drained was waterlogged except in very dry seasons. The physical link between the two names is the stream which rises on the common and flowing south turns west below the Vicarage and crosses Bell Street into the Priory. This stream till modern times ran in an open course over the street and formed a prominent feature of the town and supports the suggestion here put forward that the element Rei- derives from *ea* OE for "river or stream," or *rithe*, a word having the same meaning.

The manor embraced but was not coterminous with the parish. It overflowed into Horley and included outlying lands in Leigh, Newdigate and Mitcham. When it passed to the Warennes it attained the dignity of an honour or chief manor to which their other Surrey manors were attached as subsidiary members. The satellites were the manors of Dorking, Fetcham, Shere Vachery, Bradley, and Ashtead, though Ashtead was not acquired by the family until the thirteenth century. To these must be added the numerous petty or sub-manors carved out of Reigate itself and consisting of the Priory, the Rectory, Frenches, Redstone, Colley, Hooley and Flanchford and Combe. Of these Fetcham, Shere Vachery, Bradley and the Priory were held by knight service, a form of tenure essentially feudal though the service it involved was commonly commuted for a money payment. Dorking when not in the lord's hands was held at the yearly rent of 9s. 8d., which was paid as late as 1853. Hooley, which lay on the east side of the parish, though styled a separate manor in legal documents, descended with and or practical purposes became a part of Reigate manor. Flanchford, which lay in the south-west corner with Combe adjacent, was granted by John de Warenne in the thirteenth century to his cook Brice and Alice, his wife, at the picturesque rent of a pound of cummin to be rendered at Michaelmas.[9]

Before the end of the twelfth century the Warennes also acquired East Betchworth, a former de Clare manor, which became another member of the honour. Its tenants had every year to reap a meadow of the lord in Reigate forming part of the demesne and known as Fridaysmead, a service which in the next century was commuted to an annual payment of 1s. 3d., increased later to 2s. 8d.[10]

Queen Edith died in 1075 when her manors passed to the Crown. Shortly after the Conqueror's death and probably in 1088 William de Warenne, one of his Norman followers, was created earl of Surrey and was at the same time endowed with Edith's Surrey manors consisting of Reigate, Dorking, Shere Vachery and Fetcham. He had fought at Hastings and married Gundrada who was not, as sometimes alleged, the Conqueror's daughter though she may have been his stepdaughter. The gift was probably a reward for his support of William Rufus and may also have been designed to act as a counterpoise to the growing power of the de Clares who held Blechingley and many other Surrey manors ; but whatever its motive it made a welcome addition to his neighbouring territory in Sussex which covered the whole Rape of Lewes. He died in the same year and was succeeded by his son William, who married Isabel, daughter of the count of Vermandois. Her family arms, the famous gold and blue chequers which later were adopted as the Warenne device, are preserved in numerous inn signs and appear in the seal of our Borough Council. This earl was frequently styled earl of Warenne instead of earl of Surrey, and his successors used both titles indifferently. His son, again William, who succeeded in 1138 had seen much fighting in the civil war then raging, during which he changed sides more than once.

On the latter's death in 1149 the male line expired. His only child, Isabel, succeeded to his vast possessions and became the richest heiress in the kingdom. William of

Blois, her first husband, was the second son of king Stephen. He was invested with the earldom and his wife's lands but in 1157, acting doubtless under pressure from Henry II, who wished to remove temptation from a potential rival, he resigned all his English castles to that king. He died in 1159 and four years later his widow was married to Hamelin Plantaganet, the bastard half brother of Henry II, whose chief interest for us lies in his gift of Reigate Church to the Priory of St. Mary Overy, Southwark.

His son, William de Warenne, who on his death in 1202 succeeded as the sixth earl, played a more conspicuous part in both national and local history. In accordance with the traditional loyalty of his house, he stood by king John at periods when loyalty to that monarch was a doubtful as well as a difficult virtue. The story that the barons assembled in the cave under Reigate Castle the night before meeting the king at Runnymede is historically impossible.[11] The earl stood by the king till after the grant of the Charter and only forsook his allegiance in 1216 when Louis of France had landed, though too late to save the castle from falling to that prince. In the next reign he displayed his piety by founding Reigate Priory and by benefactions to other religious houses. At his death in 1240 he was followed by his infant son, John, who grew up to be a fierce and ruffianly character and is remembered by schoolboys as the hero of the rusty sword incident related by the chronicler, Walter de Hemingburgh. In 1279 in answer to an enquiry by what title he held his franchises he is said to have flourished " an ancient rusty sword " crying, " Here is my warranty, my ancestors came over with William the Bastard and conquered their lands with the sword, and with the sword will I defend them against any who wish to seize them."[12] This outburst was followed by a less dramatic appeal to the law. At Guildford the same year before John de Reygate and other justices itinerant he successfully claimed a prescriptive title to the castle, honour and towns of Reigate, Betchworth and Dorking, the right to hold a weekly market on Saturday and fairs on five days annually, assize of bread and ale with divers other rights including free warren throughout the manors.[13] In 1270 while

engaged in a lawsuit with lord Zouche at Westminster Hall
he savagely attacked his opponent and his son in open court
and then fled to Reigate Castle to escape retribution.
Prince Edward gave chase and threatened to besiege the
Castle, whereupon the delinquent yielded. He was fined
10,000 marks but of this he managed to evade payment of
the greater part. His tenants complained of his oppressions
and during the Barons' War, when he sided with the king,
he incurred the popular hatred and had to protect Reigate
Castle against the Londoners.

After the battle of Lewes, 1264, in which Warenne fought
for the king, Reigate Castle passed to Simon de Montfort,
who recognised its importance by retaining it in his own
hands. When in August, 1274, Edward I returned to
England as king he was entertained at the Castle by Warenne.
The earl died in 1304, over seventy years of age, an old man
for those days. His grandson, John, who succeeded as
the eighth and last earl of his house, secured a remission
of the rest of the fine imposed in 1270. In 1313 he was
granted the right to hold a Market at Reigate on Tuesday
which took the place of the Saturday Market. But his
career is chiefly remarkable for his attempts to divorce
his wife, Joan of Bar, and settle his estates on his illegitimate children by Maude de Nerford. In 1317 he fell
foul of the Earl of Lancaster, who had attempted to put
a stop to his intimacy with this lady. Warenne retaliated
by seizing Lancaster's wife at Canford in Dorset and con-
ducting her to Reigate Castle. The victim was probably
not an unwilling captive but the affair created a sensation
and led to private war between the two earls.

Warenne died in 1347 without lawful issue. His sister
Alice had married Edmund Fitzalan, earl of Arundel, and
through this union his estates in the south of England
passed with the title to the powerful family of Fitzalan whose
chief seat was Arundel in Sussex. Richard Fitzalan, earl
of Arundel, grandson of Alice and famous as a naval com-
mander in the French wars, was beheaded for treason in
1397 after being treacherously lured from Reigate Castle
where he had retired to escape the malice of Richard II.
His lands were forfeited to that monarch and were, with

the exception of Reigate, granted in the same year to Arundel's son-in-law, Thomas Mowbray, earl of Nottingham, who was created duke of Norfolk, but in 1398 suffered banishment as a sequel to his historic feud with the duke of Hereford, afterwards Henry IV.

Reigate was then granted to John Holland, duke of Exeter, the king's halfbrother.[14]. He also received the custody of Arundel's son, Thomas, whom he treated with great brutality and confined in Reigate Castle under his steward, Sir John Shelley, till the lad managed to escape. Early in 1400 Holland lost his head for conspiring against Henry IV, who restored Arundel's son to his father's estates and title. On the earl's death without children in 1415 the Warenne estates in Surrey and Sussex passed to his three sisters subject to the life interest of his widow, Beatrix, who survived till 1439. This division of the title presents the first serious complication in the descent of the manor. The three sisters and co-heiresses were Elizabeth, who married Thomas Mowbray, duke of Norfolk, Joan, married to William Beauchamp, lord Bergavenny, and Margaret, wife of Sir Roland Lenthall.[15] To avoid the complications of joint ownership their descendants agreed in the year 1440 upon a partition whereby Reigate with other manors outside Surrey was assigned to John, duke of Norfolk, in satisfaction of his share of the inheritance.[16] He took the chief Surrey manor in virtue no doubt of his high rank and his descent from the eldest sister whose grandson he was. The dukes of this line were short-lived and the title expired on the death of his son, John, the fourth duke, in 1476, who left as his sole issue a daughter named Anne. Two years later this child though but an infant of six years was married by Edward IV to his second son, Richard, duke of York, who was of the same tender age as his bride. The union aimed at securing the vast Mowbray estates for the house of York and to this end an Act was passed providing for his succession to her estates if she died without issue, as she did in 1481. Her death resulted in a second complicated division between co-heirs. The persons who became entitled to the estates, subject to the prince's interest, were John, lord Howard, and William,

lord Berkeley, two of the descendants of Elizabeth by
Thomas Mowbray, Thomas lord Stanley and Sir John
Wingfield.   The prince during his short life which ended
with his murder in the Tower, probably in June 1483,
enjoyed the profits of his wife's estates.   In the same year the
co-heirs appear to have agreed upon a partition by which
Reigate was allotted to Howard and Stanley in equal
shares.[17]

Howard, popularly called "Jack of Norfolk," as one of
Richard III's warmest supporters, played an active part in
the events which placed him on the throne.   His conduct
raises a strong presumption of complicity in the murder of
the two princes, and it is highly significant that on 28th June,
1483, he was created duke of Norfolk and Earl Marshal,
two of the Mowbray titles that had been conferred on the
little prince, Richard, while his son, Thomas Howard, was
created earl of Surrey.[18]   That crime certainly brought him
vast and immediate benefits for the prince's death removed
the only obstacle to the enjoyment of the Mowbray estates
by him and his fellow heirs.   He lost no time in asserting
his rights.   After visiting the Mowbray manors in East
Anglia he turned south and reached Reigate on Saturday,
13th September, where he put up at the Priory and lodged
his retinue at the castle.   On his arrival the steward paid
twenty pence for a pious offering on his behalf and payments
on a lavish scale were made to the prior and others for fuel,
light and provisions.   Before leaving he purchased fifty-five
horses for 28s. 2d.   On the following Monday he continued
his progress to Horsham, but he and his party were at
Reigate again on the 27th and 28th of the same month.[19]

In his zeal to secure the new régime on which his own
fortunes depended, Howard undertook to furnish 1,000
men for the king's service of whom ten were drawn from
Reigate, including John Lute, the bailiff, John Skynner,
John Pope, Richard Brewster and John Skelton.[20]   An
attempt has been made to identify the last-named with
John Skelton, the poet, but this tempting conjecture remains
unproved for want of corroboration.[21]   The name is, however, fairly common in local records of the sixteenth and
seventeenth centuries and later.   One John Skelton is

mentioned in the Court Roll, 1532, when he was fined
6s. 11d. for breaking the assize of ale, and in 1623 Rachel
Skelton, " the late wife of Thomas Skelton," held several
copyhold tenements in the manor.

Howard's vaulting career ended at Bosworth in 1485,
where probably some of the Reigate men followed him to
battle.   His lands passed to the new king, Henry VII, but
were later restored with his share in the manor to his son,
the earl of Surrey.   After Howard's death the partition of
1483 was disregarded by lord Berkeley who, in order to
disinherit Maurice Berkeley, his brother and heir, settled
his fourth part in default of his own issue on the king in tail
male, and this settlement was confirmed by Parliament in
1491.   Shortly after, lord Berkeley died without issue, and in
1504 on the petition of his brother an Act was passed revers-
ing the settlement and admitting Maurice's claim to a fourth
part.   Maurice appears to have thereupon sold this part to
the earl of Surrey, who thus became owner of the manor
jointly with Thomas Stanley, earl of Derby, who under the
partition of 1483 or subsequently had acquired the Wingfield
quarter in addition to his own.[22]   The earl of Surrey was
restored to the dukedom in 1514 and died in 1524.   His
eldest son and heir, Thomas duke of Norfolk, succeeded
subject to a life interest in the manor which Henry VIII
granted to the dowager duchess.   She died in 1545 and in
1547 the duke and his son Henry, earl of Surrey, the poet,
were attainted for treason.   The son was beheaded and the
father only escaped the block through the king's timely
death.   His half share of the manor which on his attainder
vested in the crown was in 1551 granted to his half-brother,
lord William Howard, subsequently created baron Howard
of Effingham, who held it till his death in 1573.   Lord
William was followed by his widow who survived till
1581 and held it in dower.[23]   Their son and heir,
Charles lord Howard, afterwards Lord Admiral and earl of
Nottingham, then succeeded to the one moiety and took a
lease of the other moiety from the earl of Derby.   By deed
dated 26th January, 1623, the Lord Admiral settled the
Howard moiety after his death on Margaret, his second wife,
during her life with remainder to their son, Charles, and his

heirs. In 1627, three years after his death, his widow married
Sir William Monson, afterwards viscount Monson. By deed
dated 10th January, 1632, between the son, Sir Charles
Howard, his mother, the countess dowager of Nottingham,
lord Monson and trustees, it was provided that the
countess and lord Monson should suffer a recovery to be
sued against them by the trustees to the intent that the
Howard moiety of the castle and the manors of Reigate and
Hooley should be held for the use of the countess during
her life and after her death to the use of John Eldred of
Lincoln's Inn and John Price of Kingston-upon-Thames
during lord Monson's life in trust that he should from time
to time during his life " be answered the rents fines and
profitts and not otherwise to meddle or have anie thinge to
doe with the premises or anie part thereof," and after his
death to the use of Sir Charles Howard during his life and
thereafter as he, Sir Charles, should by deed or will appoint.[24]
The countess died in 1639 and two years later Sir Charles
sold his reversionary interest in the moiety of the castle and
manors to John Goodwin of the Inner Temple, William
Methwold and Benjamin Goodwin, John's brother, for
£1,560.[25] John Goodwin was already well acquainted
with the subject of his purchase for he was at that period
steward of the manor and he and Monson were first cousins.[26]

The Derby half-share or moiety was after the death of
Ferdinand, the fifth earl, purchased on behalf of Thomas
Sackville, subsequently earl of Dorset and part author of
Gorboduc, the earliest English tragedy. His son Robert, the
second earl of Dorset, who succeeded him in 1608, founded
the charity known as Sackville College, East Grinstead, and
charged all his lands by will with a rent-charge or annual
payment of £330 for its support. He died within a few
weeks to be succeeded by his son Robert, the third earl, who
soon became notorious as a rake and spendthrift. To pay
his debts he sold part of his estates but without disclosing the
rent-charge, which the purchasers on becoming aware of
disputed. This led to protracted litigation between the
College and the owners of the estates affected which was not
finally settled until 1700. Reigate manor was saddled with
a small part of the charge amounting to £9 5s. 5d., which

was paid without dispute until the year 1927, when the Borough Council redeemed it. The earl's share in Reigate was sold in 1628 to Sir John Monson and Robert Goodwin as trustees for lord Monson, to whom they conveyed it in May, 1646, and Monson on the occasion of his second marriage in the same month settled this and his other property on himself for life with remainder to his eldest son in tail.[27]

A detailed Survey of the manor had been prepared by order of the earl in 1623 for the guidance doubtless of possible purchasers. The Survey, of which several copies exist in manuscript, was the work of Thomas Clay aided by a jury drawn from the tenants. It was apparently accompanied by a map but this has been lost. Clay, who was himself a copyholder of the manor and married to a daughter of one of the bondmen, took some liberties in order to inflate the value. The Priory, for instance, was wrongly included as part of the demesne and the manor of Linkfield was stated to be held of Reigate manor though in fact held of the Priory. He placed a yearly value on the copyholds, which bore no relation to the trifling quit rents actually paid for them, to serve probably as a guide in assessing the fine payable on the admission of a new tenant which though arbitrary was based on the annual value and was eventually fixed at one and a half times that value.

Shortly after the Restoration Monson was sentenced to life-long imprisonment as a regicide and his property was forfeited to the king Charles II, who, on 4th December, 1661, granted it to lord Berkeley, Sir Charles Berkeley and Henry Brounker as trustees for his brother, James, duke of York. The duke appointed fresh trustees in 1668.[28] He had on 21st March, 1662, appointed Edward Thurland of Great Doods, his solicitor general, to be chief steward of the manor.[29] In 1686 the duke, who had since ascended the throne as James II, purchased the other moiety of the manor from Deane Goodwin of Blechingley, and the entire interest was thus at length reunited.[30] John Goodwin, who outlived his fellow grantees, had by deeds of Lease and Release dated 21st and 22nd January, 1672, settled his moiety after his death on his grandson, Deane Goodwin.

The manor remained crown property until 1697 in which

year it was granted to Joseph Jekyll under the description of "the Mannor or Mannors of Reygate and Howleigh with all and singular the rights, members and appurten-ances within the parish of Reygate or elsewhere in our county of Surrey . . . with the scite of the ruined Castle there . . . of the yearly value of £396 2s. 3d. . . ." to hold at the yearly rent of 6s. 8d. payable to the crown.[31] Jekyll by deed-poll dated 16th July, 1697, declared himself a trustee for his brother-in-law, Sir John Somers, who had shortly before been raised to the woolsack and received this endowment to support his high office and the peerage which followed it.[32]   The grant formed one of the articles of lord Somers' impeachment by the Tories in 1701, but their attack quickly collapsed and the descent was not again interrupted by revolution or forfeiture. He died unmarried in 1716 and the subsequent history of the manor and its owners is comparatively uneventful.

Lord Somers' heirs were his two sisters, Mary, who had married Charles Cocks, a Worcester attorney, and Elizabeth, wife of Sir Joseph Jekyll. Shortly after his death the sisters and their husbands made a partition of his estates by virtue of which the manor was conveyed to Sir Joseph and his wife successively for their lives.[33] Lady Jekyll survived her husband till 1745 when the Manor passed to her nephew, James Cocks, Mary's eldest son, who repre-sented the borough in Parliament for nearly forty years. Dying in 1750 he was succeeded by his son James, who lost his life in 1758, when John Cocks, brother of James Cocks the father, inherited, and from him the manor passed in unbroken descent through successive generations of his lineal issue.   The peerage was revived in favour of Charles Cocks, John's eldest son, who was created baron Somers in 1784, and in 1821 an earldom was conferred on his son, John Somers Cocks. The third earl Somers, who died in 1883, left his Reigate estate by will to his daughter, Isabel Caroline, better known by her married name of lady Henry Somerset. She during her life made it over to Mr. Somers Somerset, her only son, who sold his interest in Reigate town by auction in 1921, and in the following year generously presented the remainder of his manorial interests to the Borough Council, which thus became lords of the manor.

The general absence of local records earlier than the sixteenth century makes it impossible to describe what may be termed the internal history and economy of the manor during the middle ages, though it was this aspect that concerned the small farmers and peasants who made up the bulk of the population. Changes of manorial ownership meant little to them. Year in and year out their never-ending task was to raise the food necessary for the subsistence of themselves and their households. The manor as they knew it was an institution for defining and enforcing the customs that regulated a large part of their lives and directing the agricultural routine of their little community. Fortunately two of the reeves' accounts have been preserved and these give some interesting glimpses of the manorial system, though at widely separated periods.[34]

The first is the account of Nicholas Santon for the year ending Michaelmas 1300. The reeve was subordinate to the bailiff, who had charge of the farming operations, and at Reigate as in many other manors, custom prescribed that the office should be filled yearly in rotation by the villein tenants holding a yardland or virgate, or a half-yardland. The duties must have pressed hardly on an illiterate bondman though he had the help of a clerk in preparing his account. Another officer obliged to serve in virtue of his holding was the bedel or beadle who was chosen from the tenants of the farthing lands and cotlands. He assisted the bailiff in serving processes and carrying out orders of the manor courts and was also entitled to certain allowances for his services. He must not be confused with the parish beadle of later times familiar to us in the pages of Dickens.

The account follows the usual form and starts with receipts. Under the heading " Rents " appear the rent of the foreign (*forinsecus*)—i.e., from holdings within the manor but outside the borough, and of the borough—i.e., from holdings within both borough and manor. The heading "Farm and tallage " includes 33s. 4d. from the farm of the market (*firma fori*) which shows that the market tolls were let or farmed to a contractor. Tallage, which was an arbitrary tax levied on the villeins for the lord's benefit, produced 46s. 8d., and Romescot or Peter's Pence 4s. 4½d. Receipts in kind include a pound of cummin as the rent of Flanchford which fetched 2d.[35] four horseshoes with nails fetching 2d. and eight ploughshares fetching 4s. Fines and perquisites of court which were a valuable source of income produced £9 2s. 1d.

The sale of corn (*Vendicio bladi*) realised £28 8s. 6d. Of this £15 6s. 0d. is for 41 quarters 9 bushels sold for the earl's expenses, and £9 14s. 9d. for 95 quarters of oats sold for the same purpose. A bushel of barley fetched 6d. Medieval prices while more variable were notoriously lower than modern prices, yet attempts to correlate them are misleading owing to the very different conditions then prevailing. The sale of store animals includes an ox from the store of Reigate sold for 16s., and a steer and cow from Herewaldeslee-Harrowsley in Horne—sold for 6s. and 6s. 8d. ; 24 cheeses from Harrowsley realised 5s. 9d., and 155 eggs 12s. 0¾d. The customary duties of ploughing and harrowing the lord's demesne were sold, probably to the tenants who owed them, and so commuted, at 6d. and 2d. per acre respectively. The close connection existing between Reigate and other Warenne manors is shown in the entries under " Foreign receipts." These contain several sums received from Stephen Bromman, reeve of Dorking, and John att Wode, reeve of Betchworth, for provisions supplied to them for the earl's " expenses," in other words for the needs of him and his entourage while visiting the manors on some of his frequent perambulations. We can picture Stephen and John hurriedly sending to Reigate for oats and herrings, chickens and eggs, to supplement their stores when they heard that the earl was expected, and obtaining from Nicolas wooden tallies as receipts for the money they paid him. There is an item of 4s. for hay bought by Stephen for the same purpose and carting it to Keniton—Kennington —another of the earl's Surrey manors. The reeve of Ditchling, one of the Warenne manors in Sussex, purchased 6 sheep at 12s. for the like purpose, so that what with supplying the earl's requirements at Reigate and meeting

these "foreign" calls Nicholas must have experienced a
big drain on his stores.

The expenses side of the account opens with the outlay
on repairs and new parts to the plough and carts, also
wages paid to the hired farm servants and to workmen
casually employed to repair the buildings.   The ploughman
received 5s. 6d. for the year and ½d. per week for his food,
the drover 4s. 6d. for the year, the carter 2s. for 38 weeks
and 14d. for his food.   Considerable sums were laid out in
repairing the great stable, and further repairs to the roof
after a great storm of wind on the day of the feast of SS.
Fabian and Sebastian (20th January) cost 4d.   A man
working five days to roof the room of the earl (*cameram
Johannis de Warrenn*) was paid 15d.   The roof of the
grange was re-tiled, for which purpose 3,000 tiles and 50
ridge tiles were bought for 4s. 6d. and 6d. respectively,
while the man employed for eight days in fixing the tiles
was paid 2s. 4d., and the boy who helped him 12d.   Roger
the Lockyer for repairing the great gate of the castle received
6d.   There is a curious item regarding the hire of a man to
close the brattice (*ad obstupandam bretascham*) of the great
wall of the bakehouse by the precept and view of Hugh
the Marshall.   A brattice was a wooden staging built
out from the top of the wall with holes in the floor for
defending the walls against attack.   Possibly the work
consisted of removing the staging and filling up the holes
in the walls for the supporting timbers.   A sum of 5s. was
paid to Peter Haweys for felling wood in the earl's wood
and converting it into 1,000 pales for the fence round the
park.   This was all paid work as was much of the agricultural labour such as mowing, tedding and gathering the
lord's hay.   Hocmead was mowed by the villeins, but
Pakkismead, Salemead, Fridaysmead and Depemead were
mown by hired labour.   Under the heading *Vadia* are
entered the wages paid to various regular servants.   William
le Warener received 37s. for the year which included the
cost of a robe.   Adam Bosoyng, in addition to his wages
as janitor of the castle, received 2s. 6d. for the expenses of
the ferets.   Patrick Scot, keeper of the earl's falcon, received
27s. 1½d. for 31 weeks' wages, while the expenses of feeding

the bird for the same period came to 12s. 0¾d. Various allowances and perquisites were granted to the reeve and other officers for the year, including the beadle, the forester, the warrener and the grange keeper, chiefly by remitting their rent and customary villein services. Of the sum received for Peter's Pence 2s. 4d. was paid to Reigate church.

Payments for the earl's expenses show that he visited Reigate on at least four occasions during the year of account and that his longest visit lasted five days.

The sum total of expenses was £113 4s. 1¾d., leaving a balance due from the reeve of £17 3s. 7½d. Of this he was allowed 20s. for sundry unauthorised expenses and he produced a tally for £4 6s. 1½d. paid to William de Capella, the receiver. But he was in trouble over a sum of £10 17s. 6d., representing half the amount of a relief paid by lady Joan Butler who held the manor of Shere Vachery of the earl. This had been paid through John de Nevile, steward of Reigate manor, in pollards or base money which had been made illegal shortly before and was now worth only half its nominal value. Nicholas explained that he accepted this money unwillingly, and he claimed and was granted the earl's indulgence for the irregularity which thus reduced his final deficit to 20s.

On the dorse or back of the roll are entered particulars of the live and dead stock belonging to the lord and of the dealings therein during the year, distinguishing between the stock remaining over from the previous year (*de remanenti*) and that of issue (*de exitu*) added during the year of account from whatever source. The customary services (*opera et consuetudines*) due from the villeins were in some cases sold, in others exacted by the lord. Thus they had to plough 20 acres " at the time of wheat sowing " and another 7¾ acres of the lord's land, while the work of ploughing 10¾ acres was sold. The entire work of threshing both corn and oats was sold, whereas weeding work was exacted. Each of the villeins holding a virgate, of whom there were twenty, had to carry three cartloads of wood, but of these 60 cartloads 55½ were sold " because the earl did not make a visit to the castle." Horse cartage (*averagium*) and the duty of the cottars to bind the lord's corn are marked " without price " (*sine precio*) and so were exacted. Most of the other works were saleable and were sold, the purchasers no doubt being as a rule the tenants who owed them.

The second account is that of Robert Ace for the year ended Michaelmas 1447, when the manor was owned by John Mowbray, third duke of Norfolk. Its most striking feature is the large amount of land let to farm, that is to say at fixed money rents and generally for life or for a term of years to tenants who held it on a commercial basis and free from the customs and agricultural routine of the manor. Much of this land, including the Great and Little Parks, was demesne land which the lord found more profitable to let than to work himself, but part was customary land which had come into his hands through forfeiture or death. Another noticeable point is that all services due from the customary tenants were by this date commuted for fixed payments and in no instance was their performance still exacted.

While it is unsafe to theorise from an isolated year yet the account contains unmistakable signs of economic distress due apparently to some external cause which may well have been the exhaustion produced by the long French war and the decline of arable farming in this century. The paragraph headed " Decrease of Rents " sets out a long list of reduced rents and lands which had fallen into the hands of the lord and remained unlet for lack of tenants. It is significant too that the farm of the market for this year dropped to 5s. 6d., " for want," it is explained, " of stranger merchants coming to the town."

Bondmen who wished to reside outside the manor had to obtain the lord's licence for which a fine known as chevage was exacted, the usual rate being 12d. per year. This was paid by Richard Bawe, Walter Pope and William Gander, but John Bouching paid 8d. only. They belonged to four of the oldest villein families in the manor. The custom known as garsenes which produced 12d. this year was the old Domesday rent in commuted form of one pig in seven due for running swine in the manor woods. Earlswood Common was let for the same purpose for 5s. 4d. but nothing was received for the pasture of le Rie—Wray Common—

because it was overrun and eaten up by the lord's rabbits.[36]

On the expenses side over £36 was paid in fees and wages to servants of the manor. The higher posts at this period were life appointments held by the lord's retainers. John Lematon, steward of the court, received £20 a year. John Timperley and his son held the offices of steward of the lordship and constable of the castle for their joint lives and the life of the longer liver of them. The Timperleys were Suffolk men who sat in Parliament for Surrey seats and stood high in the duke's favour.[37]   He was godfather to the son and had let to the father the warren rent free and the meadow known as Fridaysmead at the nominal rent of one red rose, if demanded.

The prior of Reigate had been fined 16d. at the manor court for failing to clean the ditch on the west side of "his Priory," but 6d. of this was remitted because when the fine was imposed the ditch " stood amended."

The account showed a surplus of £6 3s. o½d., which in the language of medieval book-keeping was " owing by the reeve." Of this sum 13s. 4d. was assigned for the repair of the castle and the balance to Sir Robert Wingfield, receiver general of the lord's property.

When the Lord Admiral succeeded to his father's share of the manor in 1581 there were many small farmers and labourers attached to the various manors throughout the country who had not risen to the position of copyholders, but still remained in a state of serfdom or villeinage and in theory at any rate were, with their families and belongings, at the mercy of the lords and could be bought and sold like chattels.   At Reigate there were four families in this servile condition named Gander, Ace, Pope and Botchinge, the heads of which were still paying chevage for leave to dwell outside the manor as their ancestors had done in the previous century. By deed dated 18th June, 1581, Henry, earl of Derby, seised of a moiety of the manor granted to Charles, lord Howard, " Richard Ace and Richard Gander of the Parish of Reigate, William Botching of the Parish of Nutfield, Nicholas Gander and John Botchinge, villeins and bondmen regardant belonging to the manor of Reigate their issues sons and daughters." By a subsequent deed lord Howard, seised of the other moiety of the manor, for divers good reasons manumitted from the yoke of servitude of villeinage and bondage the same Richard Gander and Bartholomew and Frances Gander, his son and daughter. In thus freeing his serfs he was merely imitating the queen, who as a shrewd business woman drove a lucrative trade by liberating the bondmen on the royal manors. Gander held a small farm called Setbys at what is now South Park and his fields adjoined the park. At a Court Baron held 6th September, 1581, Gander, who is described as "lately a bondman but now manumitted," was admitted to hold his lands as an ordinary copyholder with a reservation to the lord of one field of over eight acres lying on the south side of the park palings. So in return for his freedom he gave up one of his fields to round off the lord's park. Richard Ace, who was manumitted at the same time, occupied a farm called Bales which lay at Wiggie. The consideration for his freedom is not stated but probably consisted of a money payment.[38]

The Survey of 1623 which was prepared in circumstances already explained presents a view of the manor in decay after it had ceased to function as an agricultural organisation. The villein owing services to his lord had given way to the copyholder occupying his land for a small money payment and ranking as a yeoman. Much of the land had been enclosed or consolidated in compact holdings as the result not of parliamentary action but of voluntary forces which had long been at work, though it is probable that some of the outlying holdings like Salfords, Streters and Dobers which stood on the fringe of the manor in Horley parish and on the Weald clay had always been compact units and had originated in grants to newcomers after the better land nearer the centre had been absorbed by earlier settlement. Others like Fengates in Linkfield Street and Setbys at South Park had certainly become consolidated by the sixteenth century.

It is true that several common fields are mentioned in the Survey which refers to Lodgefield under Reigate Hill, Southfield, near Wiggie, Lesbye (Lesbourne) between Lesbourne Road and Church Walk, Great Meade with possibly two other fields near Reigate Lodge, Combe Field near Littleton and Nunersh at Trumpets Hill, which lay, it will be noted, not together in one spot but in different parts of the manor dotted along the valley from east to west. Some of the holdings are said to lie in common or intermixed in these fields but this means not that they were still cultivated on the open field system but only that they were not yet enclosed. The absence of any mention in the surviving court rolls and draft rolls of orders regulating the operations incident to common-field husbandry is a further indication that the manor had ceased to exist as an agricultural unit before the middle of the sixteenth century. The general conclusion to be drawn from a study of the available evidence is that the common fields were not limited to one set of three grouped together in the conventional pattern but consisted of several distinct groups in different parts of the manor. These, however, accounted for part only of the tenants' land, the remainder comprising more or less compact parcels each held by a single tenant and worked in severalty.

The demesne lands specified in this Survey comprised fields bordering the southern edge of Earlswood Common which had evidently been taken in from that waste. Names such as Bayes Inholmes and Petterich Inholmes indicate land thus annexed. Damask Mead and Lords Mead, the names of two small parcels at Wiggie of a little over five acres, suggest remnants of the lord's holdings in the common field there.

In or shortly after the year 1700 another Survey was prepared which may be described as a revised edition of the 1623 Survey on which it was evidently based. A remarkable feature is the greatly enhanced yearly values placed on the copyholds which in some cases are more than double those given in the earlier Survey, though these values could not be realised in practice except as fines on admission or in the few cases where holdings came into the lord's hands through forfeiture, or escheat on failure of heirs.

In 1773 Sir Charles Cocks, then lord of the manor, obtained a private Act to enable him to enfranchise the copyholds which were stated in the preamble to be " a diminishing estate " owing to the custom whereby a tenant though possessed of several copyhold tenements was liable to only one fine and one heriot on death or alientation.[39] The custom was not peculiar to Reigate and in manors where it prevailed gave rise to a movement in favour of enfranchisement to facilitate conversion of the lord's interests into more profitable forms of investment. For purposes of this Act the manor was again surveyed with the help of a jury of tenants who completed their work in 1775. The answers of the jury to the articles of enquiry are extant, but the terrier of the demesne and copyhold lands is missing though the map which accompanied it has survived. This shows the copyhold lands divided into rectangular fields after the modern fashion and there is no definite trace of common fields. Yet while much had changed in the intervening century and a half, much remained as it was in 1623, and it is possible by means of the map to identify a number of the holdings described in the first Survey.

A note in a seventeenth century hand added at the end of one of the MS. copies of the Survey of 1623 gives a list of the customary lands of the manor, according to which these were divided into six yardlands of 60 acres (or more) each, twenty one half-yardlands of 30 acres each, nineteen farthinglands of 15 acres and four cotlands the acreage of which is not stated. The yardlands or virgates of sixty acres were exceptionally large. Normally the virgate did not exceed thirty acres though its size varied greatly in different manors and even in the same manor, and units of sixty acres are occasionally met with in the Weald.[40] From the Reeve's account 1300 it appears that there were then twenty customary tenants holding a virgate each, whereas the list gives only six holdings of that size.[41] The inference is that the remaining fourteen holdings had been split up into half-yardlands and farthinglands before the seventeenth century, and this view gains support from the fact that a few of the holdings given in the list under different categories bear the same or similar names. For example, Cecely at fford is the name of both a half-yardland and a farthingland, while Robards at fford and Chert, and Robards at Hole and Chertlands, are the names of half-yardlands and farthinglands respectively. The evidence for the seventeenth century shows clearly that this process of reduction was then operating strongly, partly no doubt as a result of the parallel process of enclosure. It is noticeable for instance that Fengates which appears as a half-yardland in the list is described in the Court Roll of 1579 as a virgate for which Alice Gylman, widow, was elected to serve as reeve in that year. Dobers and Combes which appear in the list as yardlands are described in the Court Rolls of 1620 and 1628 as half-virgates. But some of the half-virgates had by then as a result of further division ceased to be so except in name. Combes, as the following incident reveals, though still nominally a half-virgate had been reduced to fifteen acres. In 1629 John Richardson who had in the previous year been elected reeve for this holding refused to collect more than half the manorial quit rents because as he swore it was limited to fifteen acres of reeveland. As, however, he had been elected to the office this excuse did not avail him and he was ordered to collect the whole of these rents for the year with the provision that Thomas Skelton, the beadle, ought to join him in the next year's collection.

NOTES TO CHAPTER II

[1] I *VCH* 297.
[2] The hide varied greatly in different manors but seems to have been this size at Reigate.
[3] IV *VCH* 412-3.
[4] *PN Surrey* 281-2.
[5] For the origin of " church " names see *PN Worcestershire* 106-9.
[6] The parish was " an area of diffuse settlement " in contrast to the " nucleated village " (Cf. Fox, *Archæology of the Cambridge Region* 311).
[7] *PN Surrey* 304.
[8] 44 *SAC* 52-3. *PN Surrey* 304.
[9] I *M & B* 305.
[10] III *VCH* 167. The payment was 1s. 3d. in 1300 (43 *SAC* 119), and had risen to 2s. 8d. by 1447. Fridaysmead lies behind The Barons and is now cultivated as allotments.
[11] See p. 45 below.
[12] Malden : *Hist. of Surrey* 110-11 ; III *VCH* 234. The incident is rejected by some authorities. Its authenticity is discussed by Mr. G. Lapsley in an article in *Cambridge Historical Journal*, 1926, p. 110, etc.
[13] I *M & B* 273 ; III *VCH* 234.
[14] *CPR* 15th Jan. 1398-9 and 3rd March 1399-1400. Custody of the castle, town and lordship of Reigate was granted 27th July, 1397, to Sir Wm. Arundle, K.G., a nephew of the late earl, who in the following year obtained a grant of the castle and lordship at the yearly rent of £106 13s. 4d. (*CPR*,

20th May, 1398).   Apparently the duke took subject to this lease till it expired on Arundle's death in August 1400.

[15] See Appendix I, Table I.

[16] Apparently the partition did not include the castle, for subsequently by Letters Patent of 11th Dec. 19 Hy. VI, Sir R. Lenthall was granted custody of (inter alia) a third part of divers houses and buildings in Reigate Castle on behalf of his son, Edmund, on whose death without issue in 1447 his third share passed to the duke of Norfolk and lord Abergavenny.   This would explain the reference to the " halvendale," i.e., half part, of the castle granted to the duke of York by the Act 19 Edward IV.   (Ministers Accts. Gen. Ser. 1120 No. 1 ; Rolls of Pmt.   (Rec. Com.) VI 168.

[17] 56 SAC 69–70.

[18] Cf. Ryan & Redstone, Timperley of Hintlesham 19 & 20, and references there given for the views for and against his guilt.

[19] Howard Household Books (Roxburghe Club) 456–7, 460.

[20] Ibid. 480–1.

[21] Skelton's Magnificence (EETS) cxxv–viii.

[22] This agrees with the account in I M & B, 276–7, except that they omit any mention of the 1483 partition.   See also 7 VCH Sussex 5–6 and references there given.

[23] Manor Courts were held in her name to 1580.

[24] These deeds from the Manor Archives have not previously been published and throw fresh light on the devolution of the Howard moiety.   They correct the inference drawn in III VCH 235 that it passed to Chas. Howard, second earl of Nottingham, instead of to his younger half-brother of the same name.

[25] By deed dated 25th March, 1641, being an appointment under the deed of 26th January, 1623.

[26] Their maternal grandfather was Richard Wallop of Bugbrooke, Northants.

[27] III VCH 236 ; I M & B 280 ; S.P.Dom. 1654, May 2nd.   From 1654–1661 Courts were held in the name of Thos. Woodford who was probably a trustee under the 1646 Settlement.

[28] Pat. 13 Chas. II 46 n. 13 ; Close Roll 20 Chas. II pt 26 No. 13 (Deed dated 11th August, 1668, appointing Henry, earl of Peterborough, Richard, earl of Burlington and Thos. Grey, Trustees).

[29] Hist. MSS. Com. 8 Rep. App. i 280.

[30] S.P. Treasury Books 1685–89, Nos. 979, 1005 & 1373.   The price paid was £4,400.

[31] I M & B 281.   Howleigh or Hooley is often confused with Hooley (Coulsdon) and Horley.

[32] The original grant and deed are among the Manor archives.

[33] The deed of partition is dated 14th March, 1717 and was followed by a deed declaring uses of the manor dated the next day.   The partition was perfected by levying the necessary fines.   Jekyll was knighted in 1700.   For the Cocks' descent see Appendix I, Table II.

[34] The original accounts are among the duke of Norfolk's muniments. (See 28 SRS 18 n. 5.)

[35] See p. 24 above.

[36] This seems to be the meaning of a rather obscure passage.

[37] The father acquired the manor of Hintlesham and was one of the duke's Suffolk tenants.   (See Ryan and Redstone, op. cit. 2 & 4).

[38] See my article Bondmen at Reigate under the Tudors, 38 SAC 149.

[39] 13 Geo. III c.5.

[40] Cf. Lambert, Banstead 53, 54 & 67.   A list of the holdings is printed in Appendix III.

[41] See p. 36 above.

CHAPTER III

THE CASTLE

THE origin of Reigate Castle, of which only the earthworks now remain, is uncertain, but it was probably constructed soon after 1088 when William de Warenne was created earl of Surrey and received a grant of Reigate from the king.[1] As he died in that year the castle was most likely the work of his son, the second earl. It was formed by cutting a deep ditch round one end of a natural ridge or plateau and throwing the excavated soil on to the inner area so as to make a broad and lofty motte or mound. Early Norman castles were usually devoid of masonry, the perimeter of the mound being protected by a wooden stockade within which stood the hall of the lord, also of wood. The spacious summit makes it evident that the castle was designed for residence and not as a purely military stronghold, though by being placed at cross-roads it occupied a position of some strategic importance. Notwithstanding its situation immediately above the town it stood just outside the Old Borough boundary.

At some time in the second half of the twelfth or possibly in the early part of the thirteenth century the wooden stockade gave way to a stone curtain wall and the buildings within were replaced by stone ones including a stone keep. Probably at the same time the outer ward, or bailey, was laid out on the east side. This was protected on the north and north-east, where, luckily for the makers, a band of clay runs through the Folkestone beds of the Lower Green-sand[2], by a wet ditch or moat of which part—about a third—still remains. On the south-east side the moat was approached by the dry ditch of the castle which was extended east and then north to complete the defences*.

*See Plan of Reigate Town.

The walls round the motte or inner ward had a crenellated parapet behind which a look-out could be kept and defenders could be posted in case of attack. Semicircular towers built at intervals in the walls and projecting over the ditch enabled the defenders to counter and outflank attempts to scale or mine the enceinte from without. Finally, in order to guard the entrance on the north or London Road side an outer gatehouse or barbican was in all probability erected opposite the west end of the moat. The low mound now used as a children's playground is thought to conceal the foundations of this structure and would probably repay excavation.

On the south the castle was approached by the broad passage that leads up from High Street. This was formerly entered through a gateway having a chamber above, and known in the seventeenth century as " The Gatehouse," and later as " The Old Building."

Little is heard of the castle before the thirteenth century. In 1216 it was captured by Louis, the French Dauphin, on his march from Kent to Winchester, apparently without resistance. He reached here on June 18th and moved on to Guildford the following day. The story that the barons met in the cave to settle the terms of Magna Carta is an evident fabrication.[3] It is, as Mr. Malden pointed out, equivalent to asserting that the Reform Act of 1832 was concocted in the cellars of Apsley House.[4] Equally mythical are the stories of underground passages connecting the castle with the Priory and Blechingley Castle. Similar tales are told of countless other old sites usually without a tittle of evidence to support them. John de Warenne's escapades in 1270 when he fled to Reigate and surrendered to prince Edward rather than face a siege, and his captor's subsequent entertainment at the castle, have already been narrated.[5]

The castle was strongly fortified by the earl of Arundel when he retired here in 1397 as narrated in the previous chapter. He was tempted from this refuge by his brother, archbishop Arundel, on the faith of the king's promise not to harm him which was broken as soon as he reached Court.[6]

The castle continued to be maintained for the use of the

lord or his family till the sixteenth century, and during the reign of Edward VI it was the home of John Foxe while serving as tutor in the household of the duchess of Richmond[7]. Thirty years later it had fallen into decay and was described by Lambarde as " the ruins and rubbish of an old castle which some call Holmesdale."[8] Its decline, however, must have been more gradual than is implied by this contemptuous reference. During the Civil War its defences were strengthened so that it evidently still possessed some military value. In July, 1648, on the outbreak of lord Holland's insurrection, the Committee of Parliament ordered the castle to be made indefensible, but the owner, lord Monson, neglected apparently to obey this order, for during the rising it was temporarily occupied by Holland and his opponents in turn, and after the rising collapsed was garrisoned without the Committee's authority at the expense of the County, a step which roused much popular discontent and obliged the Committee to intervene.[9] A Survey made in 1663 gives the following description of the property, " The scite of the Castle of Reigate together with the several parcels of ground within the cercuit of the same containing 17 acres with the houses thereupon vizt. the Tower consisting of a Hall and parlor and 2 faire Chambers overthem and 3 convenient Lodgeing Roomes in the Third Story and a Cellar with other out Buildings consisting of a Kitchen and a faire roome over it Alsoe a stable a Barn of ffower bayes of Building a Coach house with a Chamber over it and one other outhouse adjoyning unto the Barn of one lowe roome and a Chamber over it All which are in reasonable repair and usefull. There are other Buildings very large which are very much ruined and much of them ffallen downe and cannot well be repaired without re-edifying. All which premises are in the occupation of Michael Aynscome, Bailiff of the Manor."[10] The tower was no doubt the old Norman keep somewhat modernised, but the other buildings were probably of later date. Subsequently decay became more rapid for in 1686 the castle was reported to be " ruinous," only the bare walls remaining, though the Bailiff's account for 1698–9 showed a small outlay on repairs. As late as 1790 one of the wall towers with a fragment of the curtain wall on the south side still remained, but these had disappeared fourteen years later when the only buildings visible were the existing gateway and a small one-storey building described as a " summer apartment."[11] This gateway adds a picturesque touch but, as its construction betrays, is not a genuine antique. It was erected about 1777 by Richard Barnes, who rented the grounds, with material taken from the ruins, but the Latin inscription extolling the imaginary services of William de Warenne in the cause of liberty though concocted in Barnes' time was not added till recent years.

The grounds remained in private possession until last century. In 1873 after being laid out at the cost of some local residents they were granted by lord Somers to the Borough Council on a long lease, and in 1921 the Council purchased the freehold reversion from Mr. Somers Somerset. The total area open to the public is about five acres, the summit of the mound covering nearly an acre and a quarter.

As early as the fifteenth century the land adjoining the outer ward was let off at an annual rent. It was known as the Small Park to distinguish it from the Great or Old Park south of the town, which later went by the name of Reigate Park. In the nineteenth century it was called Castlefield and used for several years as a cricket field and was later acquired by the Borough Council and is now occupied by the Town Hall and Castlefield Road.

The so-called Barons' Cave under the mound is first mentioned by William Camden in his *Britannia*, published in 1586.[12] He had visited the castle and says that under it he saw " an extraordinary passage with a vaulted roof hewn with great labour out of the soft stone of which the hill is composed." The Survey of 1623 speaks of " a quantity of special white sand within the Lord's Castle," which has led to the assumption that the cave was dug for the sake of its sand.[13] Steps at the north end lead up to the top of the mound and this fact coupled with the regular plan and shaped roof seems to negative the idea that it was formed as a sand quarry. It appears more reasonable to regard it as an adjunct of the castle purposely designed to act as a store or dungeon. The sand mentioned in the

Survey, assuming it to have been loose sand, was more probably taken from the ditch and banks, for there are signs that these have at some time been lowered and cut away at various points. The ditch, for example, is considerably deeper on the west and south-west sides of the mound for no apparent military reason but owing probably to commercial causes. The castle in its declining years became a common quarry for building material, and we must be thankful that so much of its ground work has survived.[14]

The castle in medieval times was in charge of the lord's constable, and the staff included a chaplain and janitor. William Welburne, the constable for the year to Michaelmas 1300, received a wage of 2d. a day, exactly double that of Adam Bosoyng, the janitor. Master Oliver, the chaplain, performed clerical as well as religious duties and received large sums from the reeve for the expenses of the earl in that year when he visited Reigate and his other manors in Surrey and Sussex.[15] The office of constable was coupled in the fifteenth century with that of steward of the manor and was bestowed by the Mowbrays on some of their leading retainers, though the duties of steward were performed by deputy. In 1446–7 John Mowbray, third duke of Norfolk, appointed John Timperley and his son John constables and stewards for their lives and the life of the survivor at a wage of ten marks a year. Richard Felingley, the janitor, also held his office for life at the old wage of 1d. per day.[16] John Mowbray, the fourth duke, on succeeding his father in 1461, appointed Nicholas Gaynesford, one of the members for Surrey, steward and constable for life at the annual wage of ten marks, an office which he continued to hold after the duke's death in 1476 when the manor passed to Richard, duke of York.[17] In January, 1486, when the manor had passed to Henry VII by the death and attainder of John Howard, duke of Norfolk, William Clyfton was appointed constable of the castle and bailiff of the lordship with custody of the warren there.[18]

Reigate while under the Warennes received passing visits from several of the Angevin kings in the course of their constant perambulations, and they doubtless put up at the

castle on these occasions. King John came here on
10th December, 1215, and again on 22nd and 23rd April,
1216, while on his way from Guildford to Malling six months
before his death. Edward I, in addition to his early visit,
came again on 15th January, 1285. Edward II stayed here
in June, 1310, and Edward III from 2nd to 4th and 7th to
8th July, 1329.[19]

NOTES TO CHAPTER III

[1] See p. 24 above.
[2] Topley, *Geology of the Weald* 141 ; 40 *Proc. of the Geologists' Association* 241.
[3] It is recorded by Salmon in his *Antiquities of Surrey* (1736) 71, and earlier
in Miege's *The New State of England* (1699) ; and see p. 25 above. It probably
owed its inspiration to the Whigs at the time of the Revolution of 1688.
[4] *Magna Carta Commemoration Essays* XXV.
[5] See p. 25 above.
[6] See *DNB*, s.v. Richard and Thomas Fitzalan and Thomas Arundel.
[7] See p. 127 below.
[8] *Dictionarium Angliae Topographicum* (ed. 1730) 306.
[9] *S.P.Dom.* (1648-9) 157, 182, 196.
[10] It was customary at this period for the bailiff to have the use of the Castle
as part of his remuneration, but in 1687 it was let to a tenant at £16 a year.
[11] I *M & B* 293.
[12] *Op. cit.* (ed. Gough) 168.
[13] IV *VCH* 397, but cf III *Ibid.* 321.
[14] At the Court Leet in 1583 Allan Cuddington and Richard Dumbrecke
were presented for carrying away stone from the Castle without licence. Both
apparently were pardoned.
[15] Reeve's Account 1300.
[16] Reeve's Account 1447.
[17] Min. Accts. Duchy of Lancaster, Bdle. 454. No. 7312.
[18] VI *Rolls of Pmt.* (*Rec. Com.*) 352.
[19] *Itinerary of King John in Description of Patent Rolls* by Sir T. D. Hardy ;
p. 26 above ; I *Collectanea Archaeologica* 118 ; *Cal. of Patent Rolls* (1327-1330),
402-4, 410, 432.

CHAPTER IV

1. THE PARISH CHURCH OF ST. MARY MAGDALENE

REIGATE parish church, like the majority of old English churches, is a complex of various styles of Gothic architecture, and like them it suffered badly from nineteenth century restorations. Despite the silence of Domesday it is probable that a church existed on the site from pre-Conquest days. The oldest parts of the present structure are the walls of the nave which were pierced in the last quarter of the twelfth century to form the existing arcades, but a fragment of Saxon carved stone has been preserved that may have belonged to an earlier building.[1] The site was no doubt chosen because of its prominence and central position. It lies on a sandy ridge at a point approximately in the centre of the parish round which probably a little Saxon settlement sprang up to form one of the scattered groups in which the population was from an early period distributed.

The church, by the name of Crechesfeld, is first mentioned in the twelfth century when it was presented with its tithes and land by Hamelin de Warenne and Isabel, his wife, to the Augustinian Priory of St. Mary Overy, Southwark.[2] At the date of this gift the church had an aisleless nave and, it is supposed, a central tower, but before the end of that century north and south aisles were added to the nave, the walls of which were pierced by the insertion of arches.

Before 1291 the Priory appropriated the benefice to its own use and as a result the living lost the principal source of its revenue and was thenceforward served by a vicar chosen by the patron house.[3] The only remaining sign of thirteenth century work is the geometrical window with restored tracery at the west end of the north aisle. The chancel chapels or

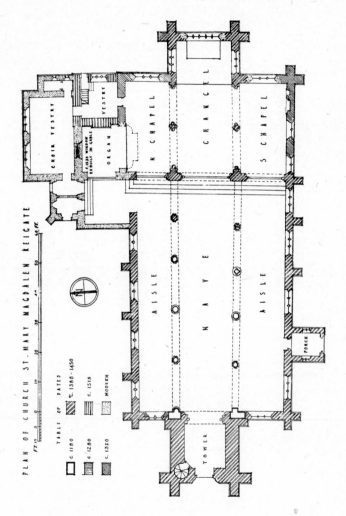

PLAN OF CHURCH ST. MARY MAGDALEN REIGATE

TABLE OF DATES
- c. 1180
- c. 1280
- c. 1520
- c. 1380 - 1450
- c. 1513
- MODERN

N

CHOIR VESTRY

VESTRY

ORGAN

C. 1835 WINDOW REBUILT IN GABLE

N. CHAPEL

CHANCEL

S. CHAPEL

AISLE

NAVE

AISLE

PORCH

TOWER

FIG. III.—PLAN OF REIGATE PARISH CHURCH.

aisles were added in the early decades of the following century.

Sweeping alterations took place towards the end of the fourteenth and during the first half of the fifteenth centuries when the building assumed its final form and came to be one of the largest of Surrey parish churches. The central tower fell or was pulled down and a new tower of fine proportions was erected at the west end. The south aisle was enlarged to bring its south wall into line with that of the chancel chapel on the east, and a south porch was added. The nave was extended one bay to the east in the space set free by the removal of the tower. The chancel was also extended one bay eastward to form a sanctuary in advance of the side chapels, and the arches between chancel and chapels were rebuilt. The fenestration was improved by introducing larger windows in the nave aisles in the contemporary Perpendicular style, and the new sanctuary was lighted by three handsome windows in the same style, of which those in the north and south walls still remain.

These alterations greatly changed the internal aspect of the church and their effect must have been heightened by the lavish use of stained glass and coloured decoration. But perhaps the most imposing feature was the triple screen stretching across the entrances to the chancel and chapels and surmounted by the great rood and its attendant figures in the central arch.[4] Images of various saints were set up about the church, two of which are mentioned in the will of John Longhurst of Reigate, 1487, who bequeathed sixpence to the light of St. Mary in " Jesyne," i.e., in childbed, and fourpence to the light of St. Antony.[5]

The only other alteration before modern times was the addition of the vestry at the north-east corner in 1513. This interesting little building is entered by a door in the north chapel surmounted by a Latin inscription in black letters which records an early and remarkable instance of enlightened piety. It bids the reader remember that John Skynner " gentylman " with various sums left to his disposal for the souls of the persons named as well as with 103s. 4d. of his own money " for the souls of his own parents hath for the honour of God caused this porch (*vestibulum*) to be built." The vestry is in two storeys, the upper of which houses the parish library. Its walls, originally of brick, have been cased in Reigate stone.

The images and decoration disappeared at the Reformation, but the reredos, though void of its statuary, and some at least of the stained glass, was spared. Fragments of the original fifteenth century glass in the chancel windows remained as late as 1828 and were not finally removed until 1845. These windows also contained a quantity of heraldic glass depicting the arms of the Warenne and later families connected with the parish which were recorded by the heralds when they visited the church in 1610 and 1623.[6]   Much of this must have suffered grievously in 1661 when a madman named " Thomas Glynn late of Reigate glasier forcibly and unlawfully smashed and tore out the windows of the parish church," for which his only punishment was a fine of 12d.[7]

In the eighteenth century a gallery was erected at the west end of the nave to accommodate the choir and instruments. The music was discoursed by a band of local performers after the manner usual in country churches at this period.[8] A document of the year 1730 is extant to show that members of the choir took their duties very seriously and went so far as to sign an agreement to attend regularly at the Sunday morning and afternoon services " to sing Psalms and any Item for the better improvement and making ourselves fitt for singing," under penalty of a fine on any who absented themselves.[9]

The south aisle was cumbered with a gallery erected by Sir John Parsons, owner of the Priory, under a faculty granted to him in 1700 on the ground that " he hath a fine house and estate within the Parish of Reigate and a wife and several children and a very large family and has no pew belonging to him for them to kneele pray sit stand and hear divine service and sermons." This continued in use by succeeding owners of the Priory until its removal after 1845.[10]

In 1770 the body of the church was re-pewed out of a legacy bequeathed by Mrs. Mary Okes of Redstone, augmented by subscriptions.[11]

Plate III.

REIGATE CHURCH, EAST END, 1833.
(From a lithograph of a sketch by Wm. Thornton.)

During the first three decades of the nineteenth century
the building was severely " churchwardenised " in accordance with the debased fashion of the time. A third gallery
was put up in 1818, this time in the north aisle. It was
erected, to quote Ridgeway, " by subscription for the use
of the familys of those that subscribed for them—eleven
pews for eleven familys."

Other disfiguring alterations carried out in this period
had less justification and caused alarming damage to the
structure. " All the external buttresses of the aisles were
removed save two at the south-west angle. . . . All the
tie beams and king posts of the great centre roof were
removed. A cornice of the meanest description was run
along the wall plate, and a plaster ceiling hid from view all
the rafters."[12] The effects of this meddlesome folly were
soon apparent and by 1828 the nave roof was in a dangerous
condition. Iron tie rods were inserted in the nave and chancel and the aisles walls were shored up with makeshift
buttresses. During the same period the east windows of
the chancel chapels were taken out and replaced by ugly
churchwarden substitutes which appear in contemporary
prints.[13] (Plate III.) The tower was extensively repaired
in 1824 at a cost of over £1,000 which was raised partly by
voluntary subscription and partly by a church rate of 1s. 3d.
in the £. The subscription list was headed by lord Somers
and his son, lord Eastnor, followed by the two members of
Parliament for the borough.[14]

The church was twice restored in Victorian times, first
in 1845 and again thirty years later. The architect employed
on the first occasion was Mr. Henry Woodyer, of Guildford,
who used the opportunity to " improve " the church in
accordance with the ideas of the prevailing Gothic school.
He had the beautiful five-light east window of the chancel
taken out and replaced by an incongruous substitute of
geometric design. He was also responsible for the east
windows of similar design in the chancel chapels which
replaced the churchwarden substitutes. The seventeenth
century monuments against the north wall of the sanctuary
were removed to other parts of the building, and the Bludder
monument at the end of the north chapel was shifted to

make room for the effigies of Richard Eliot and his son.
These fine memorials suffered shockingly in the process of
removal and have remained ever since in the same deplorable plight.   Fortunately the Ladbroke monument,
which at that date stood against the north wall of the north
chapel, escaped unharmed.   This splendid specimen of
eighteenth century monumental art is signed by James
Rose, a London sculptor whose known work is confined to
this and one other example.   Richard Ladbroke of Frenches,
the worthy commemorated, was a wealthy London distiller
who left £1,500 by will for the erection of his monument
and thoughtfully added an annuity of £5 for its upkeep, a
provision which probably saved it from spoliation.   Plate IV
shows the appearance of the interior in the middle of last
century.

The church is strangely destitute of any monument to
the Howards who rest within its walls.   Lord William
Howard, his second wife, their son, the Lord Admiral, and
several other members of the family, were buried in the
vault built by lord William beneath the chancel, but
though by his will he desired his wife as executrix to " erecte
and make one dacente tombe for me in the said Chauncell
of Reygate, as my trust is in her," this wish was never
observed.   In 1888 to commemorate the tercentary of the
defeat of the Armada a brass plate to the Lord Admiral was
put up in the chancel bearing an inscription which with slight
variations follows that upon the coffin plate.   Above hangs
an engraving of the portrait attributed to Zucchero, which
is reproduced as the frontispiece of this volume.

Below the east window of the south chancel chapel is a
block of white marble with a classical frieze and voluted
capstone but void of any inscription.   This mute monument
was designed to commemorate the Rt. Hon. William Elliot,
M.P., a son of William Nassau Elliot of Great Doods, who
died in 1818 and is buried in the family vault under the
chancel.   Differences arose in selecting the most suitable
of the numerous eulogies pronounced on the deceased and
the blank has remained unfilled.[15]

The restoration of 1874 was essentially conservative in
character and entirely free from the disgraceful and senseless

Plate IV.

REIGATE CHURCH.
Interior, C. 1850.

Plate V.

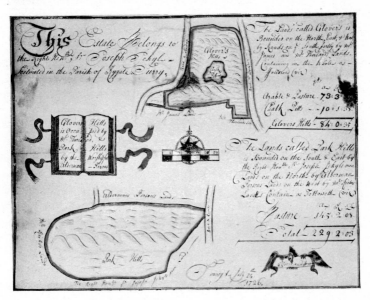

ESTATE PLAN OF REIGATE AND PARK HILL, 1726.

vandalism that had marred previous restorations. Mr. George Gilbert Scott, the architect engaged on this occasion, who is constantly confused with his father, *Sir* G. Gilbert Scott, issued an interesting report on the church and the work he recommended, which was printed in 1873. The condition of the nave and tower was so precarious as to excite the most serious alarm. These were taken down and faithfully rebuilt without any deviation from the original designs though it was thought necessary to reface the tower with Doulting stone, a variety of Bath oölite, and to renew much of the other stonework in the same " unsympathetic " material, so styled because of its failure to blend with the Reigate stone of which the church was built. In the north aisle the gallery was removed and the wall lowered to its previous height with the consequent disappearance of the tier of " meeting house windows " and the gabled roof in which they were fixed.

In 1908 the church received its latest alterations. An organ chamber was added to the north chapel with a transept to the west of it and a choir vestry built on the north side of the chamber and old vestry, the architect responsible for the work being Mr. J. O. Scott, a younger brother of Mr. G. G. Scott.

The octagonal stone font is modern gothic of feeble design, and its appearance is not improved by a series of grotesque heads carved round the bowl to give a spurious air of antiquity. Its predecessor appears in a sketch by Hassell in 1823 which shows a Renaissance font with a baluster pedestal and wooden cover.

In 1552, according to the Edwardian inventories, the church possessed four great bells in the steeple and two hand bells.[16] In 1784 the six bells then existing were re-cast to eight by Robert Patrick, founder, of Whitechapel, the expense being met by public subscription.[17] In 1811 the treble bell was re-cast by Thomas Mears of the White-chapel foundry at a cost, as shown by the churchwardens' accounts, of £23 19s. 6d. Two new bells were added in 1899 to commemorate the long ministry of the Rev. J. Newman Harrison. In 1927 one of the bells was re-cast and the other nine were re-tuned to mark the completion of twenty-five years' ministry of the late Canon Davies. The cost of new bell ropes is provided by an old charity of unknown origin which yields an annual sum of £1. This sum, until redeemed in recent years, was charged on a field in Lesbourne Road which became known in consequence as Bell Rope Field.

The Royal Arms are now skied in the tower, in company with some nice cartouches and other mural tablets, in a position which makes them hard to decipher. They are elegantly carved in wood, the shield being blazoned with the arms assumed by queen Anne on the union with Scotland in 1707.[18] One of the tablets on the south wall of the tower is to Sir Edward Thurland. Its original position was in the chancel.

The registers have been partially transcribed though not printed. They are in a good state of preservation and commence in 1556 with christenings, not in 1546 as usually stated. The burials commence in 1561.

The churchyard contains some good examples of finely lettered tombstones of the eighteenth century, and a few of the wooden " bed-heads " which were once prevalent throughout Surrey owing to the dearth of suitable local stone. Aubrey remarked in 1673, " They use no tombstones in the churchyards but rayles of wood over the graves on which are engraved or printed the inscription."[19] Just south of the church tower is a plain headstone to Elizabeth East, widow, an old inhabitant who died 27th May, 1820, in her 101st year.

The Burial Board, established in 1855, purchased land to the south and east of the churchyard for a cemetery to meet the needs of the growing population. In 1932 the Borough Council as the burial authority opened a new cemetery, known as Redstone Cemetery, and chapel at Redhill.

LIST OF VICARS AND PATRONS

The list of vicars given by Manning and Bray, which is copied on the board in the church, contains several omissions and errors.[20] These are rectified as far as possible in the following list, in which the names of the incumbents and patrons are given in parallel columns. The parish was in Winchester diocese until 1877 when it was transferred to Rochester and from that passed in 1905 to the newly-formed diocese of Southwark, of which the former Priory Church of St. Mary Overy became the cathedral. Thus after an interval of nearly four centuries the old connection with Southwark was renewed in another form.

Incumbents	Patrons
Edward de Dorking, instituted 10th July, 1311	Prior and Convent of Southwark
Alan de Cheyham [Cheam], inst. 23rd October, 1314	The same
Thomas Viel de Kershalton [Carshalton] inst. 13th March, 1325	The same
John Coleman de Chiterne, inst. 5th April, 1346	The same
Richard de Redgrave, inst. 30th May, 1346	The same
Richard Cousande or Cufaude, inst. 2nd May, 1347	The same
Robert Worcester de Colyngbourne, inst. 15th June, 1358	The same
Thomas Chapman de Orewelle, inst 25th August, 1358	The same
Richard Gregory de Kyslyngbury, inst. 11th January, 1360	The same
Robert Page, inst. 19th August, 1361 ..	The same
Richard de Ambresden or Ambrosedene, inst. 6th December, 1365	The same
William Dorsley, inst. 21st January, 1370	The same
Stephen Seylyerd, inst. 4th March, 1385	The same
John Bray, inst. 1st June, 1399	The same
Richard Wodehouse, resigned 1st March, 1456	—
William Clere or Clerk, inst. same date..	The same
John Smith, inst. 14th December, 1470..	The same
Richard Wyche, inst. 16th March, 1471	The same
William Lathes, resigned January, 1497	—
William Giddyng, A.M., admitted 23rd January, 1497	The same
Robert Michell, prior of Southwark, admitted 9th December, 1499	Prior of B.M. of Ellsyngspitall in the City of London by grant of Prior and Convent of Southwark
John Robson, prior of Reigate, admitted 25th January, 1501	Collated by Bishop Thos. Langton

INCUMBENTS	PATRONS
William Brown, inst. 12th October, 1502	Prior and Convent of Southwark
Thomas Wodenott, inst. 6th June, 1510	Bartholomew Lynsted, Sub-prior
William Major, prior of Reigate, inst. 1515	Prior and Convent of Southwark
John Lymden, prior of Reigate, inducted 14th June, 1532	—
George Clyff, resigned 1557	—
Henry Norman, inst. 10th April, 1557 ..	James Skynner
Richard Skynner, inst. 28th January, 1562	Queen Elizabeth
Richard Day, inst. 29th May, 1583 ..	John Skynner
William Cawsey, B.D., inst. 29th January, 1585	Alice, widow of John Skynner
William Hampton, inst. 22nd April, 1599	Sir Thos. Palmer and Alice, his wife, widow of John Skynner
John Hampton, presented 1636	William Hampton, brother of presentee
Richard Parr, M.A., inst. February, 1647	Dame Margaret James, widow of Sir Roger James
John Williamson, appointed by Parliamentary Commissioners 3rd July, 1654	The same
Andrew Cranston, M.A., inst. 29th October, 1697	Roger James
John Bird, M.A., inst. 16th December, 1708	Trustees of Roger James, the Younger
John Rigden, M.A., inst. 20th April, 1728	Trustees of John Bird
Francis Rogers, M.A., inst. 16th December, 1732	Grace, widow of John Bird
William Pottell, M.A., inst. 18th September, 1738	Richard Filewood and his wife, formerly Grace Bird
William Stead, M.A., inst. 2nd January, 1741	Richard Filewood
Marshall Montague Merrick, D.C.L., inst. 1781	The same
Jeoffry Snelson, M.A., inst. 1782 ..	The same
Richard Filewood Snelson, M.A., inst. 1812	Mary, daughter of Jeoffry Snelson
John Newman Harrison, M.A., inst. 1847	J. N. Harrison
Frederick Charles Davies, M.A., Hon. Canon of Southwark, inst. 18th June, 1901	A private Evangelical Trust
Richard Talbot, M.A., inst. 17th October, 1929	The same

NOTES ON THE VICARS AND ADVOWSON

In 1463 the value of the living was stated not to exceed twenty-five marks sterling in a papal dispensation granted to William Clerk to hold a second benefice.[21]

In 1536 the net annual value was returned at £20 5s. 3½d. by Henry VI I's commissioners.[22]

In 1552 Edward VI granted the rectory to James Skynner of Reigate in return for a payment of £458 4s. 9d., and since then the advowson has remained in private hands.

Henry Norman, 1557–1562, did not die in 1561 as stated by Manning and Bray, but was deprived, possibly on account of his refusal to acknowledge the royal supremacy. His successor, Richard Skynner, was also registrar to the bishop of Norwich.[23]

Richard Day or Daye, who was the first undoubtedly protestant vicar, resigned in 1585, probably to become rector of Chipstead, Surrey. He was a scholar of Eton and son of John Daye, the famous Elizabethan printer, who produced the first as well as three subsequent editions of Foxe's *Book of Martyrs*. Richard in his earlier days followed his father's calling and translated and published Foxe's *Christ Jesus Triumphant*.[24]

William Hampton was the father of John Hampton, his successor at Reigate, and of William Hampton, rector of Blechingley 1625–1677. He was chaplain to the earl of Nottingham, the Lord Admiral. Christopher Hampton, his brother, was archbishop of Armagh 1613–1625.[25]

John Hampton held a lectureship at the church as appears in a petition to the House of Commons in 1642 from the minister and other inhabitants praying " that a lecture formerly performed and frequented every Tuesday in the forenoon being their Market Day, and of late years discontinued might be revived, performed and continued by Mr. Jo. Hampton " and neighbouring ministers. The petition was granted, but three years later charges were preferred against him which were ordered to be examined by the Parliamentary Committee for Plundered Ministers for Surrey. The result of these proceedings is not recorded, but in January 1647, he gave up Reigate on being appointed by Parliament rector of Woodmansterne where he remained undisturbed until his death in 1673[26] He was also vicar of Banstead from 1623 to 1636.[27]

Richard Parr stands out as one of the few vicars of more than mediocre ability. The living was insufficient to attract men of superior parts and those ambitious of preferment. Parr was instituted in 1647 by order of the House of Lords, after taking the National League and Covenant, on presentation by lady Margaret James, his mother-in-law. From 1643 he served as chaplain to his fellow countryman, archbishop Usher, who died at Reigate Priory in 1656. He shared Usher's Calvinistic views and published a Life of that prelate in 1686. He resigned Reigate in 1654 to become vicar of Camberwell and rector of Bermondsey, being presented to Camberwell by Sir Edmund Bowyer, whose wife, née Esther Aucher, was a niece of lady James. His work entitled *Christian Reformation*, 1660, in which year he received the degree of D.D., was addressed to his " dear kindred and countrymen of the county of Cork," and the parishioners of Reigate and Camberwell.

In a Parliamentary Survey of 1658 the living was stated to be of the yearly value of £40.[28] In 1705 it was returned by Cranston at £70 per annum besides perquisites, and the vicar paid £22 for first-fruits.[29]

An action brought by the widow of John Williamson shortly after his death in 1697 illustrates some of the difficulties which the parson had to contend with in recovering his tithes. She claimed twelve years' arrears from Sir John Parsons for the Priory and land occupied by him. Evidence taken from local people showed that the vicarial tithe had time out of mind been payable in money, not in kind, and that the gardens of houses in the Old Borough were titheable by ancient custom, though the witnesses differed over the amounts that could be charged.[30]

Andrew Cranston's great achievement in founding the Parish Library is described later in this chapter. He also acted as the earliest local correspondent of the Society for Promoting Christian Knowledge which had been founded in 1698. He wrote to the Society 1st July, 1700, " That he has received the three Circular Letters and imparted them to the Neighbouring Clergy, who highly approve the Design. That Mr. Hare's illness has put great stop to their present endeavours. That as soon as he can form a Society, he will wait on the Bishop with our Letters and Papers. That the Papers and Books mentioned in the Second and third Letters to be sent are not yet come to his hands. That the way to send to him is either by the Coach on Wednesdays and Saturdays at ye Catherine Wheel in Southwark or by John Fisk or Henry Ware Waggoners on Mondays and Fridays at the Greyhound in Southwark. He recommends for Lay Correspondents John Sellyard, Esq., at his house near Bletchingley and Mr. Bromhall, near Rygate, or either of them, and adds that Mr. Sellyard is now put into Commission of the Peace." He wrote again 31st March, 1701, " That they have no Charity Schools, no Societies of the Clergy, and no Converts from Quakerism. That one Library has been set up lately and, in his Parish, Monthly Sacraments, and the number of Communicants encrease daily." " Mr. Hare " was Hugh Hare of Betchworth, son of lord Coleraine and a J.P. for Surrey. " Mr. Bromhall " was Richard Broomhall of Wonham, near Reigate. " John Sellyard "—or more correctly, Seyliard—lived at Pendell, Blechingley. All three gentlemen presented books to the library.[31]

John Bird purchased the advowson in 1715 from Roger James of Reigate for £230, and by his will dated 15th March, 1722, devised the next presentation after his death in trust for his son, John Bird, then a minor.[32] He is described by Dr. Richard Rawlinson, Aubrey's editor, as " a sensible well-bred gentleman " and " worthy Benefactor to the Church " who had " much augmented this Vicaridge by his Industry and Care."[33] The account book left by him shows that several local farmers conspired together to refuse payment of his tithes and involved him in much litigation in which, however, he generally succeeded. His nephew, Edward Bird, gained evil notoriety as the culprit in a sordid tragedy. An army lieutenant of dissolute habits, he quarrelled with a waiter at a tavern of ill-fame in Westminster in 1718 and ran him through with his sword. For his crime he was hanged in spite of frantic efforts by his relatives to gain a reprieve. An ornate monument, since removed, was erected in the church showing him clad in armour with truncheon in hand and cravat round his neck which popular fancy converted into a halter. For several years on the anniversary of his death his disconsolate mother made a pilgrimage to the monument to mourn the fate of her reprobate son.

William Pottell was a minor canon of St. Paul's Cathedral noted for his hard drinking, which is illustrated by the following amusing story told by Ridgeway : " One Sunday after Divine Service in the afternoon he came to the Swan Inn in Reigate with his black gown on, and got quite tipsy. He quarrelled with one of the Company and went out in the street and strip'd off his gown, threw it down and said ' Lay thou there Divinity until I have beat this man.' "[34]

William Stead was also rector of Woodmansterne 1751 to 1775, and of Limpsfield from 1775 to his death in 1781, an example of the pluralism then rife. Ridgeway styles him " a great oddity."

Jeoffry Snelson was also vicar of Hendon, Middlesex. He married a daughter of Richard Filewood, the third husband of Grace Bird, the widow of John Bird, the former vicar. She devised the advowson to her husband on whose death in 1786 it passed to his son-in-law. His son, R. F. Snelson, succeeded him as vicar.

J. N. Harrison continued as vicar till his death on 18th January, 1901, at the age of 85, and thus held the living for the record period of fifty-three years.

The vicarage house in Church Street was rebuilt in 1847–8 at a cost of £2,000 on the site of the earlier house.

In 1877 the advowson was offered for sale by auction when the net income of the living was given as £410 18s. od., of which the tithe rent-charge produced £373 8s. od.[35]

II. REIGATE PARISH LIBRARY

THE library, which is still housed in the upper storey of the old vestry, its original home, was formed in 1701 by the Rev. Andrew Cranston, vicar of Reigate 1697–1708, and of Newdigate 1699–1708. Its aim was to meet the difficulty of procuring books then experienced by the country clergy, but its use was not confined to them. In the old MS. catalogue it is described as " the Publick Library, Belonging to the Parish of Reigate in the County of Surrey, and for the use of the Clergy and others in the Archdeaconry [deanery] of Ewell," though the deed of 1708 widened its scope by declaring that it should be maintained "for the use & perusal of the Freeholders Vicar and Inhabitants " of the parish " and of the Gentlemen and Clergymen inhabiting in parts thereunto adjacent." The vicar started the collection with a gift of seventy theological works, and two years later presented many additional volumes. His zeal for letters must be ascribed to his northern upbringing for he was Scotch by birth and a graduate of Edinburgh University. He was remarkably successful in enlisting the support of his parishioners and the neighbouring clergy and gentry. Early donors of books, or money for their purchase, included John Evelyn, the diarist, John Flamstead, the rector of Burstow and first Astronomer Royal, the earl of Shaftesbury, Edmund Calamy, Benjamin Hoadley and the Society for Promoting Christian Knowledge, while at a later date Arthur Onslow, speaker of the House of Commons, baron Maseres and several of the nobility were among its benefactors. The townspeople showed praiseworthy zeal for the enterprise. Russell, the blacksmith, gave the bar and fastenings and Henry Ware, the waggoner, was, to quote the Catalogue, " prevailed with to carry parcells for the Library from London Gratis which accordingly he chearfully performed to the time of his death which happened August 5th, 1704," after which his son continued the same good service. Joseph Bostock, " Writing-master in Reigate," wrote the orders or rules in the Catalogue.

By the deed of foundation dated 4th November, 1708, the vicar transferred the collection to forty-four trustees, freeholders, and, in the majority of cases, inhabitants of the parish. They included lord Somers, viscount Windsor, Sir John Parsons and James Cocks, the two members for the borough, and Sir Joseph Jekyll and Jacob Tonson. The deed directed that the books should " for ever remain and be part of the Goods of the Church . . . dedicated to

the service of Almighty God and the promotion and preservation of true Religion and good Literature." The
churchwardens and freeholders of the parish after being
summoned by public notice were authorised to frame orders
and nominate new trustees and to appoint the vicar for the
time being, or other person, keeper, who was to enter into
a bond of £600 or such other penalty as should be fixed.

The death of the founder in the same year temporarily
arrested the growth of the library, but some years later
benefactions recommenced, and throughout the remainder
of the eighteenth century continued intermittently. The
rules, which are set out in the old MS. Catalogue, require
the keeper to give a bond of £500 to preserve the books from
embezzlement. He is to attend twice a week and on
holydays to lend books. Every borrower is to deposit the
price of the book borrowed or else give a written undertaking to return it within a specified time, and is to make
good any damage.

Reigate Library earned the distinction of being expressly
excepted from the provisions of the Statute passed in 1708
(7 Anne C.14) to preserve and regulate the large number of
parish libraries that had sprung up as a result of the movement started by the Rev. Thos. Bray. The saving clause
exempts the " publick Library lately erected in the Parish
of Ryegate in the County of Surrey for the use of the Freeholders Vicar and Inhabitants of the said Parish and of the
Gentlemen and Clergymen inhabiting in parts thereto
adjacent," on the ground that it was " constituted in
another manner than the Libraries provided for by the Act."
It is clear from this exemption that the Library was already
firmly established and favourably regarded. Moreover,
its description as a " public Library " indicates a wider
scope than that of the parochial libraries founded by Bray
and his Associates for which the Act was designed. Cranston
had himself foreseen the need for a measure of this kind,
and in January, 1707, he wrote to the Society for Promoting
Christian Knowledge suggesting the addition to a Bill
about to be introduced into the House of Commons relating
to Charity Schools of a clause " for the preservation of all
Parochial Libraries erected or to be erected in the Kingdom

since the Parochial Library at Reigate has now in it about 500 folios and about 1,000 small books and yet wants a settlement by Authority." The committee of the Society advised him to approach the promoters of the Bill and endeavour to get a clause inserted " for the more effectual securing and preserving the said Libraries of Reigate and of Bedford and of all Parochial and Catechetical Libraries erected or to be erected in England and Wales."[36] The Bill failed to mature, and before the Act became law the deed of 1708 had been executed and rendered it unnecessary to apply the provisions to Reigate.

In 1744 the Committee appointed by the Vestry to inquire into the Parish Charities reported that all but two of the original trustees were dead. Nothing was done to fill the vacancies till forty years later before when the last survivor had passed away.

At a Vestry held on 18th October, 1784, fresh trustees to the number of forty-five were nominated and the vicar, the Rev. Jeoffry Snelson, was elected librarian and agreed to enter into a bond in a penalty of £100. The list of new trustees included lord Hardwicke, the first lord Somers of the second creation, Sir John Hynde Cotton, Bart., Sir Merrik Burrell, Bart., Richard Ladbroke, baron Maseres and the vicar and principal inhabitants possessed of freehold property in the parish. The vicar called in all borrowed books, and had the library fitted up and the volumes arranged alphabetically.

In 1893 a carefully compiled catalogue was printed in which the contents were classified under subject headings. They are numbered and arranged by cases and shelves. The volumes number upwards of two thousand, including a small collection of MSS., mainly in Latin, of which the most important is entitled *Passio Scotorum Perjuratorum*, and contains a fierce satire on the Scots, attributed to Stephen Birchington, the fourteenth century monk of Canterbury.

At least half the volumes are theological, the remainder being miscellaneous in character. There are some early editions of famous works, but the chief treasure is an early Prayer Book which apparently belonged to lord William

E

Howard as it bears his initials and his family arms and motto.

The library has long survived its original object and is now of interest mainly to the book lover and antiquary, but it occupies an important place in the history of the library movement for it stands out as a novel and, while the need for it lasted, successful experiment in providing a free public library on modern lines. Its exceptional character was recognised by the Act of 1708. It had a wider scope and basis than the old parochial libraries and those formed by the Rev. Thomas Bray, and marked a notable advance towards the public municipal libraries of the present day.

NOTES TO CHAPTER IV

[1] III *VCH* 240. This fragment, which is in the library, probably formed part of an arm of a Saxon Cross.

[2] Dugdale, VI *Monasticon* 170. Watson (I *Memoirs of the Earls of Warren and Surrey*, 106, 108) regards the grant by Hamelin and his wife as merely confirmation of the two earlier grants, which he quotes, made to the Priory by William de Warenne, the second earl. The tithe of corn in the parish was subsequently, and apparently before the end of the twelfth century, granted by Southwark Priory to the Cluniac Priory of Lewes (43 *SAC* 86, 107).

[3] In the Taxation of Pope Nicholas, 1291, the rectory was valued at £13 6s. 8d. and the vicarage at £5. per annum (*Rec. Com.* 208).

[4] For a fuller architectural description of the church see the account by Mr. P. M. Johnston in III *VCH* 239-42.

[5] 17 *SRS* 72 No. 244. The bequests were for the purchase of candles to burn before the images.

[6] Peatling, *Ancient Stained and Painted Glass in the Churches of Surrey* 75 & 76 ; *The Topographer* No. XX (1790) 44 ; Harl. MS 1561 ; IV Brayley *Hist. of Surrey* 42. A panel with the Warenne shield has been re-set in the window of the Library.

[7] 35 *SRS* 129. In 1803 Jas. Knowles agreed to glaze " the Windows with Newcastle Crown Glass at 1s. 6d. pr. ft." (Mins. of Vestry).

[8] This gallery was removed c. 1850. An organ was installed at the west end under a faculty in 1832 (Mins. of Vestry, 5th April, 1850). In 1833 an annual sum of £3 10s. od. was voted from the church rates of the Old Borough towards the organist's salary.

[9] *Surrey Mirror*, 10th Feb., 1922.

[10] Plate IV shows this and the later gallery. In 1704, when lord mayor of London, Sir John presented the fine brass chandelier that now hangs in the chancel (See 47 *SAC* 42-3).

[11] I *M & B* 314. Pews in the chancel, a part of the church which belonged to the Rectory manor, were sometimes let at curious rents. In 1700 Sir Evelyn Alston, Bart., held a pew at the yearly rent of half a guinea and a fat turkey.

[12] II *SAC* 189 ; Mins. of Vestry, 30th April, 1828. In 1803 a committee of the Vestry resolved " that the beams in the nave of the church be removed and that the screens between the church and the chancel be taken down." The Table of Benefactions was made and put up in 1806 at a cost of £26 17s.

[13] Thornton's view of 1833 (opp. p. 52) shows the new windows.

[14] Churchwardens' Accounts and Mins. of Vestry, 1829. At a Vestry held in 1836 consent was given " to the church being warmed by Stoves or otherwise by Voluntary Contributions provided that no part of the expense be paid out of the Church Rates."

[15] *Palgrave* 64 ; *Gentleman's Magazine*, Vol. 88 Part II, 467.

[16] 21 *SAC* 64.

[17] I *M & B* 313—16 where the inscriptions on the bells are given.

[18] The arms are : Quarterly 1 and 4 England impaling Scotland, 2 France, 3 Ireland. The Beatitudes formerly appeared in the south chapel of the chancel. Some of the opening words in eighteenth century lettering are still faintly legible under the whitewash on the south wall.

[19] " A Perambulation of Surrey," MS. in the Bodleian Library.

[20] I *M & B* 322–4 ; see 38 *SAC* 100-103 for notes by the author on certain of the vicars, which are not repeated here.

[21] 34 *SAC* 117.

[22] *Valor Ecclesiasticus* (Rec. Com) II 43.

[23] I *M & B* 323 ; II *VCH* 22, 48 ; 43 *Harl. Soc. Publications* 59.

[24] Cooper, *Alum. Cantab.* II 476 ; DNB.

[25] 11 *SAC* 202, where his name is wrongly given as John.

[26] II *Commons Jo.* 807 ; IX *Lords Jo.* 624, 644 ; 9 *SAC* 299–302.

[27] 31 *SAC* 136.

[28] 17 *SAC* 96.

[29] 12 *SAC* 170. The liability for first fruits was discharged under the Act, 6 Anne c. 24.

[30] Exchequer Depositions 11 and 12 Wm. III Hil. Surrey, No. 7. This garden tithe was the origin of the present town tithe which is charged at the rate of a groat in the £ on the rateable value. The great or rectorial tithes of corn, hay and wool seem to have been collected in kind till a later period : the tithe barn stood on land called Chappel Fields near the present junction of Ringley Park Road and Reigate Road.

[31] Allen & McClure, *Two Hundred Years : The History of the S.P.C.K.* 98, 99.

[32] Abstract of title in the author's possession. Bird did not purchase the great tithes and these were sold to Sir Wm. Scawen of Carshalton in 1720. His brother, Sir Thos. Scawen, purchased the Rectory manor, house and land in 1730 (Cf. I *M & B* 321).

[33] Aubrey, IV *Hist. of Surrey* 192. Rawlinson was at Reigate in 1717 and has left a short note of his visit which is preserved among his MSS. at the Bodleian (D. 1418 II p. 156).

[34] An obituary notice of him in the *Gentleman's Magazine* (1740, p. 622) gave the value of the living at £80 a year.

[35] *Monthly Illustrated Magazine*, Oct., 1879.

[36] S.P.C.K. MS. Minute Book 4, p. 12.

CHAPTER V

THE PRIORY, THE CHAPELS AND THE MARKET HOUSES

I. THE PRIORY

REIGATE PRIORY, the only religious house in the parish, was founded some time in the earlier half of the thirteenth century by William de Warenne, fifth earl of Surrey, who died in 1240, but the exact date of its origin is unknown. It was a small house of Augustinian or Black Canons Regular who may be described as a community of clerics living according to rule. Like monks they lived a communal life and were bound by vows, yet as clergy they could when in priest's orders undertake the cure of souls, and some of the Reigate canons became vicars of the parish. Like many other houses of this order it originated as a hospital and is so styled in the early documents, but by 1334, in which year it is described as a convent, it appears to have shed its pristine character and become a purely religious institution.[1] The dedication to the B.V.M. and the Holy Cross may have given rise to the error at one time prevalent that it belonged to the Crutched Friars.[2] The error gained local currency and found expression in the name Black Fryars Alley which applied in the eighteenth century to a yard off High Street.

The Priory was endowed, probably by its founder, with considerable property carved out of Reigate manor to form a sub-manor. This comprised several tenements in the Old Borough and a number of local farms, including Littleton in Reigate and Dayhouse, Salford and Sharps in Horley. In 1317 John de Warenne granted and released to the Priory certain annual rents for the endowment of a chantry in Reigate Castle for the health of his soul and the

souls of his ancestors. The Warennes also endowed it
with the manor of Southwick in Sussex which in earlier
days formed the chief source of its income, but according
to a petition which the prior and canons presented to the
bishop of Winchester in 1335 this property was at that date
destroyed by frequent inundations of the sea from which
and other causes they were reduced to poverty. To com-
pensate for this loss the church of Dorking-with-Capel was
transferred to them by Lewes Priory, another Warenne
foundation, and they received a licence to appropriate the
revenues of the living.

The list of benefactions in the fourteenth century also
included grants of West Humble and the advowson of
Mickleham Church, and confirmation of a grant of Wonham
water-mill.³ But the revenues were never large and it
was the least wealthy of Surrey religious houses. Henry
VIII's commissioners in 1535 returned the net annual
revenue at £68.16.7.⁴

The history of so small a house is, as might be expected,
comparatively uneventful. In 1348 news reached the bishop
of abuses (*comperta*) at the Priory, which had become greatly
decayed owing to lax discipline. He directed his chancellor,
John de Usk, with John de Wolvelye, to hold a visitation of
the house on the next lawday after the translation of St.
Swithin and to correct the abuses, but the result is not
recorded.⁵

In 1374 during a vacancy in the office of prior through
the death of prior Kente, the bishop, who was the famous
William of Wykeham, directed the parishioners under
threat of excommunication to attend mass at the parish
church on Sundays and festivals. It was reported that for
some time past certain of the townspeople had been in the
habit of frequenting early mass at the Priory church and
then making off to spend the day at taverns and drinking
booths, and in other disreputable ways to the grave peril of
their souls, the prejudice of the vicar and the scandal of
many. The vicar had evidently complained to the bishop
of this defection on the part of his flock, who to save their
time and legs had transferred their attendance to the
church handiest to their doors. The sub-prior and convent

were enjoined to see that the parishioners did not in future attend their church for mass and other offices.[6]

The number of canons in residence was never considerable and often fell below six. In 1397, for example, there were five ; in 1530, when John Lymden the last prior of the house was elected, four ; and in 1499 the number had sunk to one. At the date of the Dissolution the number amounted to four, including the prior.[7] The Priory was dissolved 26th July, 1536, Lymden receiving an annual pension of £10 for life,[8] which was still being paid in 1553. He probably married and had a family ; the name which is not met with before his time occurs frequently in the Parish Registers for more than a century afterwards.

At a court of Reigate Manor held on 29th July, 1532, Thomas Owan was stated to have cut down several oak trees in the lord's wood called " le old parke " adjoining the Priory, but he alleged that he had done so by order of the prior and convent. Richard Doughty, one of the canons, denied this and said that Owan had cut the trees wilfully and in spite of the fact that the prior and convent had often reproved him and sent him away. Order was given that he be brought to answer to the lords for his trespass.

In 1535 the prior and convent borrowed £16 7s. 4d. from Thomas Stydolf, one of their tenants, and put their seal to a deed securing payment of the loan out of some of their rents. Transactions of this kind with the end fast approaching invariably aroused suspicion, for experience showed them to be often merely a ruse to secure part of the spoils for the inmates against the threatened dissolution. In 1546 Lymden, when called on to justify the deed, explained that it was delivered to Stydolf and his son more than eighteen months before the suppression and that the money was spent " about the suits of the house."[9]

The list of priors given in the *Victoria County History* can be supplemented with the names of Chandler, Michell and Robson. Twice in 1499 there was a vacancy and on each occasion John Pocatt, then the sole canon, renounced his right to elect. On 13th July bishop Langton appointed Robert Michell, late prior of Tandridge, to succeed John

Chandler, who had resigned.   Michell shortly after became
prior of St. Mary Overy, Southwark, and on 23rd November
the bishop appointed in his place John Robson, late sub-
prior of that house.   John Lymden, a canon from St. Mary
Overy, was elected 28th November, 1530, by Dr. J. Incent,
Wolsey's vicar-general, to whom the canons had remitted
their choice.   Michell and Robson were also for a short
space vicars of Reigate, though Michell became vicar after
his election to Southwark.   The connection between Priory
and church grew stronger as the end approached, the last
two priors being also the last two vicars appointed before
the Reformation.   Lymden was appointed to the living in
1532 in succession to William Major, whom he also
succeeded in the office of prior.[20]

The Priory was subject to the Bishop's jurisdiction and
the election of a prior required his confirmation.   The
procedure on an election was highly complicated and expensive, and was rendered void by failure to observe any
of the requisite formalities, for which reasons the canons
frequently took no step to fill a vacancy or else ceded their
right to the bishop.   Of twenty priors from the thirteenth
to the sixteenth centuries only one was validly elected by
the canons.   In every other case the bishop had to intervene
because of default or irregularity and appoint a new head
direct, though his choice usually fell on the candidate
favoured by the inmates.[11]

The Priory with its manor and other possessions was
granted in 1541 by the king to lord William Howard and
his wife and the heirs of their bodies in exchange for the
rectory of Tottenham, at the yearly rent of £7 4s. 9d.
The steward of the manor for part of the brief interval of
royal ownership had been lord Edmund Howard, lord
William's half-brother, and father of the unhappy girl who
later in 1541 became the fifth wife of Henry VIII.
Catherine's attainder brought temporary disgrace on her
kinsfolk and for a short time the estate reverted to the
Crown, but was restored to lord William in 1544.[12]   On
the death of his son, the Lord Admiral and earl of Nottingham, in 1624, the estate passed to the latter's widow for
her life and the Priory became her home.   In the Survey

of the previous year the Priory with the park adjoining is
stated to contain just over 200 acres, and to be " well
stored with tymber trees and replenished with deere havinge
allso in the same a faire pond well stored with fishe and a
small breede of herons " ; and the park is one of those
mentioned in a list of every park in Surrey " keeping deare,
that contains a mile in compass or more," prepared in the
time of queen Elizabeth.   In the year 1625 the countess
married Sir William Monson, who was shortly raised to the
Irish peerage as viscount Monson of Castlemaine.   In his
youth he had served as her page and later became a hanger-
on at court.   Their marriage at the parish church was an
important event in local society.. The next day the newly
wedded pair showed themselves to the townsfolk by riding
through the market and followed this up with a round of
visits at which the countess introduced her young husband
to her neighbours.[13]   Monson came of an old Lincolnshire
family and was a son of Sir William Monson, the admiral,
who lived at Kinnersley in Horley.   He was a shifty,
unscrupulous man of uncertain temper and dissolute habits
and was constantly in debt.   In right of his wife he became
entitled while she lived to the Priory and to the Howard
moiety of Reigate manor, and he later acquired the other
moiety.   He upset the tenants by attempting to enforce the
old privilege of free warren or the right to hunt game and
rabbits throughout the manor, a claim which was disputed
by the tenants and involved him in litigation.[14]   His un-
popularity received striking proof in 1629 when a jury
which had been empanelled to determine various questions
touching the lord's interest in the manor showed their
resentment by feigning ignorance of the matters submitted
to them which must have been well within their knowledge.
On the death of his wife in 1639, Elizabeth, countess of
Peterborough, succeeded to the Priory Manor as granddaughter of the Lord Admiral and next heir.   She was a
lady famed for her beauty, and like her husband, who died
in 1644, espoused the Parliamentary cause in the Civil War.
Their sons, Henry, the second earl of Peterborough, and
John, who was subsequently created baron Mordaunt of
Reigate and a viscount by Charles II, threw in their lot

with the king.   In the early days of the war Henry had
fought for the Parliament but deserted to the king in 1643,
a step which so incensed his mother that she attempted to
defeat his reversionary interset in the manor in favour of
her younger son, John, who seems to have retained her
affection in spite of their political differences.   But this
family rift was not her only trouble.   She had to pay heavily
for John's delinquency, and owing to Monson's refusal to
give up possession of the Priory she was forced into a long
and bitter struggle to assert her title.   In a series of lawsuits
he resorted to all the arts of obstruction, and at times even
to force, to resist her rights and it was not until the
Restoration that they were fully established.[15]   She lived
till 1671 and was succeeded by her second son, viscount
Mordaunt, who had obtained a grant from the Crown of
the reversion on her death.   He died in 1677, and in 1681
his eldest son and heir, the eccentric Charles Mordaunt,
subsequently created earl of Monmouth and earl of Peterborough, sold the estate to John Parsons, a wealthy London
brewer and afterwards Lord Mayor, who was knighted in
1687 and represented the borough in Parliament for many
years.   Sir John died in 1717 and was followed by his son,
Humphrey, who earned the rare distinction of being twice
Lord Mayor of London, and died in 1741 during his second
year of office.[16]   In 1766 the estate was put up by auction
under a private Act of Parliament and purchased by Mr.
Richard Ireland of Dorking, whom Ridgeway unkindly
dubbed " a miserable old cheesemonger."   Ireland died in
1780, having devised it by his will to his niece, Mrs. Jones.
Her son's trustees sold it to George Mowbray from whom it
was purchased in 1808 by lord Somers.   From that date
the estate devolved with Reigate manor until 1921 when it
was sold by Mr. Somers Somerset to countess Beatty, wife
of admiral of the Fleet, earl Beatty, and on her death it
passed by her will to her younger son, Mr. Peter Beatty,
who in 1942 sold it to the Mutual Property Life and General
Insurance Company Ltd.   In 1945 the Borough Council
decided to acquire the estate for a community centre and
playing fields.

The existing house occupies the site and incorporates some

fragments of the canons' buildings. The Howards converted
them into a Tudor mansion and demolished the church, but
the house reached its present form in Ireland's time and
since then has received no major alterations. He pulled
down much of the old structure and skilfully "Georgianised"
the appearance of the parts remaining. His work was
completed by 1771 when John Wesley visited him and
recorded in his journal the sweeping changes that had
recently been made. Nevertheless the south façade apart
from its Georgian dress still broadly resembles that shown in
a print dated 1577, though the wings have been reduced to
shallow projections. The chief ornament of the interior is
the magnificient carved oak mantelpiece which came from
Blechingley Place and is said to have been designed by
Holbein.[17]

II. THE CHAPELS AND MARKET HOUSES

LITTLE is known of the history of the three medieval chapels
of St. Thomas the Martyr, the Holy Cross, and St. Lawrence.
The first was certainly a chantry chapel and the two others
bore most probably the same character. The existence of
three such chapels occupying separate buildings in one
small town is exceptional and cannot be paralleled elsewhere
in Surrey. They had apparently all ceased to exist as
religious foundations before 1547, when the general suppression of chantries began.

In 1330 the bishop, John de Stratford, received information that on four days in the week the daily chantry in the
chapel of St. Thomas had been recently withdrawn, and he
ordered the archdeacon's official to hold an enquiry.[18] The
building stood in the present Market Place and was taken
over for public use at the Reformation when it became
known as " the New Market House," to distinguish it from
the old Market House, though it was also referred to simply
as " the Chapel." The chapel underwent some adaptation
and was fitted with an upper floor divided into compart-
ments.[19] It disappeared when the existing building was
put up.

Ridgeway, with whom dates were not a strong point,

gives two different years for the erection of the New Market House and two for the demolition of the Chapel. " The Market House," he writes, " was erected about the year 1720 or 1723 at the time that Arthur Onslow was speaker of the House of Commons. He petitioned to the Lord of the Manor to have it built on the place it now stands, to oblige a Mr. Glover who had a large shop just by it." Onslow did not become speaker until January 1728 so that if this story about him is true the erection could not have taken place before that year. As regards the chapel, he writes, " Near where the Market House now stands was a Chapel dedicated to Thomas à Becket, which was taken down about the year 1725," or, as two other versions of his History have it, " which was pulled down about the year 1728." The " Mr. Glover " referred to was William Glover, a mercer, whose shop lay on the north side of High Street just west of Mr. La Trobe's premises. He named one of his sons Arthur Onslow, a fact which seems to give colour to Ridgeway's story, and as will be seen shortly had a large hand in the erection of the Clock House. But the date invariably accepted by modern writers is that given by Bray, who states on information supplied by Ambrose Glover that " About the year 1708 the Chapel was taken down and the present building erected but upon the site of the Chapel. The Clock House was built for a prison for the Felons and others who are brought to the Easter Sessions held at *Reigate* ; and in 1801, when an enlargement of this building was made for the better accommodation of the prisoners, the workmen came to the foundation of the Chapel."[20] With this must be compared a previous passage stating that the " *Market House* was erected by Sir *Joseph Jekyll* while in possession of the Manor. Near to this site is also a smaller building serving for a Clock House, and erected on or near the site of a *Chapel* which formerly stood there, and was dedicated to *Thomas Becket*."[21]

Evidence is now available from more than one source to show that the year 1708 is not even approximately correct. The chapel was certainly standing as late as 1725, for in that year the vicar, Mr. Bird, had to make a return to his bishop and in answer to one of the questions he stated,

" There are three chapels, one is the Sessions House, one a
Barn, one a Private House," the first of these being of
course the chapel under discussion.[22]   Again, Sir Joseph
Jekyll did not come into possession of the manor until 1717,
and the deed of partition in that year included among the
property allotted to him and his wife " all those two Market
Houses and the severall rooms over the same situate in the
Borrough of Ryegate," showing that not only the chapel
but also the old Market House was still in existence. Further
evidence as to the date can be adduced from a contemporary
source.   The following is an extract from a newspaper
cutting pasted into a copy of Aubrey's *History of Surrey*
which belonged to Dr. Rawlinson, the editor of that work,
and is now in the Bodleian Library : "We have an account
from Ryegate that his Honour the Master of the Rolls
(Sir Joseph Jekyll) has caused the old Market and Sessions
House to be pulled down as well as the New, and in the
Place of the latter has caused to be erected a Market and
Sessions house, upon ten Arches, which was partly done by
voluntary Contribution, as also a Clock house which was
done by the direction of Mr. Glover, who illuminated the
Clock-house upon his Majesty's Birthday."   Unfortunately,
neither the date nor name of the paper is given but it is
possible from other evidence to fix the event within a
margin of six years.   The cutting proceeds to refer to
" Mr. Thurland of Ryegate " and the belief that he and
his friends contemplated the improvement of the Crawley
causeway and Talworth Lane.   Edward Thurland, the
" Mr. Thurland " in question, who was a grandson of the
judge and lived at Great Doods, died 18th December, 1731,
so that the disappearance of the chapel and erection of the
new Market House must have occurred before that date and
not earlier than the year 1725.   A careful review of all the
evidence leads to the conclusion that 1728 or 1729 is the
correct year and that consequently Bray's " about the year
1708 " predated the event by some twenty years, possibly
as the result of a clerical error.

The extract quoted adds to our knowledge the interesting
fact that the old Market House was pulled down at the
same time.   This building is believed to have stood in the

old Market Place which occupied a position on the north side of the Middle Row at the spot where Slipshoe Street converges on Upper West Street.* The medieval undercroft which lies beneath Messrs. Stannard's Garage in West Street is confidently assumed by Bray and by later writers who have followed him to have been a substructure of the old Market House. After describing the position of the old Market Place he adds, " there is a Vault or Crypt arched and ribbed with freestone, and there is great reason to suppose that the old Market House was erected over it."[20, 23] He fails to give his " great reason," or rather that of Ambrose Glover from whom he got this information, and there are in fact good reasons to the contrary. In the first place the undercroft appears to have been not within the site of the old Market Place but to the south of it, and on the site of premises which were known in Sir Joseph Jekyll's day as " Luck's Castle." In 1720 Sir Joseph purchased from Nehemiah Eastman of Reigate, salter, a burgage property by the description of " a messuage or tenement yard and gateroom situate in a place called the Middle Row and Abutting on the King's Highway leading from the Market-house towards Dorking on the North part." It appears from earlier deeds of this property that the messuage had been divided into three tenements and had acquired the name " Luck's Castle " after Thomas Luck, one of its former occupiers. The building came to grief in 1734 when it was destroyed by a high wind, but the site is shown on Bryant's plan of 1785 and appears to have included the undercroft. " The Market House " mentioned in the deed of 1720 was probably the new Market House or chapel and in any case did not form any part of the purchase. Secondly, it is obvious that the purchase could not have included the old Market House because at that date it already belonged to Sir Joseph, having passed to him with the manor under the partition of 1717. Finally, Luck's Castle was destroyed in 1734, not in 1728, and by a gale of wind, not by human agency.

The earlier prison stood in a yard behind Glover's shop approached from the Crown Steps, which may explain why

* See Plan of Reigate Town.

that tradesman took so active an interest in the erection of the Clock House. This building was set up on the east side of the Market Place at a distance of some 80 feet, according to Bryant's map, from the nearest part of the new Market House and about the same distance from Glover's shop.* It probably stood just within or just without the eastern end of the chapel site having regard to Bray's statement that the enlargement in 1801 impinged on the foundations of that building. Unless therefore the chapel was of altogether unprecedented length it is impossible to credit his other statement that the new Market House was erected on the site of the chapel, which is moreover at variance with the evidence that came to light in 1873 when in course of laying the sewer the foundations of the chapel were discovered beneath the paving to the *east* of the Town Hall, as the new Market House was then called.[24]

In 1922 the building, which since the erection of the new municipal buildings in 1901 in Castlefield Road has been known as the Old Town Hall, was purchased and presented to the Borough Council by the late Mr. Randal Vogan of Reigate.

A new prison was built in 1811 in Mint Yard, which thenceforth took the name of Cage Yard. The pyramidal roof and cupola of the Clock House, which appears to have been removed about this time, were set up on the Town Hall to add a striking if not imposing feature to that building. The corner chimneys were added in 1853 when extensive alterations to the Hall were carried out by lord Somers at a cost of over £750.

The chapel of the Holy Cross is assumed by Manning and Bray to have been " an appurtenance of the Priory " on account of its name, but this is not convincing and their case is not strengthened by citing a grant of part of Reigate Hill to the Hospital of the Holy Cross, which clearly was not the chapel as they suppose but the Priory under its early name. The building stood at the west end of High Street in the island block known as East Row or Island, and not on the north side of that street next the Red Cross as marked on the Ordnance Survey sheets. In the seventeenth and eighteenth centuries it was used as a barn, called " the

* See Plan of Reigate Town.

Stone Barn," and housed one of the numerous oatmills for which the town was then noted.[25]   It was pulled down shortly before 1786 and a house erected on the site.

The third chapel, that of St. Lawrence, of which alone any part of the superstructure now exists, stood on the east side of Bell Street a little below the Market Place.   Of its ecclesiastical history nothing is recorded save the fact that it was used during the last quarter of the fifteenth century as an occasional court by the archdeacon of Surrey for the exercise of his probate jurisdiction.[26]   At this period it had already lost its sacred character if, as seems probable, it was " the Stone howse " in which the duke of Norfolk stabled four of his horses on his visit to Reigate in September 1483.[27]   It was certainly known by that name in post-Reformation times when it was converted into a shop and private dwelling.   The thick outer walls form the shell of the building now occupied by Messrs. Holdsworth and Knight.   Internally the remains of a stone corbel and roof trusses betray its original character and point to a date early in the fourteenth century.

NOTES TO CHAPTER V

[1] II *VCH* 105-6.   Tandridge Priory, another small Surrey house of the same order, also started as a hospital.   Manning & Bray engrave an imperfect impression of a fourteenth century circular seal of $1\frac{5}{8}$th inches diameter which shows Christ on the cross between St. Mary & St. John within a sexfoil ornamented with crosses.   In the base is the Warenne shield of arms and in the field are branches fructed and slipped.   Round the border in Lombardic characters is the legend : S. COMMUNE PRIORATUS SANCTE CRUCIS DE REYGATE.   (I *M. & B.* opp. p. 273.)

[2] *Trans. Roy. Hist. Soc.* (3 Series) VII, 204-5.

[3] For a list of the temporalities see I *M. & B.* 294-301.   For Southwick manor see *Sussex N. & Q.* V. 176.   The manor of Linkfield in Reigate was held of the Priory and paid an annual rent of £1.

[4] *Valor Ecclesiasticus* (Rec. Com.) II. 66-7.

[5] Winton Epis. Reg. Edington II, fo. 16.

[6] II *VCH* 106 ; *Wykeham's Reg.* II 220-2 (Hampshire Rec. Soc.).

[7] *Registrum Thome Wolsey*, Vol. 32 *Cant. & York Soc.*   XI n. 4 and XVIII. For a list of the canons in 1530 see 47 *SAC* 24.

[8] II *VCH* 107.   In 1509 the priors of Reigate and Tandridge were each fined 13s. 4d. for failing to attend the chapter of their order at Leicester. This and the sums mentioned in the text must be multiplied by at least thirty to arrive at present-day values, so the prior was not ungenerously provided for.

[9] IX *L. & P.* 268.

[10] II *VCH* 107 & n. 7 (above).   The *VCH* (*Ibid.*) follows Cox's mistake of including Adam in their list of priors and repeating his story about two

London citizens, benefactors of the order, who entered the house under Adam. (See reference in n. 2 above.)

[11] *Reg. Thome Wolsey op. cit.* XVIII and XIX.

[12] III *VCH* 236.

[13] 4th *Rep. Hist. MSS. Com.* 306. The marriage is not entered in the parish Register.

[14] *S. P. Dom.* (1637) 559. Lord Monson is supposed to have cut down the trees on Earlswood, Petridge Wood and Wray Commons and converted them into rabbit warrens. (I *M. & B.* 287.)

[15] I *M. & B.* 302–3 ; *S. P. Dom.* (1645–7) 571–2 ; *5th Rep. Hist. MSS. Com.* 13, & 6th *Idem* 8.

[16] Both Sir John and his son were well-known racehorse owners and breeders. Sir John purchased the Toulouse Barb, named after the Count of Toulouse, a natural son of Louis XIV, and from him bred the Reigate Mare which became the dam of Cinnamon. This barb was also the sire of Mr. Panton's famous mare Molly. (44 *SAC* 5 ; Weatherby's *General Stud Book* i 391). Humphrey Parsons entertained at the Priory on a lavish scale. " On Tuesday last," we read in the *London Journal* of Saturday, July 13th, 1728, " Mr. Alderman Parsons made a sumptuous Entertainment at his house at Ryegate in Surrey, for the Company of *Merchants of the Staple of England*, of which he was lately chosen Mayor."

[17] His design is said to be in the British Museum but I have failed to trace it there. For the provenance of the mantelpiece see Lambert, I *Blechingley* 275.

[18] Reg. Stratford fo. 50. A chantry was a service performed at regular intervals and supported by an endowment at which masses were chanted for the souls of the founder and his family.

[19] Cf. *S. P. Try. Books* (1685–9) 1581, " Erasmus Pledge for a chamber over the new market house £1 10s. 0d."

[20] I *M. & B.* 289.

[21] I *M. & B.* 288.

[22] 39 *SAC* 98.

[23] For a detailed account of the undercroft see the article by Canon Livett, *A Medieval Undercroft at Reigate* 34 *SAC* 32. He adopts Bray's assumption that the old Market House stood above it, but was unaware of the further evidence now available.

[24] Hooper, *Guide* 73. The Plan of Reigate Town in 1786 should be consulted for the position of the chapels and other buildings mentioned in this chapter.

[25] IV *Aubrey*, 191–2 ; I *M. & B.* 288. M. & B.'s statement that it stood " in the middle of the North side of the principal Street, near the West end," is confusing owing to the inconsistent use of the adjectives " middle " and " north " in the same context. If it stood on the north side of the street to the west, it could not have been in the middle either of the street or its north side ; and if in the middle of the street then to speak of the north side is meaningless.

[26] 17 *SRS* Nos. 244 and 258.

[27] *Howard Household Books* (Roxburghe Club) 461.

CHAPTER VI

THE STORY OF THE HIGHWAYS

THE local system of ancient highways shows the general north-south tendency, in conformity with the usual lay-out of the parishes, which is so marked a feature of old Surrey highways, particularly in the south of the county. These, generally speaking, still follow the lines they have followed from time immemorial in spite of improvements and alterations by modern road engineers. To this longitudinal series the main east-west road along the Holmesdale Valley which traverses Reigate in common with other parishes under the North Downs, served as a grid or connecting link. This road is the medieval counterpart of the prehistoric track, known to modern generations as the Pilgrims' Way, which followed a more or less parallel course along the Downs some two miles to the north but lost much of its importance with the growth of settlements in the valley. In the nineteenth century the Pilgrims' Way acquired fictitious eminence as the great medieval highway for Pilgrims journeying to and from Canterbury but in the light of recent research this claim must be rejected as unhistorical.[1] Reigate certainly owes more to the valley road than to the Way and its fancied pilgrims, for it was on this road that the town had its beginning and the section along which it extended still forms the main limb.

The north-south route by London Lane—now London Road—and Bell Street was little used except by local traffic on account of its bad plight and extreme narrowness at many parts, and did not assume importance as a through communication until the later part of the eighteenth century. Till then the road system centred on the old Market Place at the junction of Nutley Lane, Upper West Street and Slipshoe Street. The two last gave direct access to London

Lane and High Street, and passages from the Market Place communicated with West Street on the south.[2]

Highway repairs were a parochial obligation, but in Reigate this duty was split up between the six petty boroughs which composed the parish, each being liable for the highways within its own borders. An official known as the surveyor of highways, usually a local farmer or tradesman, was appointed annually for each borough to supervise the roads but, as he had to serve willy-nilly and without pay and lacked any training for the job, little was done to remedy their sorry plight except under compulsion. Those boroughs which failed in their duty could be presented and fined at the Court Leet of the Manor, the Court of Quarter Sessions or the Assizes, and the offending surveyors were liable to be similarly dealt with. Proceedings of this nature were extremely common and had often to be taken repeatedly before a highway received the necessary attention. Thus in 1620 the inhabitants of Santon Borough were presented at the Court Leet on account of Park Lane being " in decaye " and were ordered to amend the same under penalty of 20s. They were presented again in 1622 for permitting Wray Lane to be ruinous and in decay and ordered to repair this within a given time under a penalty of 10s. The following year they were again presented and ordered to forfeit the 10s. for their default and were given further time to repair under a penalty of double the previous sum. This had the desired effect and at the Court Leet held in 1624 the repairs were reported to have been done.

In 1574 the Court ordered that sufficient timber should be allowed for erecting a gate at the upper end of Wray Common in White Lane (now Wray Lane) with the object, no doubt, of preventing cattle straying from the common.

Footpaths adjoining a road were part of the highway and like it repairable by the inhabitants as a whole, though in the town this liability attached to the frontagers. In 1622 for instance George Rodes, Henry Worley and others were presented for permitting the footway before their tenements in Reigate Borough to be ruinous and ordered to repair it within a month under a penalty of 3s. 4d.

A highway included a bridge along its course. In 1611

the inhabitants of Santon Borough, who evidently found their liability a grievous burden, were ordered to repair the Vicarage Bridge upon pain of forfeiting 20s., and were again in trouble in 1628 when they were ordered to repair Flanchford Bridge within two months under a penalty of 40s. Vicarage Bridge spanned the stream crossing Church Street by the Vicarage.

Liability to repair fell in certain cases on the owner of the adjoining land. Thus at the Easter Quarter Sessions for 1661 held at Reigate, Jasper Lisney was presented for neglecting to repair " the common highway leading from Kingston Hill to the foot of Reigate Hill commonly called Crabtree Bottom which he ought to repair by reason of the tenure of his lands there."³ Kingston Hill was the contemporary name for Colley Hill and the way in question is now represented by the track running eastward along the foot of Reigate Hill to the main road near the Yew Tree Inn.

Obstructions and encroachments were a fertile source of trouble to the authorities and ranged from overhanging boughs and deposits of refuse or timber to enclosing or stopping up a path or road. In 1630 Edward Ryder, gentleman, was presented at the Court Leet for stopping up the lane in Crabtree Bottom already mentioned. Old inhabitants were called to prove that this had been a public way time out of mind. John Elven, aged 94, deposed "that for all the time of his memory and knowledge which hath been for this three-score and ten years and upwards he had known the said way to be a common highway to Kingston Hill for carts and carriages without denial of any kind . . . and when the field was not sown then the way lay below the Crab tree and when it was sown then above the Crab tree between the field and the hill." On this evidence Mr. Ryder was ordered to " lay open " the way within 14 days under a penalty of £10.

The activity of the Manor courts in enforcing road repairs sharply declined in the second quarter of the seventeenth century when their powers in this and other matters of a criminal nature were being increasingly absorbed by the justices of the peace. Presentation or indictment at Quarter Sessions became the normal procedure and of this several local examples occurred during the period 1659–1666 for which the records of Surrey Quarter Sessions have now been published. One such case has already been quoted. Another local highway in a sorry state at this period was Nutley, or as it was then called Nettley, Lane. In 1661 the inhabitants of Colley Borough were presented on the count that this lane " was and still is out of repair muddy and dangerous and in such decay . . . that the lieges of our lord the King are unable to pass and ride on the said highway without great peril to the grave damage and annoyance of the said lieges." The grand jury returned a true bill, but no effective measures appear to have been taken for at the Easter Quarter Sessions 1662, held at Reigate, the inhabitants were again presented on the same charge which was repeated in the following year and again in 1664, when they acknowledged their default and were fined 2s. 6d., which seems a trifling penalty for so persistent an offence.[4]

The state of the roads before the later turnpike era and its isolating effect on the town is vividly described by Ridgeway in one of his brightest passages which, though often quoted, deserves repeating. " About 56 years back," he says, writing in 1816, " Reigate had not one good road to it and very few people came to it. The farmers used to bring their corn to market mostly on the backs of horses and as to coaches I do not think I have seen ten pass through the Town during the course of the year except Alderman Parsons' who had six of the strongest horses that could be purchased to draw him from London to Reigate." Reigate must also have frequently witnessed the spectacle described by Salmon in his account of the adjoining parish of Leigh. " The men and the horses who draw their corn to market, of which seven, eight or nine are in a team, with a weight for which four were sufficient in other places, look as if they had wallowed in the mud." In 1755 Alexander Broughton, a Reigate attorney, referring to the road traversed by the alderman and its continuation south of the town, told a House of Commons Committee that it was " in many parts so narrow that two carriages cannot pass nor a horse-

man pass a carriage . . . And that in the parish of Horley
. . . . the parishioners have performed their statute work
and raised a levy of sixpense in the pound which has been
insufficient to repair the said roads."[5]

A state of things which is accepted as natural and
inevitable in one age becomes intolerable in the next, a
truth forcibly illustrated by the history of the King's
highway. The growth of wheeled vehicles during the
seventeenth century and especially towards its close
emphasised the crying need for road reform and eventually
roused the attention of Parliament. The device hit upon
was the imposition of tolls, on the theory that those using
the roads should pay the cost of their upkeep. This expedient
made rapid headway and as a result the statute book of
the eighteenth century is thronged with hundreds of special
turnpike acts applying to roads in all parts of the country.[6]
The first turnpike road in Surrey was that authorised in
1697 between Reigate and Crawley to span the intervening
belt of Weald clay, under an Act entitled " An Act for
repairing the highway between Reigate in the County of
Surrey and Crawley in the County of Sussex."[7] This
recited that " the lanes leading from Woodhatch Borough
to Sidlow Mill and Salmons Cross . . . and the Lanes
called Horsehill and Bonehurst . . . and Petteridge being
the road from Stenning, Horsham and other Parts of great
Trade and Commerce in the County of Sussex to London,
are very Ruinous, and almost Impassable for above Three
Miles in Reigate, insomuch that it is become dangerous to
all Persons that pass those Ways." The justices were to
appoint surveyors to carry out the repairs, and receivers of
the tolls which were to be paid according to a scale fixed
by the Act " for all such Horses, Carts, Coaches, Waggons,
Droves and Gangs of Cattel as in time to come shall pass,
be led or droven in or through the said Way." Power was
given to erect turnpikes or gates at which the tolls could be
collected. These wide powers were never implemented and
the only work carried out was the construction of a bridleway
or causeway for horses with posts driven in between the
road and the causeway to prevent the use of the latter by
wheeled traffic.[8] Further Acts were passed in 1724 and 1737

for repairing the roads mentioned in the previous measure, but nothing was done to improve the approach on the northern or London side until past the middle of the century. Travellers leaving the town in that direction usually proceeded by London Lane and up Reigate Hill by the road which was the forerunner of the present main road (see Plate V), or as an alternative they could climb the hill by the track behind " The Rock." Another route led off by Nutley Lane and Colley Hill, or Kingston Hill as it was formerly called, across Walton Heath. Each of the two last routes involved a steep climb by a narrow deep-sunk track up the face of the Hill, which must have been impassable for wheeled traffic though, according to Glover, they were used as ways to Croydon and Kingston until the road up Reigate Hill was turnpiked.[9]

Traffic between London and the country south of Reigate avoided the town during the greater part of the year and struck eastward in order to follow the main road through Croydon and Godstone. Things remained in this condition until 1755, when powers were conferred on a body of trustees by the Act " for repairing and widening the road from Sutton in the County of Surrey through the Borough of Reigate by Sidlow Mill to Povey Cross."[10] The Act followed the usual form of turnpike legislation then current. It was limited to 21 years but was renewed from time to time for further periods of the same length. The trustees appointed included several of the county gentry and local people of position, including Arthur Onslow, speaker of the House of Commons, Charles Cocks and Charles Yorke, the two members for the Borough, and the Rev. Wm. Stead, the vicar. They were authorised to erect turnpikes and levy tolls on traffic using the roads under their charge. They met for the first time at the Swan Inn, Reigate, on 15th April, 1755, and this became their usual meeting place. They decided to obtain an estimate of the expense of amending the road from Sutton to Reigate as well as that from Reigate to Povey Cross, and that an estimate be made " of the different ways of rising the Hill from Reigate." This was the chief problem they had to face and involved making a new road at a higher level on the upper slope of

Reigate Hill.[11] Later the same year they decided to hire teams for ploughing up the roadways at a rate not exceeding 10s. per day for each team consisting of five horses at least. Modern roadmaking is not associated with the plough, but in the eighteenth century when metalled roads were the exception the road plough was an implement in common use.

The vicar displayed his zeal in the work at Reigate Hill as well as some ingenuity by persuading his colleagues to have a huge battering ram set up with the object of beating down the chalk on the new line of road. Ridgeway, who describes this ponderous contrivance, says that the idea was suggested to the reverend gentleman by the battering rams used against the walls of Jerusalem. The ram when set up took between twenty and thirty men to work it, but after a day's trial two men on the following day proved able to shift more chalk " than all the men and ram had done the day before." It was adds Ridgeway naively, " quite a fair, most of the inhabitants was at it. . . . They gave it the name of Ram Stead Hill and Ramfair."

The new section was finished in the Spring of 1756, when it was ordered " that the old road leading through London Lane through Crabtree Bottom up Kingston Hill to the gate on Walton Heath and the road by Croydon Hill be immediately stopped up, and that notices be given to the several Proprietors of lands adjoining such roads of the Trustees' intention to sell the same to the best bidder." Offers of a few shillings were received but not, apparently, accepted. Happily these old tracks, which have already been described, still remain to us as interesting memorials of our ancient highways.*

Part of the Pilgrims' Way, however, was diverted as an indirect result of the new turnpike. The owner of Gatton Park, foreseeing that the turnpike road would increase the traffic between Reigate Hill and Gatton and Merstham, obtained an order of Quarter Sessions in 1756 empowering him to stop up the section of the Way through the park between the present Upper Lodge and Tower Lodge and replace it by a new road to be made along but outside the north-west boundary of his estate.[12]

* See page 86 above.

One of the chief boons which the road brought in its train was the provision of improved postal facilities. In 1775 a daily post (Sunday excepted) was established between London and many provincial towns, including Reigate, served by turnpike roads.

Ridgeway states that in 1745 the road was measured from London to Reigate, but this most probably refers to its measurement under the Act of 1755. In Owen's *New Book of Roads*, 1782, the distance is given as $21\frac{1}{2}$ miles.

Several other important improvements to the Reigate portion of the road were carried out at different times during the existence of the Trust. In 1784 the Surveyor was ordered to expend £100 in paving the road through the Old Borough of Reigate. An appeal was made to Mr. John Yorke and Sir Chas. Cocks, the members for the borough, " praying their assistance as upwards of £100 or more than the above ordered will be wanted to complete the said paving." The honorable members responded generously and offered to subscribe £50 each. In 1806 it was decided to widen London Road to " the width of 40 feet or thereabouts in the clear between hedge to hedge," and to ask lord Somers to remove the two burgage tenements in High Street. These were the remains of the block of buildings known as East Island that stood in the middle of the street and formed a serious obstruction at the western entrance of the town. The buildings were demolished and the site of the Island was thrown into the street and rented of lord Somers till 1882, when it was purchased by the Borough Council.

In 1815 the little stream that flowed across the bottom of Bell Street was culverted. The road over Cockshot Hill which a few years previously had been lowered ten feet was in 1818 lowered another six feet, and again in 1830 a further three feet.[13]

Tunnel Road was made by lord Somers through the Castle rock in 1823 and ranked at the time as a wonderful engineering feat. By providing a direct link between the Market Place and London Lane it eliminated the detour along High Street and shortened the distance by a quarter of a mile. The work provoked a characteristic outburst from William Cobbett, who condemned it as wasteful and undertaken with the sole aim of attracting more of the coaching traffic. His invective was inspired by hatred of " the Jews and jobbers," but he showed how this traffic was increasing and how the turnpike roads had made it possible for a business man to live at Brighton and get up to London and back in the day.[14] The road was completed in the summer of 1824. Besides cutting through the rock it necessitated the demolition of two or three shops north of the Market Place and the filling in of a section of the castle moat. A gate was erected on the Town side of the tunnel where tolls were levied at the rate of 6d. for a coach and four, 3d. for a coach and pair or post chaise, 1½d. for a single horse chaise and ½d. for a horse. Foot passengers as usual passed through free.

During the progress of this work a somewhat similar diversion was commenced at the top of Reigate Hill. The turnpike road which there made an elbow bend past the Upper Lodge of Gatton Park was shortened by means of a deep cutting through the chalk, and the road northwards to Gatton Inn—now The Crossways—was straightened. The surveyor responsible for this and the Tunnel Road improvement was William Constable, who served the Trust most efficiently for twenty-two years until his retirement in 1837. The cutting was spanned by an iron suspension bridge erected in 1825 from his design. This lasted until 1910 when it became unsafe and was replaced by the present concrete bridge at the charge of the County Council. The erection of the suspension bridge prompted the following epigram said to have been written by Thomas " Clio " Rickman, the reformer :

" Behold the strength the power and will
    Which, on this spot, where Freedom reigns
    Have pierced the bowels of the hill
    And hung a Noble Pier in Chains.

" Thus may each iron-hearted *lord*
    His country's enemy and bane,
    Receive from freemen his reward,
    Suspended by as strong a chain."[15]

A Bill for making a turnpike road from Purley through
Merstham to Reigate was promoted in 1796 but did not
become law until 1807 owing largely to the opposition of
the Reigate Trust, which was finally bought off by a payment
of £200 a year as compensation for loss of tolls.[16]   Its
hostility had been sharpened by the proposal to make a
branch road from Gatton Point to Povey Cross which
would have entirely avoided Reigate, and this part of the
scheme had to be dropped for the time being.   The new
road was opened in June, 1808.   It involved several miles of
fresh construction, the section from Merstham to Wray
Common being formed on land taken from Gatton Park.
The branch from Gatton Point was made under a later
Act passed in 1816.[17]   Owing to opposition from lord
Somers who objected to the road cutting through the middle
of his Hooley estate the course had to be diverted to form
the present Brighton Road at Redhill instead of following
the valley as intended by the promoters, thus necessitating
a change of alignment at a point near the present Reading
arch.   By avoiding Reigate it effected a considerable saving
and diverted much of the coaching traffic from the town,
but it was never a financial success, the revenue proving
insufficient to pay the interest on the money borrowed for
its construction.   The advent of the railway dealt it a
crippling blow.   In 1848 the tolls after paying the collector
and superintendent fell to £29 despite the fact that since
1842 the upkeep of the road had been left to the parishes
through which it passed.   The Purley and Reigate
road was likewise dogged by ever-increasing financial
embarrassment.[18]

Turnpike roads though a great improvement on the old
unformed parish roads often left much to be desired, as the
following complaint shows.   At a meeting of the trustees of
the Purley and Reigate road in 1829 Mr. Robert Waithman,
a City alderman, who lived at Wray Common, alleged that
several accidents had recently occurred in which one man
had been killed and the Brighton coach overturned.   He
spoke of the impression which prevailed that part of the
road was purposely neglected and said that currents of
water in many places ran along the middle.[19]

The main east-west road across the parish was never turnpiked except through Reigate town and remained under the control of the petty boroughs, each being liable to repair the portion within its area. This division of authority was, it need hardly be said, fatal to any improvement. In 1826 the parish was presented for failure to repair the section from the bridge over the stream at Hooley to the top of Redstone Hill. At a Vestry meeting called to organise the defence a suggestion that the boroughs should be abolished since repair of the road was the common concern of the whole parish was negatived, though it was agreed that the cost of defending the proceedings should be a common charge on the parish and not fall wholly on Linkfield and Hooley, the two boroughs responsible for this section. In the result Quarter Sessions ordered the parish to put the section into immediate repair.[20]

All local public highways except those turnpike roads which were not already repairable by the parish passed into the control of the newly formed Borough Council in 1865, when it adopted the Local Government Act of 1858. In 1864 the Council by agreement with the Reigate Trust took over the repair of the road between the Reigate Hill Toll Gate, which stood just below the Yew Tree Inn, and the top of Cockshot Hill. The roads generally appear to have been in a bad condition at this period and the state of things at Redhill roused strong protests, Station Road being singled out for special complaint.[21] This road had been constructed by the South Eastern Railway Company to afford access to their station at Redhill Junction, with an eastern extension up Redstone Hill to connect with the old main road above Redstone Hollow. When taken over by the Council in 1870 it became an integral part of the east-west route and superseded the awkward detour by way of Hooley Lane and the Hollow.

The Reigate Trust was the last of the London-Brighton Road Trusts to expire. The toll houses and gates on the Reigate-Sutton road were removed in October, 1881. With the removal of the turnpike gate at Salfords, between Redhill and Horley, on the last day of that month the Brighton road became free and open throughout its entire length.[22]

The custom of giving names to roads and streets was not formerly so widespread as it is today, when the exigences of local government and the Post Office have rendered it universal. Field names, on the other hand, which were once universal, have fallen very largely into disuse since the Ordnance Survey published its large-scale maps showing each field and its acreage. But even in towns some streets went unnamed till far into the nineteenth century. At Reigate, West Street and Slipshoe Street bear modern names, the latter having been so christened about 1860 as an outcome of the Pilgrims' Way legend that was then growing in popularity. Lesbourne Lane, Nutley Lane and Church Street all bear old names which were in use by the sixteenth century or earlier, though Bell Street in Elizabethan times was also known as Priory Lane. High Street, the name of which does not appear to have been commonly used before the eighteenth century, was known as the Crossways at its west end. Park Lane was formerly Park Pond Lane or Park Pond Head Lane in allusion to the Priory pond, and the short stretch from High Street to the Priory entrance was called Workhouse Lane while the workhouse for the old borough stood there. Similarly Hatchlands Road, which did not acquire that name till after 1863, was earlier known as Workhouse Lane from the workhouse for the Foreign at the spot later known as Shaws Corner, a name which immortalises one Simeon Shaw who a century ago kept a shop and smithy there.

Upper West Street in the eighteenth century bore the ironical name of Pudding Lane on account of its foul condition. This name was also applied to a lane which formed a short cut from Chart Lane to Reigate Road behind a house at the corner. It was closed by order of the justices in 1825.

London Road, Reigate, was earlier London Lane, so called probably not because of its direction but after a family of that name. Roger de London acquired the manor of Colley in the thirteenth century. He and his successors also held half a knight's fee in Reigate manor, which came to be known as London Lands and stretched from the lower end of the Lane for some distance along its west side.

Chart Lane is called after the Chart, the name of a customary virgate near its southern end, but this is a modern application of an old name to an ancient highway which before was without one.

The name of Wray Lane applied in the seventeenth century to the predecessor of the present Croydon Road from Wray Common to Church Street and was not confined as at present to its upper section. That section was also known as White Lane.

Blackborough Road, which is a modern extension eastwards of Lesbourne Road, preserves the name of the " parcell of barren pasture ground called Blackborough " described in the Survey of 1623 and lying near Shaw's Corner.

Ladbroke Road, Redhill, was constructed about 1860 by Felix Ladbroke through land on his Frenches estate. In the eighteenth century the manors of Linkfield and Gatton became united in ownership and belonged at one time to Robert Ladbroke, and Frenches manor which adjoined also passed into this family.

NOTES TO CHAPTER VI

[1] For the Pilgrims' Way and the theory of its pilgrim use see my article in 44 *SAC*, 47–84. The east-west road is marked A. 25 on the Parish Map.

[2] See Plan of Reigate Town. West Street and Slipshoe Street, though modern names, are used for the sake of clearness.

[3] 35 *SRS* 136. For a case of alleged obstruction of the footpath from Waterlands to Le Tyler in Reigate in 1353, see *Public Works in Medieval Law* II, 178–9.

[4] 35 *SRS* 106–7 ; 36 *SRS* 181, 300 ; 39 *SRS* 171. In 1695 the justices at Reigate Quarter Sessions allowed the inhabitants of Santon borough a rate of 2d. in the £ towards repair of their highways, 32 *SRS* 82.

[5] Salmon, *Antiquities of Surrey* (1736) 71. 27 *Commons Journal* 103. J. Taylor in *The Carrier's Cosmography* (1637) states that a carrier from Reigate came every Thursday to the Falcon, Southwark.

[6] Cf. Webb, *The Story of the King's Highway*. Chap. VII.

[7] 8 & 9 Wm. III c. 15.

[8] III *M. & B. l.* The lanes mentioned included those marked A. 217 (south portion) & B. 2035 on the Parish Map. There is no direction in the Act that posts should be " put in the middle of it to prevent its use except by riding and packhorses " as stated in IV *VCH* 436. Such a provision is on the face of it highly improbable as it would have seriously impeded horse traffic using the causeway, and rendered the surveyor liable in damages for any accidents that occurred.

[9] I *M. & B.* 288 n. There was also another possible route by Wray Common and Wray Lane which joined the London Road at the top of Reigate Hill.

[10] 28 Geo. II c. 28. The roads in the parish in charge of the trust are those marked A. 217 and B. 2035 on the Parish Map.

¹¹ This quotation and most of the subsequent details about the work of the Reigate Trust are extracted from the MS. Minutes of that body.

¹² Order of Quarter Sessions held at Reigate 27th April, 1756.

¹³ " In March 1818," says Ridgeway, " the footway in Bell Street was paved with broad stones."

¹⁴ *Rural Rides*, May 5th, 1823. Tunnel Road was taken over by the Reigate Trust and freed of toll in 1858. Reigate had its own stage coach. This set out from the Grapes Inn every Monday, Wednesday & Friday at 8 a.m. and proceeded via Banstead & Sutton to the Catherine Wheel Inn, Southwark, whence it returned Tuesday, Thursday & Saturday at 4 p.m. In 1816 the proprietors, Messrs. Huggett & Crunden, sold the undertaking to Messrs. Martin & Best.

¹⁵ From a note by Dr. C. J. Grece. For William Constable (1783–1861) and his versatile career see Hooper, *Guide* 141–2.

¹⁶ 47 Geo III c. 25. The inhabitants of Reigate Old Borough also petitioned against the proposed branch road (B.M. Add. MSS. 35697 p. 113). The road is A. 242 on the Parish Map.

¹⁷ 56 Geo. III c. 30. The road is marked A. 23 on the Parish Map.

¹⁸ *Accounts and Papers*, 1850 ; *Reports of the Secretary of State presented to Parliament*.

¹⁹ *The Times*, 20th Oct. and 20th Nov., 1829. The victim of the fatal accident was Alexander Norris, a coal merchant of Merstham.

²⁰ Mins. of Vestry held at Swan Inn, Reigate, 31st Oct., 1826.

²¹ Mins. of Vestry of Reigate Foreign held at Redhill Corn Exchange, 30th Jan., 1866.

²² The Reigate Trust controlled roads with a total length of 27 miles, all in Surrey (32 *SRS* 136. Return of Ambrose Glover, clerk.) The Reigate and Croydon Trust had expired in 1872.

CHAPTER VII

INDUSTRIAL HISTORY

AGRICULTURE remained the staple industry until the nine-teenth century when the coming of the railway made land more profitable for building, and the area devoted to farming gradually contracted with the growth of urbanisation. The change may have been encouraged by the backward state of Surrey agriculture which, according to the gloomy picture drawn by (Sir) James Caird in his *English Agriculture, 1850–51*, had improved but little since the eighteenth century. Writing from Reigate March, 1850, he reported, " In the neighbourhood of Reigate, along the valley, the land is of a friable texture, fairly cultivated in some instances but not, in any one that came under our observation, with that energy and skill which are to be met with in districts of the country which have very few of the advantages enjoyed by this. Four and five horses are frequently used in a plough. The plough itself is of very antiquated con-struction . . . The course of husbandry followed, where any is adhered to, is the four field ; but we were assured on very competent authority—that of an intelligent farmer long resident in the district—that the ordinary farmers have no plan, but usually decide as to the next crop of a particular field according to the opinion of one or two neighbours, at their weekly consultations in the alehouses on market days ! "

The Surveys of 1623 and 1700 indicate that most of the farms were mixed ones with a large proportion of arable land, and that orchards abounded. Very few of the farms and houses were without their orchards, though "orcha d" at this period was often used in the general sense of a garden.

Aubrey, when visiting the district in 1673, noted that Reigate Hill had been under the plough for the last nineteen

years and that good crops were raised there. He refers to
a device used for changing " the sheer board " of the
plough at every turning so as " to turne the earth the same
way," evidently an early form of the turnwrest plough with
a reversible mould board. He also speaks of much buck-
wheat being sown hereabouts.[1]

In 1610 Reigate was reported to be one of the four chief
market towns in Surrey. Its natural situation and proximity
to London made it a favourable entrepôt for the produce of
the surrounding country despite its poor communications.[2]
Wheat was the principal commodity and was bought up
largely by middlemen known as mealmen or badgers,
though as the seventeenth century advanced the market
became an important one for oats, with the development of
the oatmeal industry.[3]

Reigate's importance as a market centre was recognised
in 1679 when, thanks no doubt to the influence of the duke
of York as joint owner of the manor, his brother, Charles II,
granted to the inhabitants of the Old Borough the right to
hold a monthly market and a yearly cattle fair on Wednesday
in Easter week. This monthly market was in addition to the
old Tuesday market and the grant conferred the right to
hold a court of piepowder in connection with the fair.[4]
Another cattle and horse fair, which according to Ridgeway
was established in 1795 or 1796, took place on 9th December
at Reigate Heath and continued till 1913, being the last
of the local fairs to survive. A pleasure fair held in connection with it at the west end of High Street expired at the
same time. The Tuesday corn market which was held in
the Market Place came to an end in 1895. The cattle
market held on the same day had expired some years
earlier. The fortunes of both had declined since the opening
of a fortnightly stock and corn market at Redhill in 1870
by the Market Hall Company, which four years later
purchased the field opposite the hall from the South Eastern
Railway Company and converted it to this purpose.[5]

Windmills to grind the corn were erected at different
times on points of vantage. Rocque's map of Surrey,
c. 1767, shows a pair of mills at Isbells on Cockshot Hill,
Blackborough Mill, and the mill on Reigate Heath. These

four, of which the last is now the sole survivor, are marked on the first Ordnance map, 1816, together with the mill at Trumpets Hill. Wray Common mill was built in 1824 on land taken out of the Common. The Isbells mills were erected towards the middle of the eighteenth century but succeeded an older one. In 1628 Theophilus Tipton surrendered the half part of one windmill and forty acres of land commonly called by the name of Cockshothill lands. In 1639 John Life, who was then the copyhold tenant of the land called Isbells, was ordered by the Court Baron to erect " upon the premises one sufficient barne of the valew of £20 in consideration of the windmill that is fallen downe and carried off " the premises. In 1747 Mary Dewdney, widow, was granted a licence to pull down the old Windmill at Cockshot Hill, she having at her own expense lately erected a new windmill near the old one. Apparently she erected a second or else repaired the old one shortly after. The first mill on Reigate Heath was erected about 1765 on land granted from the waste upon Galley Hill.[6] "Galley" is doubtless a corruption of "gallows" and recalls the time when the hill was adorned by one of those grisly structures which, as we learn from Ridgeway, formerly stood on the Heath. The existing mill was in 1880 opened as a chapel in connection with the parish church under the name of St. Cross Chapel. It is still used for this novel purpose and is now generally known as " The Mill Church."

Hops were at one time grown on a large scale not only at Reigate, but all along the Holmesdale Valley, though their cultivation in Surrey has now died out except round Farnham.[7] Hop grounds are specified among the lands of Reigate Priory in 1538, and the Survey of 1623 speaks of grounds at Hooley and Santon while several " Hop Gardens " occur in the eighteenth century field names. Even in the town oast houses could be seen and back gardens were in some cases given up to hop growing. In 1615 Allen Venne was ordered to remove his " oste " from under the house of his neighbour, Thomas Cole, to whom it caused annoyance.[8]

Hops were not extensively employed in brewing until Elizabeth's reign, when the beer-brewer came into prominence and beer began to take the place of unhopped ale as

H

the common drink.[9]   The principal local beer-brewer at
that period was Thomas Thornton, two of whose men lost
their lives in 17th July, 1569, when they were " scalded in
the mashing vat and they died."   He and Robert Thompson
were repeatedly presented and fined at the Manor Courts
from 1583 onwards as brewers who broke the assize of
drink (*potus*).   It is odd to find them serving at times on the
juries that presented these offences, and so occupying the
quixotic position of taking part in their own conviction.
The:r offence is sometimes described as selling beer not
sufficiently wholesome, and their occupation is distinguished
from that of innkeepers and tipplers, many of whom continued however long after this to brew their own liquor.[10]
In the second half of the seventeenth century John Richardson, also described as a maltman, and Walsingham Heathfeild were the leading brewers in the town.[11]   Richardson's
brewhouse stood in Bell Street, in the position now occupied
by the Regiate Garage.   He purchased the Bull's Head Inn
in High Street in 1661, but it was not till a century later that
brewers made a regular practice of buying up inns to extend
the sale of their beer which resulted in the tied-house system.

The business until recent years carried on by Messrs.
Mellersh and Neale, Ltd., at their brewery in High Street,
Reigate, was founded by Thomas Neale in 1801, though a
brewhouse had existed on the site for some years previously.
This building is described in 1786 as newly erected on part
of the Crown field, so called from an adjoining inn of that
name which had been discontinued for some time before
that date when the name had been transferred to premises
on the north side of the Market Place.[12]

Malt making was not confined to the brewers and seems to
have been carried on as a separate trade by a few maltsters
in a small way of business.

Hemp was grown in the parish in the sixteenth to seventeenth century, and flax till the eighteenth century.   We
meet with the flaxman and flax dressing in contemporary
records ; as late as 1786 there was a flax house in West
Street and Ridgeway speaks of part of the old house which
ormerly stood in the Castle Grounds being used by a flag
dresser, indicating that flax proved to be worth cultivatinx

as a regular local crop with the development of a native linen industry.[13]

Reigate never became a recognised centre of cloth making, which until 1750 was the principal English manufacture. Yet weaving both of linen and wool was carried on locally and often in combination by the same craftsman. James Baker, weaver, of Reigate, who died in 1608 bequeathed to Thomas Toothe, his servant, " one woollen loom lying in the kitchen, 4 woollen slayes and 6 linen slayes and the warping bars and huthe,"[14] which also reminds us that weaving was then and until the Industrial Revolution a domestic industry carried on not in factories and by machinery but in the home and by hand looms. It was one of the numerous small-scale occupations that ministered to local needs in an age when each town was in a great measure self-supporting and produced many of the requirements of every-day life that are now imported from without. Reigate as a non-corporate town had the advantage of escaping the fetters placed on industry by trade guilds and municipal corporations. A silk weaver is mentioned in 1616 and a hair weaver in 1707. In 1690 Christopher Lambert, who held considerable property in the manor, is termed " silke stocking frame worke knitter."

The importance of tanning was recognised by the appointment at the Court Leet of searchers and sealers of leather charged with the duty of seeing that the product reached the required standard. It was an ancient industry, dating back to the time of Edward I, when " William le Tanner de Reygate " is mentioned in a local deed. In 1577 John Taylor of Betchworth, tanner, was fined for omitting to send one hide of leather to be sealed by those officers. A charge against William Grene in 1580 was referred to a jury of experts. A few years earlier, Robert Wood of Reigate had been accused in the Court of Exchequer of exercising the art of tanning though not duly apprenticed, while other Surrey tanners including Henry and Nicholas Bray, of Reigate, were accused in the same court of employing unlawful mixtures.[15] In 1668 licence was granted to John Richardson, tanner, to let his customary messuage with the garden, orchard and tanyard in the Old

Borough. Early in the eighteenth century the currying of leather was carried on by William Ware and his son in an alley off the High Street, which took their name but later acquired the curious name of Thunderbolt or Thunder Alley.

Ridgeway mentions three local tanyards at the beginning of the nineteenth century, one in Linkfield Street (Redhill), another at Hooley, and a third adjoining Earlswood Common, at the entrance to Mead Hole, the present Meadvale. The first is the only yard to survive and the only one with a continuous history on record going back to the seventeenth century, though probably all three were working before that period. During the latter part of that century it was carried on by Thomas Blatt and his son John, who became prominent local Quakers. The premises were copyhold of Reigate Manor and remained in the Blatt family till 1748, when they were surrendered to John Baker. In 1800 they were surrendered to John Wright, and at that date comprised a messuage, barn, stable, kiln, bark mill and out-building, tanyard, garden, orchard and one close of meadow containing two acres. They were subsequently acquired by William Tosswill. He, in 1854, sold them to Ebenezer Hooper who, ten years later, sold to Samuel Barrow. In the present century the business was acquired by Messrs. G. A. Bacon, Ltd., the existing owners.[16]

The manufacture of oatmeal, which previous writers have dismissed with a passing reference, is exceptionally interesting as an industry which achieved large proportions, not in response to local requirements, but by catering for an external demand which expanded as time went on. The trade arose in the early seventeenth century and reached its maximum development during the second half of that century and the first half of the next. Aubrey found the trade flourishing when he visited the town in 1673. Francis Ridley, John Mathew and George Charlwood are the three earliest oatmeal men mentioned in local records, and later references show that women also took part in the trade. Charlwood's mill was in West Street, adjoining the stream from the north that crosses the road there and so may have been worked by water. Another mill, that of Francis Hatcher, stood on high ground at the south end of Nutley

Lane and appears to have been a windmill, but the remainder of the mills, of which at one time there were no fewer than twenty, were in lower situations about the town and among other buildings, a clear indication that their driving force was supplied, not by wind, but by manual or animal power. Frequent references to the millhouses in which they were lodged support this conclusion. Charlwood, who died in 1639, left his millhouse to his wife for five years and then to his son. Hatcher, who died in 1699, gave his " oatmeal mill the millstone and two mill troughs to the same belonging " to his wife for her life and then to his son, George " to the intent the said mill and materials shall remain and continue appurtenant to my said dwelling-house for making oatmeal." Oatmeal was not then a common article of domestic diet in the south of England, so that the trade could not have relied on local demand. According to Aubrey, London was the chief market, the meal being used in making ship's biscuits. At first the merchant service seems to have been the principal customer but in the last quarter of the seventeenth century the Navy entered the field. Oatmeal did not become a general and regular ration in the Navy until the opening of the eighteenth century, but as early as 1676, and even before, it was occasionally issued by the victuallers in place of the ration of salt fish, to which it was usually preferred by ships' crews while serving in the West Indies and other hot climates. The names of some Reigate makers appear among those who contracted with the victuallers. Others less substantial could not afford to shoulder the risk of long-deferred payment which dealings with these officials involved. The Navy, like other Government departments at this period, was usually in financial straits and unable to pay its way, with the result that the victuallers, and in their turn the contractors, had often to wait years for a settlement of their accounts and charged exorbitant prices to cover the delay and uncertainty of payment. A glaring instance of delay came to light in 1697, when Matthew Johnson of Reigate appeared before the lords of the Treasury at Whitehall and complained that he had received only half the sum due to him for six loads of oatmeal which he had

delivered six or seven years before on Sir John Parsons'
account, and that a sum of over £20 had been owing to his
daughter for the same period. Sir John had purchased
Reigate Priory in 1677, and in the same year became one of
the victuallers to the Navy under a new and rigorous
contract drawn up by Pepys. Six years later he was
appointed a Commissioner for victualling the Navy under
the system of direct victualling then inaugurated, an office
which he retained until 1688.[17] It was probably to him
that the local makers owed their introduction to this new
source of trade, though to such of them as could not afford
long credit it must have proved a very doubtful benefit.

Occupations concerned with clothing included those of
the point-maker or pointer, who made points or laces with
which, in the sixteenth to seventeenth century, garments
were fastened, and the embroiderer who garnished the
elaborate attire then in fashion. Other lost crafts are those
of the trencher maker, who made trenchers or platters, and
sieve-bottomer, who is mentioned in 1729.

A glassman died in 1593 on Redhill Common and was
buried there by consent of the parish. He was probably
a glazier. John Goldsmith, ripyer, who died in 1602 may
have been a fishmonger or a reaper. In 1581 William
Lyfe is described as smith and horse-leech, and in the
year after occurred the death of Robert Hayes, barber and
surgeon, callings familiar in an age when the blacksmith
and barber practised a crude from of surgery. The rootman
was one that, to quote the Parish Register, 1589, " doth sell
rootes," though of what kind is not stated. Probably they
were culinary vegetables such as carrots and turnips.

Between 1648 and 1672 tokens, usually of copper or brass
and of the nominal value of a halfpenny or farthing, were
issued in vast quantities by towns and shopkeepers throughout the country to serve as small change in the absence of
an authorised copper coinage. At Reigate, farthing tokens
were issued by William Castleman, 1652, by Margaret Catt,
bearing the Tallowchandlers' arms, and by Thomas Heathfeild, bearing a sugar loaf. Margaret Catt was the widow
of Nicholas Catt, tallowchandler, and carried on the
business after his death ; Heathfeild was probably a grocer.[18]

Castleman owned the Red Cross Inn. His token is stamped
on the obverse with his name and W K C, the initials of
him and his wife, Katharine (Cuddington, who died the
following year), as was usual on tokens issued by married
tradesmen.

Some occupations became more or less hereditary, like
that of the collier or charcoal burner, which was followed by
families named Pope and Stevens for several generations.
It is possible that Smoke Lane got its name from the burning
of charcoal. Cronks Hill, which rises to the south, was the
home of John Stevens, collier, who died in 1590. The trade
was of great antiquity, and Hugh, the collier (*carbonarius*),
is mentioned in 1241 in proceedings concerning the death of
John de Reygate and his sister, Hawisia, who were found
murdered at Reigate.[19]

Reigate was formerly noted for its timber and contained
far more woodland than nowadays. It was from an early
period, one source of supply of the wood for fuel and building in the metropolis. In 1347 John de Warenne received
a request by the Black Prince to supply him with timber
from his park of Reigate and forest of Worth, to help build
a hall and other chambers at Kennington and a kitchen at
Byfleet. Earlswood was heavily timbered with oak until
lord Monson cut down the trees in the seventeenth century.
Woodhatch and Wray Common were other wooded tracts.
In 1346, Reigate with other places had to provide " timber,
stone and other necessaries " for completing the chapel of
St. Stephen in Westminster palace—an instance of the
ancient prerogative of purveyance which victimised the
subject for the benefit of the sovereign and provoked constant
complaint till its abolition at the Restoration. In the
Lord Admiral's time the parish gained some relief from this
arbitrary exaction by being excused from liability to furnish
wood and coal (i.e., charcoal), and in 1619 he persuaded the
authorities to continue this exemption for the rest of his life.[20]

The variety of geological formations in the parish with a
commercial value gave rise to a number of industries, some
of which are still carried on. Fuller's earth is the most
important natural product of the locality owing to the
presence of rich beds which occur in the sandy ridge between

Redhill and Nutfield and contain the finest earth to be found in England. Yet information as to workings before the sixteenth century is disappointingly absent, a fact seeming to imply a strange neglect to exploit these rich deposits in spite of the demand for the earth during the middle ages as an essential agent in the manufacture of English cloth. The first reference I have been able to trace occurs in a deed of 1583 by which the manor of Redstone was conveyed to John Husee. Among the lands conveyed were " Fulling Earth Field " and " The Grove lying on the south and south-east of Fulling Earth Pitts," which, with other land, were then let to " Anthony Gilmin, gent," for sixty years at an annual rent of £4. These pits were probably identical with the " certayne pitts of fullers earth " mentioned in the Survey of 1623, which lay on the north side of the Nutfield road and subsequently formed part of Copyhold Farm. The custom of Reigate manor forbade a copyhold tenant to dig and remove fuller's earth without a licence from the lord, and this may have hampered its output. As late as 1808 Mark Wood, the squire of Gatton, forfeited his copyhold land called Shipley Field for a breach of this custom.

" In Ryegate," wrote Aubrey in 1673, "is plenty of Fullers earth adjoining to Nutfield parish but 'tis in Ryegate parish 4d. per sack and 6s. per Loade." The price seems to have remained nearly constant for over a hundred years. In 1809 and 1814 the price at the pits for either the blue or yellow variety of earth was 6s. the ton, the cost of carriage to London being 18s. to 20s. the ton. There it was sold at the wharfs in Tooley Street, usually at from 24s. to 26s. the ton. Much of it was carried from Merstham to Wandsworth by the iron railway which had recently been extended from Croydon to Merstham, but this means of transport was said to be almost as expensive as carriage by road and to cause irregularity in the demand. The sole pit worked in the parish at that time was one opened by Mr. Morris on Copyhold Farm, and there were only two pits working in Nutfield.[21]

The industry has been greatly expanded during the present century, and is now in the hands of the Fullers Earth Union,

Ltd., which owns and works pits in both parishes. The chief pit at present working within Reigate parish is that at Copyhold Farm, on the north side of the main road, on which side the best deposits are found. The old pits were bell-shaped shafts about thirty feet in depth, but modern workings are carried much deeper in order to reach the main seam of hard rock. The present supply is said to be sufficient for at least another 100 years. The earth is still employed for fulling woollen cloth, though its principal use at the present day is for refining, decolouring and deodorizing oils of various kinds.[21]

Chalk quarrying and lime burning were carried on until recent times and attained considerable dimensions. The Survey of 1623 speaks of " great store of marle and chalke digged yearly at Reigate Hill." The largest pit, though now disused, still scars the face of the Hill below The Beeches, and in its later period resembled the figure of a huge lion cut in the escarpment. This part of the hill was in 1700 held on lease by Mr. Edward Thurland, and said to contain " a large chalk pit and a quarry of freestone." A smaller pit to the east, near Wray Lane, formerly known as the Wray Pit, was rented in 1700 by Anthony Best for £1 10s. a year. The low rent may possibly be explained by the custom which allowed the freehold and copyhold tenants of the Manor to help themselves to small chalk at Wray Hill for use on their lands.

Reigate stone is historically famous, though the name is a generic one applied to stone quarried in several parishes along the North Downs. This calcareous sandstone which is found in the Upper Greensand below the chalk was in wide demand for building until the end of the nineteenth century. During the middle ages it was used extensively in churches and other buildings and was much esteemed for images and ornamental work on account of its free-working properties. Among the many important buildings in which it was employed at different times were Westminster Abbey and Palace, the castles of Windsor and Rochester, Hampton Court and Nonsuch Palace and St. Paul's Cathedral. In 1365–6, thirty-eight cartloads of the stone were shipped from Battersea for Hadleigh Castle, Essex, at 2s. a cartload including the carriage to that port, and eight cartloads of the stone were put in a ship at Battersea for 18d. The stone for Westminster was also carted from Reigate to Battersea and thence taken by boat up the Thames.[22]

The names of some of the quarrymasters have come down, the earliest on record being Roger of Reigate, who, in 1253, supplied large quantities of stone to Westminster Abbey. Rogerus le Carieur, possibly his son, sat for Reigate in the Parliaments of 1295 and 1300. In 1360 Henry Pouke and John Langlond were appointed masters and keepers of the quarry at Reigate and empowered to " take as many masons and other workmen as shall be necessary for digging and cutting the stones in the quarry for the king's works in the castle of Wyndesore and put them to work in the quarry at the king's wages." The quarry was evidently requisitioned for the royal use and worked by pressed labour in accordance with the policy energetically pursued by William of Wykeham as chief keeper and surveyor of the royal castles. John Prophet also supplied stone from the Reigate quarries to Windsor Castle at various times between 1350 to 1351 and 1365 to 1366. In 1531-1533 " Richard Aynscombe of Rygate, quarryman " was paid " for 33 tonys of Rygate stone of hym bought and delyvered at Hampton Court " for the building of the Great Hall.[22] The bad weathering and friable quality of the stone have brought it into disrepute especially for external work, though it remained in favour for lining furnaces on account of its heat-resisting property, whence the name " firestone."

The hearthstone used by so many generations of housewives for scouring their hearths and front steps occurs just above the firestone of which it is a softer variety. It is still mined at Clears under Colley Hill by Reigate Mines, Ltd.

Reigate sand has long been dug for building and other purposes. In the Survey of 1623 the jury reported the existence of " a great quantity of special white sand within the Lord's Castle." In later times this white or silver sand for which the parish is famed was used for, among other purposes, glassmaking, hour glasses and writing, and some of the caves which run into the Castle Hill behind the houses in High Street were formed or extended to meet this demand.

In recent years the demand for building sand has led to increased production, and several new pits have been opened, often, it is to be regretted, at the expense of the amenities.

The beds of Wealden and other clay that outcrop in various parts of the parish have from early times been turned to account for brick, tile and pottery making. Large quantities of tiles were made here in the middle ages and clay for this purpose was dug on Earlswood Common, which is formed of Weald Clay. The Reeve's account of 1447 mentions the receipt of 4s. for 1,000 tiles made of clay taken from a certain pit on the lord's soil there, the rent for which had not been paid by the tenants. In 1372-3 Robert de Sybthorp, clerk of the king's works in Banstead and other Surrey manors, bought 10,000 tiles of John Tilere, of Reigate, at 4s. a thousand. In 1377 the prior of Merton bought 1,000 tiles "called pleyntylles" of John Tylere, of Reigate, for 3s. 8d. with a quarter of lime for 12d. for repairing the Lodge in Banstead Park.[24] Tile-making, combined later with brick-making, was probably carried on continuously from the middle ages to the present century. The Parish Registers of Elizabethan days contain entries relative to the family of "James Staplast of the causey tyler." Staplast, correctly Staplehurst, occupied a copyhold tenement on the southern edge of Earlswood Common, below the New Pond, where he no doubt followed his calling with clay supplied from the Common and water drawn from the little wayside and still existing pond in front of his dwelling.

The entry in the Reeve's Account, 1300, of the receipt of an annual rent of 2s. 8d. of the potters (*De firma figulorum per annum IIs. VIIId.*) shows that these craftsmen were at work here in the middle ages. The discovery some years ago of a medieval pitcher and jug on Earlswood Common pointed to that conclusion, but documentary evidence in support was not then to hand.

The pitcher, which is now in the British Museum, cannot be dated precisely, but is probably not later than the twelfth or beginning of the thirteenth century, and if so, is one of the earliest pieces of native medieval pottery bearing evidence of its date found in England. It is described as having "an oviform body of coarse red clay and lead glaze of a pale greenish yellow tone." The neck has been broken off, and " the main ornament consists of an applied frieze of roughly modelled clay representing a hunting scene, which includes two mounted men, one with a horn and the other with a club, four hounds and two stags," but these figures are too roughly formed to justify a more definite date.

The jug (see Plate VI), which is now in Guildford Museum was found on the eastern edge of the Common near the railway on ground now occupied by the golf house. It lay some three feet below the surface, at the bottom of a hole paved with ironstone. Several potsherds were turned up nearby. the vessel is described as "buff earthenware with decoration produced partly with a roulette in the form of vertical stripes and trellis-work, and partly with a circular stamp applied in rows between the stripes. The greater part of the surface is covered with a mottled yellow lead glaze, which in one patch has been fired to a blood-red colour. . . . The jug is a ' waster,' having burst during the firing, as is shown by the fact that the glaze has run over the edges of the wide break in the neck." It is assigned to the fourteenth century.[25]

Another possible site of an early pottery is suggested by the name Potteriches which looks like an expanded form of "pottery." The name, which was that of one of the farthinglands, attached to a field mentioned in the Survey of 1623 on the west side of Cockshot Hill, at Woodhatch. A small brickyard and pottery existed here in 1861 and continued working till the early part of this century, and it is possible that they had a long antecedent history.

In spite of the prohibition against digging soil on the Commons without the lord's licence it became a common practice for unauthorised persons to help themselves. Thus, in 1686 Israel Lynn was reported for taking several loads of clay from Earlswood Common, and in 1734 Thomas Dodge, brickmaker, was presented for digging clay and earth on several places on that Common without a licence. Bricks and earthenware have till recently been made upon the Common at the old-established brickfield of Messrs. W. Brown & Sons, and at their brick and tile works at Meadvale. At the latter works a pit in the *Perna* bed of the Atherfield clay was utilised for over 100 years. Formerly,

Plate VI.

MEDIEVAL JUG, EARLSWOOD.

ricks were also made at Woodhatch. In 1700 Israel Lynn,
e brickmaker already mentioned, held a house and land
and a brick kiln lately built thereon " which lay on the
ast side of Cockshot Hill.

The spread of brick earth which lies between Redhill and
outh Merstham has in modern times been extensively used
r brick and tile making. The works in this part of the
arish formerly engaged in the manufacture were the
attlebridge Brick and Tile Works and the Siding Brick
/orks at Holmethorpe of Mr. Richard Trower.[26]

NOTES TO CHAPTER VII

[1] Note in Aubrey's MS., " *A Perambulation of Surrey*," in Bodleian Library.
[2] 21 *SAC* 173, 180, 190.
[3] Note in Aubrey's MS., *op cit.*
[4] Pat. 31 Chas. II, pt. 3, No. 16.
[5] *Report of Royal Commission on Market Rights & Tolls*, IX (1891), 9–13.
[6] Manor Archives.
[7] Hall and Russell, *Report o ɩ the Agriculture and Soils of Kent, Surrey and Sussex*, 29.
[8] I. *M & B.* 299 : Ct. R.
[9] II. *VCH* 381–7.
[10] Ct. R. Thornton, with other Surrey beer brewers, was also prosecuted in the
urt of Exchequer for selling his beer at excessive rates (II *VCH* 387).
[11] For Heathfeild, see p. 148.
[12] Bryant's Survey, 190. T. Neale was also in business as a maltster (*Ibid.*,
6). For the Crown Inn see further p. 148.
[13] The vicar, it may be added, claimed his tithe on flax.
[14] 15 *SRS* 276.
[15] Ct.R. II *VCH* 333–4.
[16] Ct.R. Copyhold property was transferred by surrender and admission.
e outgoing tenant verbally surrendered it at a Court Baron to the lord,
resented by his steward, to the use of the new tenant who was then admitted
his place, and the transaction was recorded in the Court Rolls. Though
minally held at the will of the lord, copyholds were usually hereditary.
e tenure was abolished by the Law of Property Act, 1922.
[17] Aubrey, *op. cit.*: I, *M & B*, 289. Admiralty Records P R O : *Descriptive*
talogue of the Naval MSS. in the Pepysian Library (Navy Records Society),
ls. I and IV : XII *Calr. of Try. Books*, 10, 17. Croydon was another centre
the industry.
[18] Boyne, *Trade Tokens* (ed., 1891), II 1145.
[19] Assize Roll No. 867. Colley, the name of one of the tithings and sub-
anors, is thought to denote " charcoal clearing or wood " (*P.N. Surrey*, 305).
lliers Meadow and Colemans appear as old field names in the same
ighbourhood.
[20] I *Black Prince's Register*, 64 : I *M & B.* 287, 324 : Hooper, *Guide*, 17–18 :
mbert, I *Blechingley*, 198.
[21] II *M & B*, 266–7 : II *VCH*, 279–80, and references there given : *Geology*
the Country around Reigate and Dorking (Memoirs of the Geological Survey)* 59, 65,
1–3 : Local information.
[22] Salzman, *Medieval English Industries*, 85–6 : II *VCH* 277–8 ; Taylor,
r Lady of Batersey*, 45 : *The English Medieval Quarry* (*E:onomic Hist. Rev.* IX
. 1, 17–39) : Lane, I *History of Hampton Court Palace* 361.

[23] Hooper, *Guide* 62 : Topley, *Geology of the Weald* 141 : Palgrave, 4–9 Aubrey in his MS. speaks of the sand " being used over a great part of England for Scouring, and for Hower-glasses." In 1860 a cave behind the Red Cross Inn fell in, causing the partial collapse of five cottages erected above it, though all the occupants escaped with their lives. (*Illustrated London News*, 19th May 1860, with sketch of the disaster).

[24] Lambert, I *Banstead* 129, 131.

[25] 58 *Archæological Journal* (1902) 5, and illustration Plate I. For jug see 37 *SAC*, 245.

[26] There was in the earlier part of last century a brickfield in London Road, Reigate, on a site now occupied by premises of Wray Park Garages, Ltd. It supply came from the clay band of the Folkestone Beds which occurs at this horizon.

CHAPTER VIII

PARLIAMENTARY HISTORY

THE history of Reigate as a parliamentary borough commenced in 1295, when it sent two members to Edward I's model Parliament at Westminster.[1] It was one of the four Surrey towns represented in that assembly, the others being Guildford, Southwark and Blechingley. Reigate and Blechingley were selected, not because of their importance nor at the wish of their inhabitants, but in recognition of the influence of their overlords, John de Warenne, earl of Surrey, and Gilbert de Clare, earl of Gloucester and Hertford. "The members for Reigate," says Mr. Malden, "must be looked upon as the nominees of the earl of Surrey as in after days they were nominees of the families of Hardwicke or Somers. . . . The King and the Earls and Bishops were the leaders of organised opinion. It was as necessary that men should be elected who could act with them as it is now necessary that men should be elected who will act with the recognised leaders of great parties."[2] Unfortunately an expedient necessary to the success of Edward's great experiment was prostituted to selfish ends and became in course of time the chief obstacle to political reform. Thus from the start Reigate was a pocket borough, though nominally the right of election was in the freeholders.

It was already a borough for fiscal purposes and is mentioned in 1290, when the local sub-taxers for the subsidy of a fifteenth granted in that year were fined for offences committed by them in levying the tax. From 1332 it was subject, with other boroughs, to taxation at the higher rate of a tenth, which nominally amounted to a tenth part in value of the movable belongings of the townspeople, whereas the Foreign, or extra-burghal portion of the parish, escaped with a fifteenth.[3] The early borough, it must be remembered, was a small area of a little over 400 acres confined chiefly to the main part of the town and excluding the castle on the north side and the Priory on the south whereas the entire parish embraced nearly six thousand acres.

The number of boroughs represented in 1295 was 116, but of these several ceased to send members again, and the regular number dropped to below 100 until the creation of new boroughs by Henry VI and later monarchs. Reigate was one of the boroughs that continued with some intervals to send members until 1832. The gaps occur mainly in the fourteenth century, and are most numerous in the earlier part during which they are divided fairly evenly between Parliaments at Westminster and those summoned at other places. At other periods, however, Reigate was generally represented in the Westminster Parliaments and returns are occasionally found for more distant assemblies. At York, for example, in 1298, at Lincoln two years later, and at a few fourteenth century Parliaments convened outside Middlesex, Reigate was, nominally at least, represented, though the existence of returns for these early Parliaments does not necessarily imply that the burgesses elected actually attended.[4]

A large proportion of the earlier members were local men, of whom several, as their names indicate, were tradesmen or artisans. Roger le Carreuer, or Quareur, one of the members elected in 1295, has already been met with as master of the Reigate Hill quarry, and he was one of the sub-taxers fined in 1290. Hugo le Tailleur was returned for two Parliaments of Edward II, and one of Edward III, and in the same reign appear John le Smyth, 1325, John le Colyere, i.e., charcoal burner, 1346, and William le Baker, 1348 ; and other occupational surnames, such as Skinner, 1350 and later, Page, 1357 and Cook, 1366. Among burgesses named after the places where they dwelt or hailed from were John de Bocham, 1298, William de Maldon, 1331, John at Redeston, 1350, and John atte Cherchgate, 1346 and 1348.[5]

Other news of some of these worthies sheds a curious light on them and their times. In 1301 a party of sixty-five men from Reigate and neighbourhood raided the farm of John de Beauchamp at Chipstead by night, cut and carried away his corn and drove off a large flock of his sheep. The raiders included Hugh le Taylleur, probably the future member, Simon Blaundis, the name of a member elected in 1311 and 1312, and John, son of Joan and Roger de la Redestone. Escapades of this kind, in which priests as well as laymen often joined, were common in that lawless age.[6] Adam of Usk, a distinguished lawyer who became rector of Merstham in 1411, was some years earlier convicted of stealing a horse and had to flee the country.

The election of burgesses, or borough members, during the middle ages took place as a rule in the County Court at Guildford. One writ of election was issued to the sheriff covering the county and its boroughs. The actual election was probably made by a few of the borough electors deputed to attend the County Court, or in some instances by the sheriff himself if no electors appeared or the men of their choice were unacceptable to him. So far as any local choice was allowed, it probably took place in the Court Leet of the manor and was made from a list of the lord's nominees.[7]

As a curb on the arbitrary methods of the sheriff an Act passed in 1406 directed the names of the elected members to be written on an indenture which was to be sealed by the voters present at the County Court and then tacked to the writ of election and returned with it by the sheriff. Prynne gives the indenture for Surrey in 1415. The names of the two knights of the shire are followed by those of the burgesses chosen for Reigate, Blechingley and other boroughs. To these are appended the names of nineteen men, all of them apparently county electors who sealed as voters or choosers. The practice of final election in the County Court continued till the middle of the fifteenth century. Its decline was hastened by an Act of the year 1415 which directed the sheriff on receipt of the writ to issue a precept to the mayor or bailiff of every borough in his county enjoining him to choose burgesses. After that separate indentures were entered into, the sheriff and the bailiff and nineteen, or at times eight, persons of the community of Reigate recording that the bailiff and community had elected.[8]

Parliamentary representation in its earlier days was

G

regarded by the boroughs not as a privilege but as an irksome duty and one to be evaded whenever possible. A borough returning members had to find the money to pay their wages and was, as we have seen, subject to a higher rate of taxation than the county.   The rate of pay was two shillings per member for each day spent in going to, attending and returning from Parliament.   For attendance at Westminster two days were allowed for travelling there and back.   Thus, in 1352, William Taillour and William de Maldone, the local burgesses, were allowed £6 8s. for thirty days spent in attending Parliament at Westminster and two in travelling.[9]   The candidates elected were as a rule as reluctant to serve as their fellow townsmen were to send them and precautions had to be taken to secure their presence.   The attendance of a member was vouched for by two manucaptors, or sureties.   Sometimes the members acted as sureties for one another, as in 1302, when William Kyterel was manucaptor for his colleague, John Godwyne, who in return acted in a similar capacity for Kyterel.   A member who failed to answer his summons at the assembling of Parliament and his manucaptors were liable to be fined for his default, though it seems that the penalties were seldom, if ever, enforced.[10]

The borough members drawn from home against their will and consisting usually of petty tradesmen and yeomen must have felt strangely out of place rubbing shoulders with their social superiors, the knights of the shire.   But their position greatly improved towards the end of the middle ages.   The growing esteem for a borough seat was shown by the return in 1453 of John Timperley, one of the leading retainers of John Mowbray, third duke of Norfolk, and like his master, a warm supporter of the Yorkist cause, though yielding a transient loyalty to Henry VI.   He owned the manors of Flanchford and Gatton, and was signally favoured by the king in 1451, when Gatton was created a parliamentary borough.   He, or his son, John Timperley, junior, sat for Reigate again in 1460.   It was said of this duke by his wife that he needed the election of " such persones as longe unto him and be of his menyall servaunts," and the political subservience of the borough was even more forcibly demon-

strated in 1468 when return of writs was granted to his son,
the fourth duke, though nominally the returning officers in
and after the fifteenth century were the two constables or the
bailiff, chosen annually at the lord's court.[11]

As the fifteenth century advanced the local members,
though usually servants and nominees of the lords of the
manor, were men of position who in a number of cases held
crown appointments.   Thus John Lemington, or Lematon,
member in 1442, besides being steward of the manor was
employed in the exchequer and other government posts,
while his colleague, John Beket, was keeper of Westminster
Palace. William Shirley, who sat in the succeeding
Parliament, was yeoman of the crown, and his colleague,
Geoffrey Goodlok, held an office in the chancery.   Henry
Langton, elected in 1449, is returned as "armiger," the
equivalent of esquire, or one entitled to armorial bearings,
which his position as yeoman of the royal household would
account for.   John Stodley, or Studley, who sat in 1450,
appears in the Reeve's Account, 1447, as one of the auditors
of the accounts of Cuckfield and Reigate manors.   A letter
from him with news of the Court is contained in the Paston
correspondence.[12]

After the first quarter of the fifteenth century the seats
were more often than not filled by outsiders.   The improvement in the status of borough members made it difficult at
times to find local men of sufficient education and standing,
though this difficulty diminished in the course of the sixteenth
century.   John Timperley, the elder, and some of the other
members had local interests, but the outstanding exception
is the long political connection of the Skinner family which
commenced in 1351 and continued at intervals for over
200 years.   The family is met with at Reigate early in the
fourteenth century.   In the fifteenth century its representa-
tives acquired a coat-of-arms and ranked as gentry.   John
Skinner I, who sat for Reigate, 1450-1, improved his
fortune by marrying the daughter and heiress of Richard
Calcock, a wealthy landowner of Chipstead.   His son,
John II, entered the law, was clerk of the Green Cloth and
with his brother, Richard, sat for Reigate in the Parliament
of 1491-2.   He built the church vestry in 1513, and left two

sons, James and John III, who followed the same profession and held the stewardship of various Surrey manors. They quietly accepted the Tudor religious changes, and as men of substance whose loyalty could be trusted in all political weathers, they were employed on a number of important commissions.[13] In 1541, when the fall of queen Catherine Howard brought disgrace on her kinsfolk, John Skinner III was appointed to take an inventory of the money and goods of lord William Howard at Reigate Priory and was given the custody of that house.[14]

John III sat for the borough in the Reformation Parliament, 1529–36, and James in 1541 and 1554. His colleague in 1541 was his nephew, John Skinner IV, who also sat for the county in 1556 and 1557. He was a clerk in queen Elizabeth's household and left an only son, John V, who died without issue in 1584 when the male line expired.

On the outbreak of Wyatt's rebellion in 1554, James and his nephew, John IV, assisted lord William, who was then in high favour with queen Mary, to arrest Sir Thomas Cawarden at Blechingley for suspected complicity in the rising, and Cawarden was lodged as a prisoner in James' house at Reigate.[15]

Parliamentary representation in the sixteenth century was openly engineered in the interests of the court. The owners of the boroughs were expected to see that the right persons were nominated. Under Elizabeth elections were as little free as in her father's reign. The Privy Council exerted itself to secure the return of men who were well affected to the government and went so far as to direct the sheriff to arrange that the results should be favourable.[16]

Lord William Howard acquired the Priory in 1541 and, ten years later, the Howard moiety of the manor forfeited by the attainder of his kinsman, the third duke of Norfolk. For the next sixty years he and his son, Charles, the famous admiral, directed the political destiny of the borough and secured its steady allegiance to the crown. They played a leading part in county as in national affairs. The father was lord-lieutenant of Surrey from 1559 till his death and was succeeded in that office by his son, who had previously served as a knight of the shire and a J.P. for Surrey.[17]

(Sir) William Howard of Lingfield, lord William's second son, occupied one of the borough seats in the first and subsequent Parliaments of Elizabeth, except those of 1589 and 1597, when he sat for the county. His son, Edward, succeeded him in the borough. Sir William's fellow burgess from 1563 to 1566 was his cousin, Sir George Howard. Edmund Saunders, his old colleague in the Parliaments of 1584 and 1586, belonged to an old Charlwood family and was a J.P. for the county. Walter Haddon (1555), the civilian, and Julius Cæsar (1588), judge of the Admiralty court and later master of the rolls, were the first outsiders of real distinction to be elected.

In the seventeenth century difficulty seldom arose in finding suitable candidates among the local gentry. Sir Thomas Bludder, of Flanchford, occupied a seat in the last Parliament of James I, and was re-elected to the first Parliament of Charles I in company with Sir Roger James, who lived at the Parsonage—later Reigate Lodge—and rented from the manor the ruined castle which adjoined that property. Sir Thomas retained his seat until the Long Parliament, from which he was excluded as a pronounced Royalist. Robert Lewis, a burgess in 1621 and 1624 for the last two Parliaments of James I, was a barrister of Gray's Inn and steward of Reigate manor. The number of members who in the course of this century also held the stewardship is such as to suggest that this office carried with it the choice of one of the seats.

The election for the Short Parliament, 1640, gave rise to the first recorded contest. On a petition being lodged it was reported that three candidates had been returned, namely, Edward Thurland, Sir Thomas Bludder and Robert Goodwin. Thurland's election was declared to be clear on inspection of the indenture of return. The case of the other two was referred back to the committee, but no further report appears, owing probably to the early dissolution of this Parliament.[18] Thurland was, like Bludder, a Reigate man. Goodwin came of an East Grinstead family which owned property in Blechingley and Horne, and he had an interest in Reigate as one of the trustees of the manor for his cousin, lord Monson.

Monson sat for Reigate in 1626 and again in the Long Parliament in which he at first sided with but later opposed the court, though he owed his Irish peerage to the king. His colleague, after Bludder's exclusion, was young George Evelyn, elder brother of the diarist, who had just succeeded to the Wotton estate. He preferred the life of a country gentleman to politics, though after the Restoration he was persuaded to sit for the county.

The first of Cromwell's parliaments, which met in 1654, was elected by popular suffrage under the Instrument of Government. The smaller rotten boroughs were totally disfranchised, and Reigate was deprived of one of its seats. Edward Bysshe, junior, was elected to the remaining seat. He was the son of Edward Bysshe, the builder of Smallfield Place, and held the office of Garter king of arms under the Commonwealth. He lost that office at the Restoration, but in 1661 was appointed Clarenceux king of arms and knighted. Cromwell's second parliament was elected on the old basis. John Goodwin of Blechingley, a brother of Robert Goodwin, the member in 1640, was returned for both Reigate and East Grinstead, and chose to sit for the latter. He was steward of the manor and a strong Parliamentarian.[19]

Royalist influence became dominant in the borough at the Restoration with the fall of lord Monson and the passing of his interest in the manor to the duke of York, afterwards James II. In the Convention parliament of 1660 the borough was represented by John Hale, who had lately purchased Flanchford, and Edward Thurland. Thurland was a rising barrister, a native of the town, who lived at Great Doods, and had sat twenty years earlier. He attracted the notice of the duke, who appointed him his solicitor-general and steward of the manor, and he also became the first and, as it proved, the only recorder of Reigate. Re-elected in 1661, he continued to sit till 1673, when he was created a judge. He was succeeded by Sir John Werden, the duke's secretary. Werden was re-elected to the parliament of 1685, which was packed with supporters of the court, but deserted his master at the Revolution. Deane Goodwin of Blechingley, son of John Goodwin elected in 1656, represented the borough in the last three parliaments of Charles II. He owed the seat to his ownership of the other half share of the manor which he subsequently disposed of to the crown. Ralph Freeman, the squire of East Betchworth, was returned as senior member in 1680, but Goodwin petitioned and he was reported not duly elected. John Parsons, who first appeared in 1685 as junior member to Sir John Werden and sat for the borough with two short intervals until his death thirty years later, gained a footing in the town by his purchase of the Priory in 1681, and with it a number of burgage tenements carrying votes. As a high Tory of Jacobite hue, he was acceptable to the duke and he established a hold on the borough strong enough to withstand the determined Whig attack which he had to face after the Revolution.

The manor passed to William III at the Revolution and was granted to Joseph Jekyll for the benefit of his brother-in-law, John, lord Somers, the eminent lawyer and Whig statesman. The rivalry of the two parties led to several keenly contested elections in the new reign. The borough was roused to fresh political life and the vote acquired a new importance and value. The first of these contests occurred in the election for the Convention parliament of 1689. The unsuccessful candidate was Thomas Vincent, of Fetcham, who petitioned against the return of Parsons. The new House of Commons, which was overwhelmingly Whig, declared in favour of Vincent, who accordingly gained the second seat. In the election for the following parliament he was again at the bottom of the poll and again petitioned, on this occasion against John Parsons, junior, who had been returned with his father. Illegal practices were alleged against the son in having induced the bailiff, Allen Dewdney, to return him with his father. The petition apparently failed, as six months later Vincent petitioned again but with no better success as the Parsons retained both seats. Their election to the next Parliament, that of 1695, was unavailingly challenged by the two unsuccessful candidates who complained that the majority was obtained by undue means and incompetent votes and also by undue influence with the bailiff. This series of petitions forcibly illustrates the advantage possessed by the party which could secure the bailiff. Nominated by the lord from his tenants and subject to annual election at the manor court, this official usually deferred to the lord's wishes, except on rare occasions when rival influences gained the ascendant. Hence there could be little hope of his acting impartially, and his power of admitting or rejecting disputed votes often turned the scale at the poll.

One notable effect of this rivalry was to create a brisk market for burgages or vote-bearing tenements. Freehold premises in the borough let at two or three pounds a year or even less, acquired adventitious values and readily changed hands at prices much above their intrinsic worth. Several men of note purchased burgages during the Whig struggle for ascendancy, among them being Philip Yorke, afterwards lord Chancellor and earl of Hardwicke, William Congreve, the dramatist, and Sir Godfrey Kneller, the artist. Congreve bought a house in West Street which he sold later to Sir Godfrey, who also owned a burgage in High Street. Another burgage in High Street was acquired by Spencer Cowper, grandfather of the poet, and a third passed in turn through the hands of Jacob Tonson, junior, Joseph Addison and his friend Tickell, the poet. Tonson was the nephew and successor of Jacob Tonson, the celebrated Whig bookseller, who himself owned a burgage in West Street for which he voted in 1698. This adjoined the property of Congreve, who voted at the same election and, like Tonson, in the Whig interest. Shortly before this election a large number of burgages were bought up by lord Somers' secretary, one George Adney, and transferred into the names of Whig supporters.[20]   As a result of these efforts Sir John Parsons and his son were defeated by the Whig candidates, Stephen Hervey and Edward Thurland.[21]   Hervey lived at Betchworth and was steward of Reigate manor ; Thurland was a grandson of the judge. Hervey retained his seat till his death in 1707. Sir John regained his seat at the general election in 1701, and held it without further interruption till his death in 1717. The general election of 1713 witnessed the strange spectacle of the Tories and Whigs joining hands against a third candidate. Parsons and James Cocks were the official candidates and each received the votes of both parties. The third candidate, Thurland, who had been successful in 1698, stood apparently as an independent. The poll was a heavy one. The number voting reached the high total of 150. Parsons headed the poll with 143 votes, followed by Cocks with 115. Thurland came a bad third with 34 votes. This party arrangement continued while Sir John lived, and at the general election of 1715 consequent on the death of queen Anne he and Cocks retained their seats unopposed.

Lord Somers died unmarried in 1716, leaving his estates to his two sisters, one of whom had married (Sir) Joseph Jekyll, later master of the rolls, and the other Charles Cocks, a Worcester attorney. So commenced the long connection of the Cocks family which was to last for over two hundred years. Sir Joseph held one of the borough seats from 1722 until his death in 1738. The election of 1722 was notable for being the last fought during the unreformed Parliaments and marking the final triumph of the Whigs. Sir Joseph and his nephew, James Cocks, were opposed by alderman Humphrey Parsons and Richard Mead. Parsons followed the Jacobite leanings of his father, Sir John, the former member, and later sat for Harwich and the city of London. Jekyll and Cocks were declared elected, but a petition, subsequently withdrawn, was presented by their opponents containing the usual charges of favouritism by the bailiff, and accusing Sir Joseph as lord of the manor of having procured the appointment of that official by improper means.[22]

Henceforth, until the Reform Act, Reigate remained the undisputed preserve of the two Whig families of Cocks and Yorke, and its quiescence was unbroken except by occasional squabbles that broke out between them. The Yorke or Hardwicke connection arose from the marriage of Philip Yorke, first earl of Hardwicke, to a niece of lord Somers. For forty years on end three of his sons in turn held one of the seats. Charles Yorke, the second son, who sat from 1747 to 1768, filled in succession the offices of solicitor-general and attorney-general. A man of splendid parts, his character was marred by a fatal weakness which finally betrayed him

and led to his tragic death a few days after he had received
the great seal from George III.

Charles Cocks, grandson of Charles Cocks, the Worcester
attorney, held the other seat for nearly forty years until 1784,
when the barony of Somers was revived in his favour. The
two families thus shared the representation between them
except in the Parliament of 1784, in which William Belling-
ham and Edward Leeds sat as their nominees. Each family
steadily consolidated its position by buying up the burgages
that still remained in other hands. This competition provoked a rivalry that in course of time threatened to break up
the family compact. In 1786 both families prepared for a
contest at the next general election. The local agent of the
Yorkes at this period was a young Reigate attorney named
William Bryant, the son of a prosperous tallow chandler in
the town who held the important office of bailiff. No official
list of electors then existed and many of the votes claimed
were open to dispute. To repair this defect the younger
Bryant drew up a list of all burgages and alleged burgages
for which votes had been exercised or claimed in 1698 and
subsequent elections with a detailed account of their history
and ownership. This MS., which contains invaluable
evidence of the state of the town in the seventeenth and
eighteenth centuries, is entitled " A Particular of the Borough
of Reigate in the County of Surrey with the Names of the
former and present Tenants, and to whom the Tenements
now respectively belong made out from antient Surveys
and books and from Modern Inspections and Inquiries.
By W.B., 1786." To illustrate the list a large scale map of
the borough was prepared, copies of which are extant. The
number of possible votes according to his summary was 267,
of which 135 were assigned to lord Hardwicke and 132 to
lord Somers, but of this total no fewer than 63 are marked as
doubtful. The Somers party retaliated by supplanting the
elder Bryant as bailiff with a nominee of its own—a step
which resulted in a lawsuit and turned the younger Bryant
into a bitter and implacable enemy of that family to the end
of his long life. Wiser counsels at length prevailed, and the
rupture which seemed inevitable with the ruinous costs to
both sides of a contested election was in the end averted.

Proposals for a settlement were put forward by lord Somers, the most important being to refer the question in dispute to the decision of two barristers and in the event of an election occurring before a decision was reached to allow each family to nominate one candidate as before. These proposals were well received by the other side though the terms of final settlement are not on record. Yet as each family continued until 1832 to enjoy one of the seats a lasting agreement was evidently reached.[23]

After the death of Sir John Parsons in 1717, the members elected were with few exceptions non-resident. They had in fact seldom occasion to show their faces in a constituency where the vast majority of the electors were absentees like themselves and the excitement of an election campagin was a thing of the past. But they were expected to contribute handsomely to local objects, and it became a recognised practice for new members to present a volume to the Parish Library.

The Reform Act, 1832, cut off one of the seats and extended the parliamentary borough to include the area known as the Foreign and so embrace the whole parish. It would have been better for its good name if Reigate had, like the neighbouring boroughs of Gatton and Blechingley, lost both seats. The number of resident electors had sunk to eight, but the inclusion of the Foreign and the widening of the franchise produced only a slight increase of the electorate for several years to come and by 1851 the number had reached only 332. The passing of the Act was celebrated by a dinner to 1,200 persons in the Castle Grounds at the expense of lord Somers and the local gentry. The gathering was treated to a hearty meal of roast beef and plum pudding, washed down with copious draughts of beer and enlivened with music by the local band.[24]

The remaining seat fell to lord Somers, who bought out lord Hardwicke and so acquired undisputed sway. Members of the family represented the constituency until 1857, when lord Somers abandoned his prescriptive claim on the seat. Between that year and 1865 there were no fewer than six contested elections. The borough became the unhappy hunting ground for a tribe of political aspirants with results that led to its complete demoralisation. The candidates were for the most part of irreproachable character and included men of distinction like Sir Henry Rawlinson, the eminent Assyriologist, who twice contested the seat, on the second occasion with success, and (Sir) Edmund Monson, who later became our ambassador in Paris. The elections were embittered by the circumstance that the candidates as a rule professed the same Liberal faith and fought each other largely on personal grounds. They were, moreover, wealthy men, prepared to spend lavishly, so that Reigate soon became a byword for venality and corruption, and its last state was worse than its first.

At the election of 1865 the retiring member was Mr. Granville Leveson-Gower, the young squire of Titsey. He was opposed by Monson, and there was a third candidate named Richardson, who may be disregarded as he polled only 11 votes. Leveson-Gower secured the votes of 473 of the 912 electors and headed the poll with a majority over Monson of 197. A petition was lodged against his return on the grounds of bribery and corruption and after investigation by a committee of the House of Commons the return was suspended and a commission appointed to examine the charges. The commissioners sat at the Town Hall from August to October, 1866, and took the evidence of 500 witnesses, which was published in two bulky blue books. They found that bribery and treating had extensively prevailed at every election since 1857 and that of the persons who voted at the election of 1865, 346 were bribed. In the result the borough was deprived of its seat by the Representation of the People Act, 1867, and merged in the Mid-Division of the county. Over 400 voters who had been guilty of bribing or receiving bribes at the various elections were disfranchised and rendered incapable of voting in respect of any qualification in the borough.[25]

NOTES TO CHAPTER VIII.

[1] For the names of the members see *Original Writs and Returns Printed by Order of the House of Commons, 1878* ; and J. E. Smith, *Parliamentary Representation of Surrey*, 97 etc., where a complete list is given.

[2] H. E. Malden, *History of Surrey*, 142.

[3] XVIII *SRS*, xxxiv 5 and 39.

[4] A. F. Pollard, *The Evolution of Parliament*, 2nd ed. 316-20.

[5] " Bocham " was the early form of Bookham (Surrey). " Redeston " was of course Redstone Hill.

[6] Lambert, I *Blechingley*, 173. For similar outrages in 1313 and 1335 at Blechingley and Merstham see *ibid*. I, 178-9, and *CPR* (1334-8), 205. Blaundis no doubt belonged to the Reigate family of that name which appears among early tenants of the manor.

[7] Stubbs, III *Constitutional History*, 427-8, 431.

[8] Prynne, *Brevia Parliamentaria Rediviva*, 258-9. *History of Parliament, Register of Members, 1439-1509*, 690. In 1453 the indenture was between the sheriff and John Skynner and John Jurdan, constables of the borough of Reigate, and declared that "the said constables with common consent of all the borough hade chosen John Tymperle and John German burgesses for the said borough" (Orig. Ret. to Parl., 31 Hy. IV).

[9] Prynne, I *Brief Register*, 220.

[10] Green, *Short History*, 178-9 ; Pollard, *op. cit.*, 378-9.

[11] I *Paston Correspondence*, 337 ; III *VCH*, 234 : VI *CCR.*, 223-4.

[12] For notes on these and other members at this period see the recent *History of Parliament : Biographies of the Members of the Commons House, 1439-1509*. There is a gap in the returns between 1477 and 1529, but an unofficial list gives Richard and John Skinner as members for Henry VII's fourth parliament, 1491-2 (III *Bulletin of Inst. of Historical Research*, 172).

[13] James Skinner in 1552 received a grant from Edward VI of the Rectory Manor, formerly the estate of the Priory of St. Mary Overy, for which however he paid the cash value. John Skinner and his descendants of that name are numbered for the sake of clearness.

[14] XVI *L & P*, Hy. VIII, 1432 & 1447 ; VII *P & O of Privy Council*, 280.

[15] Lambert, *op, cit.*, I 265-6.

[16] I *VCH*, 378 ; 39 *SAC*, 55-7.

[17] Cf. 40 *SAC*, 41.

[18] *Commons Jo.*, 20th April, 1640.

[19] According to Browne Willis (*Notitia Parliamentaria*), Sir Thomas Pride, whose name is immortalised by his purge of the House of Commons in 1648, and Col. Jerome Sankey were elected in Goodwin's place.

[20] In 1738 and later years when a contest threatened, burgages were transferred to political supporters of the two families for life in return for a small payment. This created a sufficient freehold estate to confer a vote. In the eighteenth century the burgages consisted of those properties for which a vote had been allowed at previous elections, but they were not pure burgages since burgage tenure did not apply to the freeholds of the manor.

[21] " The election at Reigate is to be to-morrow : and instead of Adney and Hetherington they put up Messieurs Harvey and Thurland." (Letter from G. Follett to Robt. Harley, 21st July, 1698. *Hist. MSS. Com.* (*Duke of Portland MSS.*) *14th Rep. App.*, *Pt. II*, 598). " Lord Somers is mustering his

last list against the Reigate election but he will hardly be able to exclude
Sir J. P[arsons] " (T. Bateman to Robt. Harley, 19th Dec., 1700—*ibid.*, 639).
At the latter election Hervey and Parsons were returned unopposed as the
result of an arrangement between the parties (*Ibid., 15th Rep. App., Pt. IV*, 11).

[22] *Commons Jo.*, 18th Octr., 1722.   Mead, who is described as a citizen of
London, is wrongly identified by *M & B* (I, 292 n.) with Dr. Richard Mead,
the celebrated physician, who was a staunch and life-long Whig.   Those
polling at this election numbered 127.   In 1717 at a by-election on the death
of Sir J. Parsons, 227 polled.   Humphrey Parsons led with 117 votes, but as
26 of these were refused he was defeated.

[23] This is the MS. referred to as Bryant's Survey.   It also gives the poll lists
for all the contests from 1698 to 1722.   For the family dispute and settlement
see Hardwicke Estate Papers in British Museum, MS., 36, 232.

[24] Reigate after 1832 was a polling station for the Eastern Division of Surrey,
one of the two divisions created by the Reform Act, and shared the excitement
of contested elections for the county. (See report of action Holdsworth *v.* King,
Times, 6th August, 1842).

[25] *Report of Commissioners on Disfranchisement of Reigate, 1867*.   The Borough
Council vainly petitioned against the disfranchisement (*Times*, 27th March,
1867).

CHAPTER IX

REIGATE IN THE SIXTEENTH, SEVENTEENTH AND EIGHTEENTH CENTURIES

THE religious changes of the sixteenth century appear to have been accepted locally, as they were in other parts of Surrey, without exciting serious opposition. The influence and example of Lord William Howard, who accepted the changes without demur, must have had a steadying effect on local opinion and the teaching of John Foxe, the martyrologist, during his six years' sojourn at Reigate, did much to popularise the new faith. His patroness, the duchess of Richmond, was entrusted with the care of the five infant children of her brother Henry Howard, earl of Surrey, the ill-fated poet who had been put to death by Henry VIII in 1547. She engaged Foxe, whose protestant convictions she fully shared, as their tutor and set up her household at the castle. The three eldest children were Thomas, who became fourth duke of Norfolk and contracted a life-long friendship with his teacher, Jane, afterwards countess of Westmoreland, and Henry, afterwards earl of Northampton. Another pupil of Foxe in the town was lord William's son, Charles, the future Lord Admiral, and second cousin of Surrey's children.

Foxe while at Reigate put forth some tracts in support of his views and was, to quote Wood, " the first man (as 'tis said) that ever preached the gospel in that place, even when the Roman Catholic religion was in great strength." This statement rests on the evidence of Foxe's friend, Richard Day, for a short while vicar of Reigate, who adds that he converted many and was instrumental in abolishing the worship of Our Lady of Ouldsworth, a local Madonna credited with miraculous healing powers, whose image was an object of superstitious devotion[1].   Ouldsworth, a local corruption of " oldwarke " (the old work), was the name given to the bridge that spanned the little stream which, after skirting the Vicarage and Fridays Mead, flowed across Bell Street into the Priory grounds to feed the Priory pond.   Probably a wayside shrine set up hereabouts attracted the devotion and offerings of passers-by.   His engagement terminated on the accession of queen Mary in 1553, when he left the town and shortly afterwards fled to the Continent.

In 1551 Reigate suffered from a minor earthquake shock which also affected Dorking and some other places in Surrey and caused much alarm without doing any serious damage[2].

Henry Norman, appointed vicar in 1557, was deprived in 1562 possibly for recusancy, though if so he was one of the few Surrey incumbents removed on that ground. His successor, Richard Skinner, accepted the Elizabethan settlement unreservedly.   He was presented by the queen and retained the living till his death twenty years later. The advowson belonged to his brother, John, a member of the queen's household who probably ceded his right to present for this turn out of regard for his royal mistress.

The reign of Elizabeth, who occupied the throne from 1558 till 1603, a space of forty-four years, is an important era in our annals because of the help that local records now begin to afford.   The Parish Registers start in 1556 and are continuous from 1561 ; the Court Rolls of the manor are extant with a few breaks from 1571 onwards.   These and other contemporary sources enable our history from this time onwards to be treated on a much fuller scale than has been hitherto possible.

The neighbourhood at this period was already growing in favour as a residential centre, for which its natural attractions have always recommended it, and several members of the court and household of Elizabeth and later sovereigns had houses in the parish.   Despite the difficulties of travel, the locality was sufficiently near London to attract city merchants and gentry of the official class on the look-out for a country seat amid unspoiled surroundings.

The earliest Register of christenings shows that it was common to bestow the queen's name on infant girls and a further sign of her immense popularity appeared at her passing. It is seldom that the Registers allude to national affairs but the queen's death was an event of such outstanding importance as to prompt the following entry : " The 23 day of Marche beinge thersday morninge between 1 and 2 a clock departed this lyfe of the great renowned Queen Elizabeth late Queen of England ffraunce and Ireland defender of the faythe. She deceased at Ritchmounte and her body was buryed at Westminster Abbey the Thursday in easter week beinge the 28 day of Aprill and her funerall that day was solemly kept Ano. 1603."[3] The death in the preceding February of her old friend and cousin the countess of Nottingham, the Lord Admiral's first wife, had plunged her into a deep melancholy which hastened her own end.

The first state lottery to be organised in England appeared in 1567 under the queen's authority. It aimed at raising money to improve the harbours and for other public works, but proved a failure in spite of all efforts to set it going. In a letter dated 21st August, 1568, John Johnson, who had been appointed surveyor of the lottery, complained to William More of Loseley, treasurer of the money collected in Surrey, that Croydon had subscribed for only three lots and Reigate for only two. But their backwardness was typical of the general apathy of the queen's subjects who fought shy of risking their money in this novel venture[4].

Reigate in the age of Elizabeth and indeed until the nineteenth century though classed as a town was no greater than many country villages of the present day. Exact statistics are unobtainble but its population could not have numbered a thousand and fell, there is reason to think, considerably short of that figure. The Protestation Rolls of 1641 give a list of 404 names, being those of practically all the male inhabitants of the parish above the age of eighteen and representing probably about a third of the total population. The returns for the hearth tax, which was first imposed in the reign of Charles II, show

I

that in 1664 there were 158 inhabited dwellings in the
Old Borough which roughly coincided in extent with the
town. The majority of these dwellings were charged for
one or two hearths only and contained probably not more
than two or three living-rooms. If we allow four and a
half persons per dwelling the result is a little over 700
which is probably not far from the actual figure. The
number of dwellings in the Foreign was returned at 170
which, multiplied by the same figure, gives a total of 765
as the population of that part of the parish.[5]

Though early marriages and large families prevailed
among all classes, the growth of population was checked by
the high death-rate. Houses in the town were for the
most part packed tightly together and frequently dove-
tailed into one another in a manner that left little space
for light and ventilation though except on the north side
of High Street, where they backed on the Castle, many
of them had the benefit of large gardens. Deaths from
epidemics were appallingly frequent and whole families were
often involved, so that it is not uncommon to read of the
burial of a husband and wife and one or more of their
children at the same time.

The number of houses converted into two or three
tenements, and the persistent disregard of the law against
" inmates," i.e., lodgers, points to some increase of the town
population during the later part of the seventeenth century
which the contemporary growth of the oatmeal industry
may have accounted for.

Plague is first mentioned in 1582 but was probably
suspected four years earlier when " searchers " are referred
to. Searchers were persons appointed to view corpses
with the object of ascertaining the cause of death. A
terrible outbreak occurred in 1603, and from June of that
year to May following 184 deaths were ascribed to the
plague. Some of the victims were buried in gardens or
fields to avoid spreading infection. One pathetic entry
relates how " Thomas Alyf labourer and his wife and a
chrissomer of her newly borne " were " buryed all together
in a pyt in their own backsyde by earls wood." A
chrissomer or chrism child was one who, dying within

a few days of birth, was buried in a chrism or christening cloth. Burials of these infants are very numerous in the early Registers, and there are also frequent entries of the burial of nurse children, that is children, usually from London and of illegitimate birth, who were put out to foster parents in the country.

In May, 1637, the town was so badly infected that the Privy Council ordered the justices to put off the fair shortly due to be held there.[6] The last visitation occurred in 1665 and the following year when 107 victims perished. The year 1665 is memorable for the great plague of London and it was from there probably that the disease spread to Reigate. In the wake of this scourge came the smallpox which broke out in 1667 causing fourteen deaths, followed by intermittent attacks during the next hundred years. The seventeenth century closed with a heavy mortality from fever of an unspecified kind.[7]

Several of the Lord Admiral's servants died of the plague in 1603 and 1604. He maintained a large establishment at the Priory in keeping with the style demanded of a man of his rank and position in that sumptuous age, though this was only one of his seats and Haling House, Croydon, was his favourite residence. We read of my lord's clerk of the kitchen, brewer, butler and several cooks and, among the outdoor staff, a park-keeper, warrener, falconer, horse-keeper, mason and rent gatherer.

When we turn to the Court Rolls the cause of these ravages is soon apparent. They reveal an unsavoury picture of streets littered with heaps of malodorous filth and other obstructions, of swine roaming at large and routing in the garbage, of unscoured ditches discharging into the highway and of unmended roads often deep in mud. Thus at the Court Leet held in 1616, " It is ordered that Anthonie Lewce " and eleven others " doe remove their dunghills out of the streets before Allhallowtide next upon paine to forfeite to the Lordes every man that shall make default 3s, 4d." Again at the Court held in 1619, " It is ordered that if Thomas Paskyn, Allan Venne, John Feist and Andrew Tooth shall suffer their dunge to lye in the streete at any one time above 14 days then hee

or they soe offending shall forfeyt for every time wherein
he or they shall so offend Xs."

The Court Leet came at length to recognise the futility
of trying to stamp out the evil in the absence of any provision for refuse disposal. Accordingly in 1655 and
subsequent years it appointed scavengers and passed a
by-law, which was repeated in 1659, empowering them to
remove " dunge soyle and compost " from the streets after
four days. Anyone who obstructed them was to forfeit
2s. of which 1s. 6d. was to go " towards the amendment
of the streetes " and the remainder to the scavengers.
It is to be feared that these officials badly scamped their
duty for as the century advanced the nuisance showed no
sign of abating. Indeed at the Court Leet in 1676 John
Life, one of the scavengers, was fined five shillings for
failing to remove the dunghills lying in the streets of the
Borough with the threat of a further fine of fifteen shillings
if he did not carry out his duties within a fortnight. Sadder
still to relate, in 1679 Thomas Munnyer, senior, one of the
scavengers for that year, was himself fined for amassing a
dunghill in the highway before his house. He got off very
lightly with a fine of twopence and a further fine of 2s. 6d.
if the heap was not removed within two weeks. To
complete the humour of the situation Munnyer was again
elected scavenger for the ensuing year, probably as
additional punishment for his offence.

The Court Leet, or View of Frankpledge, whose proceedings have been quoted, dealt with a wide variety of
business and exercised some of the powers of a modern
police court. In theory every male resident in the manor
of fourteen years and upwards had to attend the Court
and was liable to be fined if absent without excuse. The
lord's steward presided and empanelled a jury of twelve
to hear and decide the causes. The first business was the
election of the officers to serve for the following year.
These consisted of the bailiff, three constables—two for
the Old Borough and one for the Foreign—and five
tithingmen or headboroughs to serve the five tithings or
petty boroughs into which the Foreign was divided. Then
came the election of two ale tasters, two fish tasters and

two searchers and sealers of leather. The offences dealt with ranged from breaches of the assizes of bread and ale —which fixed the price and quality of those articles—and non-repair of a bridge or highway, to wrongs of a more personal kind like assault and encroachments on a neighbour's property. Cases of assault, of which the following is a typical instance, were numerous. In 1577 Robert Hadlow was presented for assaulting Thomas Pilkington and drawing blood with his fists and was fined 40s. But the contest had not been unequal and Thomas seems to have given as good as he got since he was fined a like sum for drawing blood from the said Robert. Encroachments and nuisances of various kinds frequently called for the Court's intervention. Allen Venne was in 1615 ordered to lay out the land which he had encroached out of the land of Thomas Cole within thirty days upon pain of forfeiting 20s. But Venne was an obstinate fellow for at the next year's Court the encroachment was again reported and he was ordered to remove it under a penalty of 40s. A case of eavesdropping occurred in 1611 when John Wood of the White Hart was directed to mend his leads that the water falling from them " doe not annoye his neighbours," and this was to be rectified by Christmas or a fine of 20s. incurred. If the fines seem low we must remember that money at this period was worth many times its present value.

Perusal of the Court Rolls quickly dispels the idea that contempt for the law is a modern failing. By an Act passed in 1589 it was forbidden to erect a cottage on less than four acres of land and to take " inmates," i.e., lodgers. The division of houses into separate tenements was also prohibited.[8] The Act was inspired by the fear of overcrowding and that lodgers if permitted would increase the number of paupers chargeable to the parish. In 1627 William Ridley and two others were each fined the heavy sum of £10 for erecting cottages on Earlswood Common without the lord's licence and with less than the required acreage. Throughout the seventeenth century Reigate householders were repeatedly hauled up for letting rooms to inmates who were not members of their family.

Another law constantly infringed was an old statute of Edward I which enjoined on the inhabitants of every borough the duty of keeping watch and ward. The offending boroughs in the parish were regularly fined a shilling and continued calmly to ignore the statute.

The Court was no respecter of persons ; the lord if he offended was liable to be presented and fined like lesser delinquents. In 1617 the jury, in terms milder than usual, presented " that our Caege and Pillorie are fallen into decaye wch we desire maie be repaired by the Lords of the Mannour." In 1627 Sir William (afterwards viscount) Monson was presented for obstructing " the Common Sewer " through Reigate Park.

The Court in exercise of its power to make by-laws issued orders at various times directed against such matters as the ever present nuisance of dunghills in the streets, serving of swine in the Old Borough and letting them out unringed, making gates or stiles into the castle grounds from adjoining premises, and playing unlawful games and drinking in times of divine service. The order against drinking or gaming in service-time appeared in 1596, and under it Anthony Heathfeild, innkeeper, was in 1613 presented for permitting unlawful games in his house on Sunday within the prohibited hours.

As the Court met only once a year and had no power to imprison it was ill-fitted to deal with petty delinquencies. Its functions in this respect gradually faded out, and by the end of the seventeenth century it had tacitly resigned them to the justices of the peace. During the eighteenth century it met very infrequently, the only business transacted being the election of the officers. The last Court was held in 1811.

The other Manor Court, known as the Court Baron, usually met twice a year in the spring and autumn. This like the Court Leet was thoroughly democratic in character and played until the eighteenth century an important part in local government, but differed from it in being the court of the lord and not of the sovereign. It was largely concerned with the business of transferring the customary or copyhold lands of the tenants when they died or disposed of their holdings, but it also declared and enforced the customs of the manor, made by-laws and entertained claims for the recovery of small debts and for trespass and other civil injuries. It also dealt with offences against the manor of which the commonest were encroachments on the waste. The steward presided but the tenants present in Court, who were styled the homage, or a jury drawn from them, acted as the judges and it was they who decided the questions that arose.[9]

Reigate until the reign of George I was an assize town on the South Eastern, or Home, Circuit[10]. The Parish Registers occasionally refer to the assizes. Thus on 15th March, 1700, is recorded the burial of "John Peters a felon that dyed on the road in coming to his tryall at the Assizes," and on 23rd March of " Humphrey Hannael at the Assizes hangd for clipping and coining," and three other men hanged for burglary, " William King hangd for sacrilege and felony, Elisabeth Pilkington burnt there for clipping and coining." Burning was the barbarous punishment inflicted for offences regarded as treason, but the victim was mercifully strangled before being burnt. In 1698 a man hanged for burglary and felony was buried in the churchyard, and three men and a woman hanged at the same time were buried under the gallows. " They all seemed penitent," is the vicar's comment on these unhappy wretches.

In 1697 Reigate was the scene of a sordid crime, memories of which lingered till Ridgeway's day. He gives some of the bald details and these can be supplemented from other sources.[11] The victim was a single woman named Anne Edwards who kept house for Richard Rhodes, an oatmeal-man in a good way of business in Bell Street. Finding the woman to be pregnant he murdered her and fled to Ireland after burying her corpse in the garden. The crime was quickly detected and the relatives of the murdered woman offered a reward for Rhodes' discovery in the *London Gazette*, in which he is described as a " thin man of Middle stature, long Visaged, wearing his own Hair of a dark brown colour, curled at the ends, having light grey Eyes, and often Bloodshed, and a scar from the corner of one of his Eyes downwards, aged about 40." Shortly afterwards one of the guests at an inn near Drogheda, who happened to have read the advertisement, was struck by the waiter's resemblance to the description and asked him to write his name. Rhodes, for he it was, became confused and wrote his own name instead of " Francis Hatcher," his adopted alias. He was arrested and brought to England and found guilty at his trial which took place at Reigate assizes, and was hanged on a tree before the house in which the crime was committed. From there his body was conveyed to Redhill Common and hung in chains, but according to Ridgeway " was stolen away the same night." Nearly a century later the skeleton of a man thought to be that of Rhodes was dug up in a tanyard at the foot of the Common. The murderer was a man of some means and these included a sum of £500 due to him from the Admiralty. This with his other effects was claimed by the lord of the manor under an ancient custom which entitled him to the possessions of a felon found in the manor. The burial probably took place in a field known as Dedmans Cross which was later attached to the tanyard and is now the site of property called Earlswood Mount.

Ridgeway also gives an account of two other murders. His story of the stabbing of Mr. Poor, keeper of the White Hart, by the officer of a foot regiment may possibly be a misapplied version of the fate of Nicholas Castleman of the Swan, who according to the Parish Register " was stabd by a coronet of Dragoons on the 4th June, 1695." The other story relates to the exploit of a local highwayman nicknamed Roly Poly who " about the year 1728 " at Cockshot Hill killed and robbed a farmer named Colcock in mistake for a Mr. Charrington, his intended victim. Highwaymen continued to infest the main roads till the nineteenth century. In 1799 Daniel Bliss of Bell Street, whitesmith, was attacked on Reigate hill while returning from Ewell and left in a ditch. He died two years later from his injuries. Over fifty years later his great-grandson, Henry Willis of Ewell, was held up on the road at Kingswood while driving home one night from Reigate, but managed to shake off his assailants.[12]

The spring Quarter Sessions for the county were held at Reigate until their removal to Newington in the nineteenth century. Interesting light is shed on the work of a Surrey magistrate in the early seventeenth century by the note-book of Mr. Bostock Fuller, an important local magnate who lived at Tandridge Court.[13] The office of a country justice in those days was no sinecure involving as it did constant travelling on horseback over bad roads in all weathers. His multifarious duties ranged from the licensing of ale houses and the swearing in of constables and head-boroughs to the trials of delinquents for a great variety of offences both trivial and serious. Rabbit poaching was a common failing, and in 1612 Robert Richbell and Richard Mathewe were charged with hunting and killing my Lord Admiral's conies in Reigate Park. In 1618 Robert Cotes was charged with the murder of Wm. Darye of Reigate and committed to prison by Mr. Fuller after taking the evidence of seven persons.[14]

Sometimes a special session was held to deal with urgent cases as in 1664 when a jury of twenty-four local men was summoned to the White Hart to try a charge of riot against John Digge, John Heathfeild and George Heath, for forcibly entering the house of Luke Chinnell, miller, and assaulting him.[15]

Throughout the sixteenth and seventeenth centuries the belief in witchcraft remained rife and thousands of innocent women were sacrificed under laws inspired by this hoary and hideous superstition. Reigate contained some sus-pected witches who were at times harried by the law, though I have not found any case locally of infliction of the death penalty. In 1611 Jane Roberts of Reigate, spinster, was bound over by Mr. Fuller to appear at the assizes on suspicion of committing " divers felonious wytchcrafts." In 1630 Margery Brotherton of Reigate, wife of Francis Brotherton, yeoman, was indicted at the Surrey summer assizes for bewitching John, the infant son of Thomas Crust, on 1st October, 1620, who " languished until 20th October when he died." No fewer than thirty-three local witnesses appeared against her. She was found guilty and sentenced to be hung but was afterwards reprieved, possibly because of the staleness of her offence. She and Elizabeth Brotherton were charged at the same assizes with having seven years earlier fatally bewitched an infant named Elizabeth Beckwith. All but four of the same cloud of witnesses gave evidence for the prosecution against the accused who were found guilty but reprieved after sentence. Another case occurred in 1651 when three Reigate women, two of them widows, were accused of bewitching Jonas Humphrey, " who was much weakened wasted and consumed."[16]

Reigate was a centre of resistance to ship money, the fiscal expedient which made Hampden famous and brought the country a step nearer to civil war. In 1636 the parish was charged with £60 of the £3,500 to be raised in the county. In 1637 the sheriff complained that he found " so much contempt from the constable and church-wardens of the parish that unless the Lords make them a present example, and that with much severity, he doubts many other parishes will follow their courses." He also reported that he could find nothing on which to distrain for £8, the portion due from lord Monson.[17]

Some of the many religious movements and experiments of the seventeenth century are reflected in local history. In 1642 a lecture at the parish church that had been instituted some years earlier and allowed to lapse was revived.[18] Lectureships were a Puritan innovation for the extension of preaching. They had been suppressed by archbishop Laud but reappeared after his fall.

In 1648 Parliament attempted to organise the churches of Surrey on a Presbyterian basis. Episcopacy had been abolished and the Presbyterians, who were then dominant, aimed at imposing their system of worship and belief as the national faith. Presbyteries had already been set up in London and two other centres. Surrey was divided into six *classes* or presbyteries of which the sixth or Reigate *classis* comprised the town of Reigate and other towns and villages in the hundreds of Reigate and Tandridge. The local members included Mr. Parr, the vicar, and Messrs. Roger James, John Parker and John Beauchamp. But the scheme never took root and, with the possible exception of the Reigate *classis*, had none but a paper existence. The overthrow of Parliament by the Army later in the year ended any chance of its success.[19]

During the Commonwealth and Protectorate the religious ceremony of marriage was abolished and after 1653 weddings were celebrated before a justice of the peace. These civil unions, of which several are recorded in the Parish Register, were performed at the church after publication of notice on three successive Sundays in church, or on three successive market days in the Market Place. Two local magistrates, John Beauchamp and Thomas Moore, usually officiated. Beauchamp was a Presbyterian and Moore, who lived at Hartswood, an early member of the Society of Friends.

The history of local nonconformity begins with the rise of Quakerism about the middle of the seventeenth century when the doctrines of George Fox, its founder, attracted a following in the district. Fox himself visited Reigate in 1655 and wrote in his Journal, " At Reigate Friends told me of one Thomas Moore a justice of the peace that lived not far from Reigate and was a friendly moderate man, whereupon I went to visit him at his house, and he came to be a serviceable man in the Truth."[20] Shortly after a meeting was started at his house. A monthly meeting for Dorking, Reigate and Capel had been founded by 1668 and when held at Reigate took place at the house of one of the local members. Prominent among these were Thomas Blatt, or Blott, and his sons John and Thomas. The father owned the Redhill tannery, and occupied the house and farm opposite to it in Linkfield Street known as Fengates. In 1656 he was chosen bailiff of the manor at the Court Leet but for refusing to take the oath of office was fined £5 for contempt. On his death in 1667 he was succeeded by his son, John, at whose house some of the early meetings were held. Meetings were also occasionally held at the houses of Thomas, the other son, a tallow chandler by trade in Reigate, Dr. George Vaux, a physician practising in the town, and John Bicknell, husbandman. In 1687 steps were taken to find a permanent meeting house, and Thomas Blatt was " desired to make a diligent enquiry about Linkfield Street if some house barn or ground may be purchased as a convenient thing for that purpose." Some years earlier, however, a piece of land of half an acre forming part of the present burial ground had been purchased by Thomas Moore and leased to the Society for 2,000 years at a nominal rent and on part of this site a meeting house was erected about 1688. This building, with an enlargement made about 1798, stood till 1857, when it was pulled down and replaced by the present building.[21]

The faith and practice of the early Quaker conflicted with the law at a number of points and made him an easy target for persecution, of which local Friends had their full share. Two of the commonest charges against them were abstinence from the parish church and attendance at their own meeting. Time and again the brothers Blatt, Rowley Titchbourne and Ralph Holdsworth, two Reigate shoemakers, and other local adherents and their wives, were indicted for these offences at Quarter Sessions, though often apparently the proceedings were not pressed and seem to have been instituted merely with the object of singling out the more notorious offenders.[22] The Conventicle Act, 1664, which made it criminal to hold a religious meeting of more than five persons not of the same family for worship not in accordance with the Prayer Book, was more rigorously enforced. In September, 1664, for instance, Rowley Titchbourne and two other local Quakers appeared before Roger James and Edward Thurland, two of the justices, at Reigate for attending "an unlawful meeting at the house of Thomas Blatt, Reigate, with forty-seven other evildoers," and received sentence of six days' imprisonment or a fine of 5s.[23].

William Penn, the eminent Quaker, visited Reigate in 1672 and again in 1688 and 1710. Another well-known Quaker, Ambrose Rigg, the tale of whose sufferings would fill a volume, spent the closing years of his long life at the house in Church Street where he expired in 1705.[24] By his will he directed Nathaniel Owen and George Vaux, senior, the physician, to collect his books, papers and epistles and cause them " to be printed in one booke bound

and sent abroad for the service of truth and friends thereof."
Dr. Vaux survived his friend by only a few days. He had
been excommunicated in 1683 for practising physic without a licence from the Ecclesiastical Court.[25] The Church
at that date controlled the faculty as it controlled learning.
Rigg while living at Gatton had been excommunicated for
teaching without the bishop's sanction, and had suffered
from the malignity of the rector, Robert Pepys, who on one
occasion threatened to murder him and had to be forcibly
restrained by his own servant. Robert was the son of
Richard Pepys, a London mercer, who was one of the
numerous cousins of Samuel Pepys, the diarist.

Dr. Vaux's son, George, continued to practise as a doctor
at Reigate for several years after his father's death. He
occupied premises in the Market Place which, until recently
demolished to make way for Burton's establishment, were
for many years occupied as a chemist's shop, and as he is
described in the Parish Register as " apothecary " he
probably dealt in drugs. He also rented part of the house
then standing in the Castle for a dissecting room.

The Congregational Church in High Street, Reigate,
claims a history going back to 1662, though James Waters,
the first minister on record, did not commence his pastorate
until 1687 and left after five years. Possibly Edward
Hubbard, who died of fever in 1700 and is described in the
Parish Register as " an Independent preacher," succeeded
him. For many years, however, the cause was Presbyterian, in name at least, and was probably " another of the
Presbyterian meetings which for want of a real Presbyterian
organisation passed into Congregationalism."[26] In returns
made in 1715 and 1725 a Presbyterian meeting is recorded
at Reigate, but not an Independent one.[27] In 1725 the
chapel or meeting house was a barn in High Street known
as Blatt's barn after the name of its owner. By 1731 another
building near this was in use as the chapel.[28] In that year
Jane Hoadley of Reigate devised to her nephew, Thomas
Blatt, her freehold barn " near the Meeting House in
Reigate Borough," and part of her " Orchard near it which
was purchased of his Father." She also gave him " her
right and interest in the pew I usually sit in in the Meeting

House," and left £100 to maintain the ministry there.   By 1801 the barn had gone and a new meeting house had recently been erected, probably on its site, though the old house was still standing.   In the latter part of the eighteenth century when English Presbyterianism merged into Unitarianism the cause declined, and for twenty years the old meeting house remained closed.   The new building had apparently been erected by Thomas Wilson, the nonconformist benefactor, who in 1801 purchased the site together with the orchard on which the barn formerly stood. He also purchased from William Ware, the heir at law of the last owner, who was imprisoned for debt in Newgate, the old Meeting House " formerly used for the worship of God."   The new chapel was opened in 1801 by the Rev. Rowland Hill but met with violent opposition from a faction of the townspeople who endeavoured by rough horseplay to break up the services.   The preachers were boycotted and the chapel had to be closed for a time.   Mr. Wilson built another chapel in 1819 but local prejudice still ran so high that the first minister was forced to seek lodgings outside the town.   The new church seems to have made but slow progress.   A few years later Mr. Wilson with undaunted zeal again came forward and built the existing chapel which was opened in 1831 but was so constructed as to be convertible into two cottages in the event of failure. The Rev. Thos. Rees ministered here from 1835 to 1856 when he was succeeded by the Rev. G. J. Adeney, a man greatly esteemed and beloved who may be said to have established the modern church.   Under his long ministry of forty-two years the membership greatly increased, the chapel was more than once enlarged and a new schoolroom added.[29]

The first Sunday School to be established at Reigate was started in the chapel by a Miss Apted and two other enterprising ladies about the year 1803.   This unorthodox attempt to educate the children of the working class so alarmed the magistrates that they caused their clerk to write to the ladies " telling them that the Magistrates had discussed the fact that they were teaching reading and writing as well as religious knowledge, and the Clerk begged to inform these ladies that such proceedings were most dangerous and that the Magistrates would not be answerable for the peace of the town if they continued in these ways." This egregious epistle failed to daunt the ladies and the school grew and flourished under their management.

Roman Catholicism had little chance of asserting itself in Surrey after the Reformation, though a few prominent families clung to the old faith. The story that the Lord Admiral adhered to it is a modern fable. The leading Catholic family in the immediate neighbourhood was that of the Copleys of Gatton and Leigh. Thomas Copley owned freehold land in Reigate Manor and strengthened his association with the parish by purchasing the manor of Colley in 1566. He sat in Parliament for his pocket borough of Gatton under Mary and Elizabeth but later discovered scruples against conformity which he voiced in an outspoken letter to the sheriff and justices of Surrey in 1569. After serving a term of imprisonment he migrated to the Continent, entered the service of the Spanish king and died in Flanders in 1584. His son, William, succeeded to his estates and compounded for his own recusancy by an annual payment of £240. William's granddaughter, Mary, married John Weston of Sutton, near Woking, a member of another old Surrey family with Catholic traditions. She lived till 1694 having acquired Colley Manor by partition on the death of her grandfather in 1643.[30]

John Wesley preached at Reigate in 1770 and 1771 and again in 1774 and 1775. On two of these visits he was the guest of Mr. Ireland at the Priory and held services there. On the first occasion his audiences proved apathetic and he wrote in his Journal, " Wed. 19 Dec. . . . about an hundred attended at Ryegate in the evening and between twenty and thirty in the morning. Dull indeed as stones." Under 17th December, 1771, he wrote, " I preached in the evening to a small company on ' It is appointed unto men once to die.' All seemed moved for the present. They saw that life is a dream, but how soon will they sleep again ! " His later visits drew larger congregations but bore no permanent fruit, and nearly a century elapsed before the establishment of a Methodist society in the parish.[31]

England possessed no standing army until Parliament fashioned the New Model in 1645. Under the Tudors troops were raised from each county in times of emergency by means of militia levies called musters to which every hundred and parish had to supply its quota. All able-bodied men were liable to serve and if, as constantly happened, the numbers who volunteered were insufficient they were brought up to strength by forcible enlistment. In 1544, when the French attempted an invasion, a general muster of the county was ordered under which Reigate hundred had to supply four archers and eighteen billmen toward the 400 men required. In 1569 the Surrey musters were called out in consequence of the rising of the northern earls, and William, lord Howard, the Lord Lieutenant, was commanded to hold the whole force of the county ready to march at an hour's notice. The list contains the names of nine men from the Old Borough and five from the Foreign. William Poyntz of Woodhatch was disqualified for serving as a captain because he owned no estate in the county. The musters were summoned again in 1580 by the Lord Admiral, who had succeeded his father as Lord Lieutenant, when the beacons were fired under a false alarm of the sailing of a Spanish Armada. Eight years later when the Armada at last sailed Surrey was again called to arms and 836 foot, about one-eighth of the total levy, were ordered to assemble at Reigate. Fortunately the danger passed without this force being put to the test for, if opposed to regular troops, its prospects would not have been bright.[32]

The militia was called up by Parliament in 1642 on the outbreak of the Civil War. Surrey was one of the first counties to respond but its levies saw little actual fighting. After the Restoration the force sank into a state of inefficiency which continued until the Militia Act of 1757 brought about a reorganiation. Under this measure Surrey had to raise 800 men of which the quota for Reigate Hundred was 80. In June, 1759, the Reigate company numbered 60, or 20 below full strength, with a captain, lieutenant and ensign, four sergeants and two drummers. In November following, the regiment was divided into East and West Surrey battalions each made up of five companies, the

Reigate company being included in the former of the two.

The ominous course taken by the French Revolution led to the embodiment of the militia in 1792. The Surrey Volunteers and Yeomanry were raised in 1794 for home defence against the threat of an invasion. The Holmes-dale Volunteers with headquarters at Reigate numbered 208 and had the credit of being by far the strongest of the 24 companies raised in the County. Lieut.-Col. John Petrie M.P., of Gatton, was the company's commanding officer and Ambrose Glover served as a captain.[33]

During the Civil War which raged from 1642 to 1646 little fighting took place in Surrey. Reigate lay outside the zone of conflict ; it was too near London, the centre of Parliamentary influence, to be drawn into the struggle though there were Royalists in the town who became marked men during the Commonwealth.[34] Yet it had to provide its share of the sinews of war and of these the most galling and oppressive was the free quartering of troops, a practice which continued long after the main hostilities had ceased. Reigate suffered from this exaction like the rest of the county, and Parliamentary troops were quartered here in 1647 and the following year. In February 1648 a serious outbreak occurred between the troops and townsmen resulting in loss of life and much bloodshed. Two civilians, Nicholas Marden and William Preist, were fatally injured. Both were wounded, according to the entry of their burial in the Parish Register, " by some of the souldiers in Capt. Winthorps Troope in Coll. Harrison's Regiment in Sir Thos. Fairfax Armie," who " being quartered in the Town fell out with the Country men and these two murdered by them and many more dangerously wounded."

This affray was merely one of the many riots that were breaking out all over the country. Discontent was general, and in the summer of 1648 Surrey became the scene of a formidable rising under the earl of Holland which aimed at restoring Charles I. It was wretchedly organised and quickly suppressed but has a local interest because some of the fighting that occurred took place in the parish. Holland on 6th July marched from Kingston to Dorking and from there to Reigate, where some plundering took place and

one man was shot for refusing to surrender his pistols.   The
Royalists occupied the half-ruined castle and stationed outposts on Redhill Common to watch for the approach of
Parliamentary troops which were advancing from Seven-
oaks.   At the same time Major Lewis Audeley with three
troops of horse advanced from the north and in a skirmish
on the Common drove in the outposts.   The same night
Reigate was abandoned by Holland, who withdrew to
Dorking, and was occupied next day by the Parliamentary
forces.   The day following Holland tried to return to
Reigate but finding the enemy there in strength he made
off in aimless retreat towards Kingston hotly pursued by
his opponents who overtook and dispersed the remnant of
his army between Ewell and Surbiton.   " So ended,"
remarks Mr. Malden, " the last real fighting which has
taken place in Surrey, and the last serious skirmish of the
Civil Wars south of the Thames."[35]   A few Reigate men
took part in the rising and lived to regret the sequel.   Lord
Peterborough, the countess' elder son, who was one of the
leaders, escaped abroad " in a totally ruined condition,"
and her younger son, John, was also implicated.   Mr.
Pistor of the White Hart was accused of having " set forth
John James of Hourne, Surrey, with money and arms."
The charge lagged till 1652 when James, who had been
kept in prison, was ordered to be brought up to give evidence.
John Bill, a printer of London and Reigate, who had
previously fought for the king as a major of horse, had to
compound a second time for joining lord Holland.[36]

The death of Charles I in 1649 fired the vicar to record
that momentous event in the Parish Register : " January
30.   This day King Charles was put to death by separating
his royall head from his shoulders at White Hall in Westminster about two of the clock in the after noone in the 24
yeare of his reigne : Anno Domini 1648."   The entry
appears under 1648 as the legal year then ended on
24th March.

Eleven years later Redhill Common was chosen as the
rendezvous for another Royalist insurrection.   Timed to
take place in the early morning of 1st August, 1659, it was
one of a series of risings which had been planned for that

day in various parts of the country. Richard Cromwell had recently resigned the office of Protector and royalist hopes were mounting. But the government got wind of the design and sent orders to Major Audley, who had acted so efficiently in the earlier rising, to occupy the ground the day before. This he did and succeeded in catching most of those who tried to assemble, and the few who did collect were quickly driven off in flight to Shelwood, beyond Leigh, and dispersed.[37] John Mordaunt was the arch-plotter of this as he was of most of the royalist risings during the Commonwealth and Protectorate.

Reigate was lavishly supplied with inns and taverns during the three centuries under review. In the seventeenth century these included the White Hart, Swan, Bell, Cross Keys, Queen's Arms, Crown, George, Plough, Ship, Red Cross, Red Lion, Bull—later the Bull's Head—Fleur de Luce and Five Bells. The two leading ones were the White Hart and Swan which both stood in the Market Place until they were swept away in recent years. The White Hart, or Hart, the name usually applied to it in the sixteenth and seventeenth centuries, was kept between 1582 and 1611 by John Wood and later by William Pistor, who was charged for six hearths in the Hearth Tax Assessment, 1664, in which he is described as " gent." It reached its zenith in the palmy days of the stage coach between 1756 and the advent of the railway. The Prince of Wales, afterwards George IV, often patronised it on his journeys to Brighton. "At the White Hart," says an account written in 1789 " the Traveller is certain of meeting with every Accomodation he can wish, good Post Horses, an excellent larder, geuine Wines, etc., which have rendered Mrs. Sully worthy the Encouragement she meets with. His Royal Highness, the Prince of Wales, in his Excursions to Brighthelmstone, frequently dines here." He continued to patronise it after he had come to the throne as George IV. A guide to Dorking and neighbourhood written in 1823 declared, " The most interesting route of road to Brighton—the *Daphne* of the Metropolis—lies through Reigate ; and, by the superiority of its accomodation, it enjoys the patronage and decided preference of *Royalty*.

In truth, *Relf's* may be styled the *Clarendon* of the Brighton road." The allusion is to James Relf, the proprietor at that period.[38]

The Swan was conducted in the seventeenth century by Nicholas Castleman and his brother, William, and later by William's son, Nicholas. The elder Nicholas lay under suspicion during the Commonwealth when inns were closed or controlled by Cromwell's major-generals as centres of Royalist disaffection. The younger Nicholas met a tragic end in 1695 as previously related.[39] The original Crown Inn occupied a position in High Street which now forms the site of Sainsbury's shop, but in the eighteenth century the name, which survives in the passage known as the Crown Steps, was transferred to an inn on the north side of the street now replaced by Lloyds Bank. The premises had previously borne the sign of the Three Horse Shoes and were in 1647 conveyed by that name to Thomas Blatt of Fengates, tanner.

Walsingham Heathfeild, brewer and innkeeper, who was another suspected malignant, occupied the Red Lion at the corner of West Street and Park Lane with a field at the rear called Red Lion Close which included part of the present Priory cricket ground. He purchased the property in 1671 just before his death, by which date the house had been divided into three tenements. By 1729 it had ceased to be licensed.[40]

The Queen's Arms which stood on the north side of High Street was owned for some years by Thomas Blatt, the Quaker tallow-chandler. He sold it in 1656 and the deed of conveyance set out the rooms in detail including " the cold harbour "—apparently the larder—and " the signe chamber."[41]

Three of the oldest public houses to survive are the Bell, the Bull's Head and Red Cross. In the seventeenth century the Bell Inn or " Hostry " lay on the west side of Bell Street. It belonged at one time to Edward Bysshe of Smallfields who sold it in 1627. His uncle, Erasmus Bysshe, was a mercer in the town and prominent in local affairs. Many of these houses were alehouses and not inns in the legal sense. The Court Rolls draw a distinction between the innkeeper who found food and lodging as well as drink, and the common tippler or alehouse keeper who dealt solely in liquor. A tippler it should be remembered signified originally not a man who over-drank but one who sold or tippled beer.

The parish church after a common English fashion had its attendant inn which stood on the opposite side of Chart Lane and bore the appropriate sign of the Five Bells. This was closed before 1770 and a house, latterly known as " Cherchefelle " and now used as offices by the East Surrey Gas Co., was built on the site by Mr. Robert Scawen of Great Doods.

At the east side of the parish the oldest surviving inns are the Red Lion in Linkfield Lane and the White Lion in Linkfield Street. The White Lion, there is reason to think, though severely modernised, dates from medieval times. Ridgeway styles it " the principal Inn between Croydon and Sussex " and adds that the landlord laid out a bowling green on the top of Redhill Common for the entertainment of his guests. Its importance declined after the construction of the Reigate turnpike.

The Bottle House was an inn of copyhold tenure at Santon on the other side of the parish which passed to the Rev. John Bird, afterwards vicar of Reigate, through his marriage in 1703 to Mrs. Grace Arnold, widow of John Arnold, the previous owner.

The Angel at Woodhatch stands on ground that was originally part of the waste and is described in the Survey of 1623 as the " Bowling Alley lying before the gate of the Tenement called Woodhatch " ; and held by Mr. John Oade as copyhold of the manor. The present building may date back as far or farther but did not apparently come into use as an inn till the following century when it bore the sign of the White Horse. I have not traced its present name before 1814.

Education was by no means neglected at Reigate after the Reformation. No fewer than six schoolmasters and teachers of children are mentioned in the Parish Registers between 1562 and 1616. For some years in the early half of the eighteenth century Benjamin Smith, writing master, kept a school in the High Street. A girls' charity school, one of the many set up in the early years of the eighteenth century under the aegis of the newly formed Society for Promoting Christian Knowledge, was opened in 1715 ; but it had only a brief existence and appears to have expired after a few years, probably for want of local support. Surrey clergy as a body were " very averse " to this early movement for educating the children of the poor.[42]

The Parish Registers sometimes throw an interesting light on contemporary laws and customs. An Act passed in 1695 imposed a tax on births, marriages and deaths, supplemented by an annual tax on bachelors and widows. The yield from this taxation was disappointing and in 1706 it was abolished, but while in force the parson was charged with the duty of collecting the tax on marriages and burials and for this purpose had to keep a record of all deaths that occurred in his parish, and not merely the burials as was commonly the practice. Thus the Register of burials during these years is fuller than usual, as it includes the deaths of Quakers and other nonconformists. Payment of the tax is sometimes noted by the entry " K 4s. payd," " K " standing for King's tax. Another curious law respecting burials, passed in 1666, required corpses to be buried in woollen under a penalty of £5, with the object of encouraging the native woollen industry and checking the use of imported linen. This enactment was largely evaded until 1678 when its operation was tightened by a measure requiring an affidavit to be delivered to the minister within eight days of the burial to prove that the deceased had been buried in woollen. Notices of these affidavits frequently occur in the Register between 1708 and 1715. Occasionally expense was avoided by burial in herbs. John, the son of Mary Steward, " Traveller," was buried in this manner in 1709. For the luxury of burial in linen the fine was sometimes paid, in which case half went to the poor of the parish and the other half to the informer. Thus on the burial in 1710 of Ursula, lady Windsor, of Flanchford, 50s. is noted as " paid to ye poor " and the same is repeated later the same year against the entry of burial of her infant son, who like her had succumbed to the smallpox.

Anthony Ashley Cooper, third earl of Shaftesbury, made Reigate his home for a few years at the beginning of the century. He was a friend of lord Somers, owner of the manor, and like him a firm Whig. His interest however lay in philosophy rather than politics. He lived at a house in Church Street then known as Little Doods and later as The Wilderness, and while there published a collected edition of his works entitled *Characteristics of Men, Manners, Opinions, Times*, a copy of which he presented to the Parish Library. He married to please his friends and carry on the family succession, and did not see the lady chosen for him till the match was settled. In spite of this the union proved a happy one. Their eldest son, afterwards the fourth earl, was born here 9th February, 1711.

Little Doods belonged to Nathaniel Owen, one of Ambrose Rigg's literary executors and an active Quaker who kept the records of the local meeting. He had purchased the property of Edward Thurland, grandson of the judge, in 1698, and subsequently went to live there.

A more notorious resident was the ill-fated and accomplished Eugene Aram. Ridgeway, who is our authority, states that Aram was, about the year 1755, assistant to Mr. Alchin who kept an academy for young gentlemen at a house in Church Street called Repentance, and described him as " a very gay man who wore his gold laced hat and ruffles." Aram was hanged at York in 1759 for the murder of Daniel Clerk, a shoemaker of Knaresborough. The house stood on the north side of Church Street on land now occupied by modern shops.[43]

In the next decade another Reigate schoolmaster won transient fame as inventor of one of the earliest forms of cycle. About 1766 John Vevers of Woodhatch Place " Master of the Boarding School at Ryegate in Surrey," constructed a horseless vehicle described as a " Travelling Chaise." This cumbrous " machine apparently weighing several hundredweight was worked by an unfortunate footman who stood in a sort of box at the rear and, by standing on lever planks, alternately depressed each lever—propelling the vehicle by a rack and pinion sort of arrangement." Seated in front was an occupant who steered by reins, " the most complicated and indirect system ever designed." The invention excited great interest for a few years but was not a commercial success though imitated in France.[44]

Ridgeway also states that Robert Hill, the literary tailor who taught himself several languages, worked for his father, Thomas Ridgeway, for a short while in 1744 or 1745.

An exceptionally fine specimen of early eighteenth century architecture is the house known as The Barons in Church Street. It was erected about 1710 by Richard Devon, its first occupier, but took its name from a later tenant, Francis Maseres, Cursitor Baron of the Exchequer, who lived there for over 50 years. Born in the reign of George II, he wore the dress of that period till his death in 1824 and must have cut a quaint figure when he appeared abroad in his three-cornered hat, wig and ruffles. He lived to a patriarchal age and in his latter years was on friendly terms with that most pugnacious of mortals, William Cobbett, who left an amusing account of one of his visits to the Baron.[45]   In 1820 the Baron founded an afternoon sermon in Reigate Church which is still maintained. The Rev. Dr. Robert Fellowes, Ll.D., to whom he left his immense fortune, raised a handsome stone monument to his memory in the churchyard.

Dr. Fellowes in 1838 bought Great Doods, the former home of the Thurlands. In 1755 it had been purchased from the descendants of Sir Edward Thurland, the judge, by Robert Scawen who was also the owner of the neighbouring estate known as the Rectory Manor, or Parsonage, of which the Reigate Lodge estate is a remnant. This estate originally extended to Wray Park and included the advowson and chancel of the parish church and the great tithes. After being in the possession of Sir Roger James and his family for over a century it was purchased from his descendant, Haestreet James, in 1730, by Sir Thomas Scawen, a wealthy London merchant and alderman who, dying in 1730, left it after the death of his widow to his son, Robert. Shortly after Robert's death in 1778 it was sold by his trustees to Mr. Gawen Harris Nash but without the tithes. Nash bequeathed the remainder of the property to his cousin, Charles Goring of Wiston, Sussex, the planter of that well-known landmark, Chanctonbury Ring. Goring in 1786, the year following Nash's death, sold the bulk of the estate including Wray Farm to Charles Birkhead, whose name survives in Birkheads Road.

The pest house for the Old Borough, which served as a primitive isolation hospital for infectious diseases, stood at the northern corner of Chart Lane and Cockshot Road. In 1749 a lease of this property was granted for 41 years at a rent of 30s. a year to six Reigate tradesmen who were already in occupation, among them being Thomas Ridgeway, staymaker, father of William Ridgeway our local annalist. The Foreign had its own pest house which is mentioned in the minutes of a vestry held in 1791 and appears to have been situated in Littleton Lane on or near the spot that was later occupied by the Reigate waterworks. The field adjoining was formerly known as " Pest House Field," and is so named in Eve's map of the parish, 1861.

Fanny Burney, the novelist, passed through Reigate in the spring of 1779 on her way to Brighton in company with her friends the Thrales of Streatham and gave her impression of the town in a letter written at the end of the journey. " The road," she writes, " from Streatham hither is beautiful . . . Reigate, the first town, is a very old half-ruined borough in a most neglected condition. A high hill leading to it afforded a very fine prospect of the Malvern Hill nature though inferior." " Our journey," she continues, " was delightfully pleasant, the day being heavenly, the roads in fair order, the prospects charming and everybody good-humoured and cheerful."[46] Bryant's Survey of the Old Borough seven years later shows that of some 270 properties about 220 were occupied, while 14 are described as in ruins and the remainder consisted of vacant sites. On the other hand, 12 of the houses and shops including several in Bell Street are described as " newly erected." Of these the most important was the new White Hart Inn which had been rebuilt and greatly enlarged. Another and more imposing building was the house known as Browne's Lodge which stands in West Street at the end of the island site then known as Middle Row. Its occupant in 1786 was Mr. Charles Browne, whose name it perpetuates.

It had been purchased by Bryant for £2,300, probably as agent for lord Hardwicke. These new buildings followed the Georgian style of architecture then prevailing. In the course of the eighteenth century, particularly in the latter half, several other premises in the town had been partly or wholly rebuilt in the same style. The town could also offer some good shopping facilities at this period. Plate VII shows the trade-card of Thomas Pickstone, stationer, at the sign of the Bible in the Market Place. It is produced in the ornate rococo style of the third quarter of the eighteenth century and bordered with miniatures of some of his principal wares. On the other hand, a large number of the older buildings, the rents of which seldom ran to two figures and could have left no margin for repairs, showed evident signs of neglect and it was no doubt these that provoked Miss Burney's disparaging comment.

The Reformation, though it did not create them, aggravated the problems of poverty and unemployment. The relief of the indigent poor was at first left to local charity and vagrancy ranked as a serious offence, though by an Act of 1531 the impotent poor were allowed to beg if they obtained a magistrate's licence. Possibly Robert Silvester who fleeced the good people of Reigate in 1544 was a licensed beggar punished for straying outside his allotted beat. He was " set on the pillorie in Cheapside by the commandment of my Lord Chancellor and others of the Kinges Counseill and was burned with a hot iron in the cheeke with a letter of P. and after had his ears cut off hard by the head and had written on a paper set on his head ' For misusinge of the Kinges' Commission and powelinge of his subjects ' which the sayd person had done at Reigate in Surrey."[47]

Hospitals and almshouses for the aged and impotent were erected in many parts of the country by public-spirited benefactors. The movement began in Elizabethan times and grew in strength during the seventeenth century. In 1631 an effort was made to obtain local almshouses as appears from the minutes of the Court Leet at which the tenants requested the lords of the manor to grant a piece of the waste for this object. It was left to the steward to con-

Plate VII.

Homer
Virgil
Ovid
BIBLES
PrayerBooks

Day Book
Leidger
Journal
DUTY of MAN
Primers

WAFERS
Pounce
PENS
Wax
CARDS
Quills
TESTAMENTS

THO.ˢ PICKSTONE
Stationer & Bookseller
at the Bible Opposite the
Town Hall in Ryegate
SURREY
Makes and Sells allsorts
of Stationary Wares
Wholesale & Retail
At Reasonable Rates.
Money for Raggs or
Goods in Exchange.

PENCIL
Paper
INK
Slates
PLAYS
Novels
Spelling Books

TRADE CARD OF THOS. PICKSTONE.

sult the lords, who were at that time lord Monson and his wife, but nothing more is heard of the matter. Another favourite mode of charitable help was to bequeath money by will for the relief of the poor, though the effect of these gifts, which usually took the form of bread and clothing, was often to encourage mendicity rather than to relieve genuine want. Reigate benefited from several such gifts of which the principal were those derived from alderman Henry Smith of Wandsworth, the famous philanthropist, who died in 1628. He left legacies by his will to nearly every Surrey parish including £1,000 to Reigate. He had also in his lifetime settled a large part of his estate on charitable trusts and from this the parish received an annual grant. His example prompted many lesser imitators. Two local ladies, Mrs. Philippa Booker, who died in 1666, and Miss Susanna Parsons, who died in 1718, bequeathed sums for the relief of poor widows of the parish. Here as elsewhere at this period the proportion of widows seems to have been abnormally high.[48]

But voluntary methods proved inadequate to cope with the problem. Before the end of Elizabeth's reign overseers of the poor were established for each parish with power to raise money compulsorily by a rate on the inhabitants, and the parish became the unit of poor law administration. The chief concern of the overseers was to keep down the number of persons likely to become a public charge. As a result of legislation passed in 1662 and 1697 the working man was not free to leave his own parish, though assured of work in another locality, unless he obtained a certificate from the authorities acknowledging that parish to be his place of settlement. Armed with this he could migrate to another parish so that if he applied for relief there he could be deported to the parish which had certified him. The Parish Library contains a register of certificates given to the Foreign between 1713 and 1784. The law of settlement had far-reaching and pernicious results in checking the fluidity of labour and pegging the industrious workman to one place though that had no employment to offer him.

The provision of workhouses was sanctioned by Parliament in 1723. Relief could be refused to persons who declined to enter the house and those admitted were, if able, required to work for their keep. A workhouse for the Old Borough was opened in 1730. By a lease of that year premises in Park Lane at the entrance to the Priory were taken for a term of 21 years at the annual rent of £5 in the names of Richard Kay, draper ; Richard Martin, apothecary ; William Glover, draper ; William Saker, Senior, innholder ; Thomas Snelling, maltster ; John Wood, waggoner ; John Alexander, butcher, and Abraham Smith, distiller. The lease recited that the inhabitants of the Borough proposed to set up a workhouse for the poor of the borough and had chosen the lessees with the church-warden and overseers for the time being as governors or directors of the same. In a later document the premises are described as a large old messuage with several outhouses and a large garden.[49] Reigate Foreign, as a parish distinct from the Old Borough, maintained its own workhouse which stood at Shaw's Corner.

Workhouse inmates were frequently farmed to a con-tractor for so much per head or a lump sum. The former method was that adopted by both the Borough and Foreign. At a Vestry for the Foreign held at the Five Bells, 4th November, 1771, the parishioners present agreed with John Humphrey for the maintenance of such poor as they shall think proper to send to the Workhouse at the rate of 2s. per person per week, except infants under one year for whom he was to receive 1s. per week. He was also to be allowed £16 per year for firing and £1 1s. for each woman " who shall lay in of a child," and was to have the benefit of the labour of the inmates. Humphrey on his part agreed " to take good and sufficient care of such persons as shall be committed to his charge," and to take care that all " as are able do duly and constantly attend Divine Service on Sundays." In 1773 a committee appointed to inspect the Workhouse reported that the poor " were not sufficiently kept or decently clean," and that they might be maintained in a much better manner for the price allowed. The churchwardens were directed to order Humphrey, the master, " to feed the poor better and keep them cleaner." As a result of this reprimand he gave six months' notice to determine his contract. For the next few years the house was managed by a committee of the Vestry, and John Shearing was appointed master at a yearly salary of £7. In 1781 however a fresh agreement was come to with Humphrey for three years on terms almost identical with those of the former one. In 1772 John Hinton, surgeon and apothecary of Reigate, agreed to attend the poor of the Foreign " as shall want his assistance in surgery or physick " for £12 12s. for one year. In 1791 at a special Vestry called to " determine on a proper mode of contracting for the Surgery, Physick and Midwifery of the Poor " of the Foreign, Mr. Stringer agreed to do the work for the ensuing year for £15.

The practice of the Foreign as regards pauper children was to place them out with the principal inhabitants who were expected to maintain them free of charge. In 1772 thirteen children aged ten or more were allotted by ballot to that number of inhabitants occupying houses of the annual value of £50 or upwards who were to be allowed 40s. each for clothing the children.

In 1793 the parishes of the Old Borough, the Foreign, Horley, Nutfield and Headley, formed themselves into a poor law union under a measure passed in 1782, known as Gilbert's Act, which enabled two or more parishes to unite in providing a common workhouse. By deed of 11th May, 1793, lord Somers, as lord of the manor, and certain of the tenants consented to " the inclosing of ten acres of land lying at a place called the Broad Plain being on the south part of Redhill near Little London . . being part of the waste or common land of the Manor by the Guardians of the Poor of the united parishes for the purpose of building thereupon a Poor House or Workhouse." The new house described as " a large fair brick building," was completed in 1794 and as a result the poor rate in the united parishes showed a considerable reduction. A woollen industry for the manufacture of coarse blankets, rugs and waggon tilts was set up within its walls for the employment of the inmates.[50]

The five parishes though united for indoor relief remained separate in other respects. A proposal by the Vestry of the Old Borough in 1790 that the Borough and Foreign should be united for rating purposes and have one set of overseers was resisted by the Foreign Vestry and came to nothing.

The Reigate Vestries were, in later times at least, democratic assemblies open to any rate-paying inhabitant who cared to attend. They met as a rule separately, but united at Easter for the annual vestry and occasionally at other times when important matters touching the whole parish arose. The ordinary monthly meetings were but thinly attended, but the annual meetings and those called for special business drew larger numbers.

The powers of Vestries were never clearly defined nor subject to the control of any central authority. In the course of the eighteenth century they engrossed more and more of the civil business of the parish and assumed a number of functions which rightfully belonged to the parish officers, who were however only too glad to be relieved of their responsibility by " the inhabitants in vestry assembled." At Reigate the two Vestries acting separately or together elected the overseers, guardians, and people's churchwardens, and, after the Court Leet fell into disuse early in the nineteenth century, the head-boroughs. They also appointed the paid officials of the parish such as the vestry clerk, beadle and sexton. In the exercise of their multifarious activities they administered the parish workhouse and pesthouses, controlled the parish charities, appointed the head master of the Free, or Grammar School, maintained the church and its fittings, passed the churchwardens' accounts, made the assessments for the poor rate and fixed the amount of that rate and the church rate, dealt with applications for out-relief, found substitutes for the militia and repaired the town clock and cage. Acting quite irregularly the Foreign Vestry resolved in 1797 that the church rate should be paid " as in the past " out of the poor rate, on account of the difficulty of collecting a separate church rate. Equally irregular, though less excusable, was the expenditure by the Vestries in equal shares of a sum of £15 on an annual feast styled " the parish dinner " in which members and officials indulged after the Easter meeting.[51]

Local Freemasonry originated in 1784 with the founding

of the Holmesdale Lodge of Freedom and Friendship which met at the Bell Inn, Bell Street. Little is known of its history and it expired in 1813. Possibly the introduction of politics led to its decline. On 19th July, 1788, a resolution was passed : " That this Lodge shall celebrate the approaching Hundredth Anniversary of the Glorious Revolution, and that some of the neighbouring Lodges be invited to join with this one in so laudable a Festivity." The letter of invitation to dine with them at the Swan Inn, Reigate, on the ensuing 15th September—subsequently postponed to 4th November—was interlarded with high-flown phrases, such as " emancipation from religious and civil tyranny " and " sooner than so meritorious a Gala should pass without its just hallelujahs," which offended several of the brethren and brought some sharp replies to Mr. Alexander Broughton, secretary of the Lodge.

The Surrey Lodge of Freemasons, the third oldest existing Lodge in the Province, was established in 1834 under a warrant granted by the duke of Sussex as Grand Master to Frederick John, lord Monson and others. The first meeting took place on 15th January in that year at the White Hart Inn with lord Monson as the first master, and the Rev. J. C. Wynter, rector of Gatton, and Thomas Hart, the younger, of Reigate, attorney, were elected treasurer and secretary. The death of lord Monson in 1841 dealt the Lodge a severe blow, and after adjourning the meetings for a year it remained in abeyance till 1856. Meetings were then resumed at the Swan Inn and continued to be held there until 1862, when the Lodge moved to fresh quarters in the newly erected Public Hall in High Street. There it celebrated its jubilee with a banquet given in 1884.[52]

NOTES TO CHAPTER IX

[1] Wood, I *Athenae* cols. 529 and 530 ; Day's *Epistle Dedicatory* to William lord Howard of Effingham in his translation of Foxe's *Christ Jesus Triumphant* (1607). See also Mozley, *John Foxe and his Book*, 30 and 31.

[2] 14 *SAC* 2.

[3] She died at Richmond Palace, Surrey, 24th March, 1603.

[4] *Hist. MSS. Com.* 7th Rep. 179. For a full account of this lottery see C. L'Estrange Ewen, *Lotteries & Sweepstakes*, Chap. II.

[5] Surrey Hearth Tax 1664, 41 and 42 *SRS* CXXI and CXXII.   The area of the old Borough was 434 acres, of the whole parish 5,994 acres.

[6] *S P Dom* (1637) 110.

[7] After 1742 the burials Register ceases to specify the cause of death.   In 1665 Quarter Sessions ordered a special assessment of the poor rate to relieve Reigate and other plague-stricken parishes in Surrey (39 *SRS* 75).

[8] Offences under the statute were also dealt with at Quarter Sessions. In 1661 Chas. Parsifall of Reigate was presented for building a cottage without the agreed acreage. (35 *SRS* 107, 156).

[9] For a fuller account of manorial courts see Webb, *The Manor and The Borough,* 13 etc.

[10] I *M & B,* 289.   The last assizes appear to have been held in March, 1717. (Assizes 34, Misc. Books No. 3).

[11] Psh. Reg. ;   *London Gazette* 18th Jan., 1697 ;   *S P Dom* (1697) 41.

[12] Willis, *History of Ewell,* 103–4.

[13] 9 *SAC* 161, etc.   The records of Surrey Quarter Sessions for the years 1659 to 1666 have now been transcribed and published in Vols. 35, 36 and 39 of the Surrey Record Society of which I have made extensive use.   The removal took place in 1864.

[14] 9 *SAC* 195, 218.

[15] 36 *SRS* 297–8.   The accused pleaded guilty and were fined.

[16] C. L'Estrange Ewen, *Witch Hunting and Witch Trials,* 215–6, 238 ;   9 *SAC* 191.

[17] *S P Dom.* (1636–7) 501, and (1637–8) 198.

[18] See p. 59 above.

[19] II *VCH* 35–6 ;   Shaw, *History of English Church,* II, 434–5.

[20] T. W. Marsh,   *Early Friends in Surrey and Sussex,* 2.

[21] Marsh *op. cit.* 3–5 ;   MS. Minutes of Monthly Meeting of Dorking Capel and Reigate 1668–1715.

[22] 35, 36 and 39 *SRS passim.*

[23] 39 *SRS* 190.   For other instances of prosecution see Marsh *op. cit.*   79, 83 and 90.   Titchbourne though a shoemaker by trade came of a good family. His father, John Titchbourne, was a mercer of Reigate.

[24] For Penn and Rigg see *DNB.*

[25] Marsh *op. cit.* 91.

[26] III *VCH,* 232.

[27] 14 *SAC,* 217 ;   39 *SAC,* 98.

[28] See Plan of Reigate Town, 1786, where its position is marked.

[29] This account is based principally on Cleal's *Story of Congregationalism in Surrey,* 377–82 ;   the title deeds of the property and a MS. History of the Church by the late Mr. F. G. Davies.

[30] I *VCH* 586 ;   I *M & B,* 312–3 ;   II *SAC,* 153 etc.

[31] Hooper, *Guide* 39.

[32] I *VCH* 390, etc. ;   II *Ibid,* 133 etc. ;   2 *SRS,* 7.   Lists and documents respecting Surrey Musters in the sixteenth and seventeenth centuries are contained in Vols. 2, 10, 11 and 13 *SRS.*

[33] III *M & B,* 676–7 ;   II *VCH,* 145–6 ;   Davis, *Historical Records of the Second Royal Surrey Militia,* 80 and 82.

[34] For a list of suspected persons in Surrey in 1655 see 14 *SAC,* 186–9. Princes Rupert and Maurice stayed the night at Reigate, 2nd July, 1646, on their way to Dover after the surrender of Oxford (*13 Eng. Hist. Rev.* (1878) 741).

[35] I *VCH* 420.

[36] Carlyle II *Cromwell's Letters and Speeches*, 128 ; *Committee for Advance of Money*, Pt. II, 1045 ; *Committee for Compounding*, 1191.

[37] I *VCH*, 423. Palgrave (pp. 27 and 28) quotes two of Fleetwood's letters to Audeley. Audeley's reply dated 1st August, 1659, is in the Tanner MSS. (li. 107) at the Bodleian Library.

[38] The quotations are from *An Excursion to Brighthelmstone made in the Year 1789* by H. Wigstead and Thos. Rowlandson which contains an aquatint engraving of the inn by Rowlandson, and from Timb's *A Picturesque Promenade Round Dorking*, 253.

[39] See p. 136 above.

[40] The division can be seen in the illustration of West Street opp. p. oo.

[41] See *Notes and Queries*, 1st April, 1939, for a note by the Author on this novel use of the term " coldharbour."

[42] Information extracted from the early records of the S.P.C.K. kindly placed at my disposal by the Society. See also M. G. Jones, *The Charity School Movement in the XVIII Century*, 63. Susanna Parsons, who died in 1718, left 40s. a year to the school, and if that failed then for the benefit of decayed widows. The Grammar School is dealt with in Chapter X.

[43] " Repentance " sounds like a Puritan name. The earlier name was " Lomith." The property was occupied in the latter part of the seventeenth and early part of the eighteenth centuries by Benjamin Bonwicke and his son, both of whom were barristers and practised as lawyers in the town. The house was taken down before 1775. The adjoining house on the west, now converted into shops, became the office and residence of Ambrose Glover early in the nineteenth century.

[44] *London Magazine*, 1769, pp. 408–9, which gives illustrations of the chaise and its mechanism ; H. H. Griffin, *Cycles and Cycling*, 3rd edition, pp. 3–6.

[45] *Rural Rides*. (Letter from Reigate, 20th October, 1825.)

[46] *Diary and Letters of Mme. D'Arblay* (1842) I, 209.

[47] *Wriothesley's Chronicle* (Camden Soc.) I, 149.

[48] For list of the parish charities, see I *M & B*, 329.

[49] The site is now that of a house known as " Makepeace."

[50] *Ct.Rs.* ; I *M & B*, 309.

[51] The Vestry Minutes, from which I have quoted, are extant for the Foreign from 1771 onwards, for the Borough from 1780 onwards. One book of Churchwarden's Accounts for the years 1788–1858 and a Vestry Order Book for the Town of Reigate, 1726, have also survived. All but the purely ecclesiastical functions of vestries have now been transferred to the local authorities.

[52] John Lees, *The History of the Surrey Lodge* (1884).

CHAPTER X

THE GRAMMAR SCHOOL

THE history of the school begins in 1675 with the purchase of a piece of ground, forming part of the present site, for the erection of a school-house. A large part of the purchase money consisted of a sum of £150 bequeathed to Reigate by Henry Smith, the philanthropic alderman of London, who died in 1628 and disposed of much of his vast fortune for the benefit of various parishes in Surrey and other counties.[1] The remainder was raised by local subscriptions, and the purchase made in the name of Sir Edward Thurland of Great Doods, a judge of the Court of Exchequer (Plate VIII). After the erection of a school-house the property was conveyed to trustees ; but it does not appear to have been opened for teaching until 1684, when the Rev. John Williamson, vicar of Reigate, was appointed master. The start was not auspicious. Two years later we find the vicar and churchwardens suing the trustees for possession of the school premises and to establish the trusts, the real issue being whether the election of the master lay with the trustees or the parishioners. The Plaintiffs alleged that the vicar was elected by the parishioners and was put into possession by one of the trustees and the parishioners, " the Plaintiff's Williamson's Diocesan having to that end granted him a licence, and he and his usher lived in the house and was making preparation for boarders, and was encouraged so to do by several gentlemen living near who promised to endow the school house with a yearly salary so that ten or more poor children of the Parish might be taught gratis, in case the trust was declared, and the school brought to perfection, that Sir Edward being dead and there being some declaration of trust made on the conveyance in the hands of the Defendants they concealed the same and denied to

Plate VIII.

SIR EDWARD THURLAND
(*From the painting by Michael Wright in the Guildhall Library*)

discover the trust, and that the Defendant Thurland [son of the judge] had violently forced the Plaintiff, Williamson, to quit the possession of the school house." Thurland in his answer professed ignorance of most of these matters and " thought himself in duty bound to oppose Williamson being school master being a person of an ill life, and denied he ever forced him out of the school house, because he was never in, and oppose his teaching school there." Blackening of one's opponent was a common form of flourish in Chancery pleadings of that age, and this reflection on the vicar's character need not be taken seriously. In the result the Plaintiffs virtually succeeded in their claim. The Defendants were ordered to convey and deliver possession of the school premises to a new set of trustees to be nominated by the vicar and churchwardens, and though this was never done the vicar enjoyed possession for the rest of his days without further interference.[2]

The school was not in origin a grammar school and did not assume that character or name until modern times. " Grammar " denoted the Greek and Latin classics and these formed no part of the early curriculum—at least for the free scholars. It was one of a numerous class of non-classical schools established in the second half of the seventeenth century on a charitable basis for the purpose of teaching " the three Rs," subjects usually omitted at the older grammar schools. On the other hand, the master had permission to supplement his income by taking day scholars and boarders on his own terms and these received the orthodox grammar school education.

The school benefited under the wills of two local residents, Robert Bishop, who died in 1700, and John Parker of Frenches, who died in 1720. Bishop left a house in Linkfield Street, which subsequently became an inn called the Red Lion, on trust to pay the rent every year " to the Master who should teach school in the school house wherein Mr. Joseph Young did heretofore teach school in the Parish of Reigate and wherein after him Andrew Cranston Clerk now Vicar of Reigate did teach school for and in satisfaction of the free teaching of 4 poor boys," two to be chosen from the Borough and two from the Foreign.[3] Parker left £500 for the purchase of lands to be settled in trust " for the support of the School then carried on at Reigate for educating poor children in the principles of the Church of England." His executors failed to carry out this bequest and it was not until nearly fifty years later and after lengthy Chancery proceedings that the School derived any benefit from the gift. The land at length purchased consisted of two fields known as Heaths and Longs upon which St. Anne's Schools at Redhill were afterwards erected, together with a barn and yard, and four acres called the Workhouse Field owing to its proximity to the Workhouse for the Foreign of Reigate which stood at the spot now known as Shaw's Corner.

The Rev. Andrew Cranston mentioned in Bishop's bequest had married Williamson's daughter and on his father-in-law's death in 1697 succeeded to the dual rôle of vicar and master of the school.[4] Cranston, who showed his zeal for learning by founding the Parish Library, was at his death in 1708 followed as master and vicar by the Rev. John Bird, B.A., who occupied both offices concurrently for the next twenty years and proved to be the last incumbent of the parish to hold the mastership, though his successors for over a century to come were invariably clerics and officiated occasionally as curates at Reigate and elsewhere, or held neighbouring livings.

Mr. Bird showed a better head for business than most of his cloth. He kept an account book which has been preserved and contains entries of the fees charged for the private pupils under his care. For a day boy taking ordinary classical curriculum the fee was 10s. per quarter, for a boarder £18 per year, excluding the cost of books. These included such time-honoured favourites as *Sententiæ Pueriles* and Ovid's *Metamorphosis*, works on which Shakespeare had browsed when a boy at Stratford Grammar School. The right of the parishioners to appoint the master was not again challenged, and from 1728 the Vestry for the whole parish regularly elected him. Mr. Bird was followed in rapid succession by the Rev. Marmaduke Downes, M.A., fellow of St. John's College, Cambridge, who resigned within a few months, the Rev. Samuel Rossell, 1729–30, and the

Rev. Thos. Jenkins, B.A., 1730–32. The cause of these quick changes was the inadequacy of the income to support men who had no other means of eking out a living. The "rot" was stayed by the election of the Rev. John Martin of Stepney, who made ends meet by doing duty as parish curate.[5] How long he continued is uncertain. He was still in office in 1744 when a committee of the Vestry reported that Mr. Martin in consideration of his appointment "and of £60 and upwards laid out in repairing the School house for his reception . . . has constantly taught and continues to teach 4 poor boys of this Parish to read, write and cast accounts." In return for the rent of the house in Linkfield Street then amounting to £5 a year he also taught 4 poor boys chosen by the trustees of Bishop's Charity. This rent, small as it was, seems to have been paid very irregularly and at the date of the Report was over a year in arrear.

There is a gap in the Vestry minutes respecting the school affairs between 1744 and 1778, but at some intervening date Mr. Martin resigned and the Rev. Thos. Pooler was elected in his place. By the latter year the school premises were so badly dilapidated that the churchwardens felt obliged to appeal to the Vestry. Further, Mr. Pooler had recently thrown up his duties and put in Mr. Sisson as a substitute without the sanction of the Vestry. This news was broken to a meeting summoned at the church on Sunday, 15th November, 1778. The Vestry, feeling no doubt that the business was too disturbing for the day and place, promptly decided to adjourn to the more stimulating environment of the Swan Inn on the following Monday week. At the adjourned meeting "the Inhabitants present," to quote the minutes, " upon taking the adjourned business concerning the repairing the Free School of this Parish into consideration find that many more papers and matters of Intelligence to bring this business to a proper issue will be necessary than can be conveniently introduced in a public Vestry." Thereupon a committee was appointed which after holding several meetings reported that the necessary repairs would cost £70, but could not suggest how the money was to be found. They recommended that future masters on appointment should give an undertaking to keep the school in repair and teach four boys of the foundation. The average number of day scholars was found to have been thirty, in addition to the foundationers and those elected by the two charities who numbered apparently ten in all. The Vestry met in the following January to consider this Report and directed an advertisement to be inserted in the *London Evening Post* and *St. James's Chronicle* that they would elect a master " on Sunday, the 7th day of February next, and that no candidate can be admitted without being in Orders and that all applications by Candidates must be directed to the Church-Wardens."

When the Vestry next met it appeared that the time of election had been omitted in the advertisements. The only candidate forthcoming was the Rev. Thos. Sisson, who was unanimously elected after he had signed the following undertaking :—" First. To keep the School-House and Premises in tenantable Repair, after the same shall be repaired for him. Second. To take 2 boys of the town and 2 of the Foreign to be from time to time named by the respective Vestrys in consideration of possessing the said School and Premises. Third. To teach all the Boys coming to the said School the Church Cathechism twice a week. Fourth. To take care the Boys attend divine Service at the Church, as well on Sundays, as on Holy Days, and Prayer Days. To give 6 months Notice of Resignation and to resign on 6 months Notice of an Order of General Vestry."   Mr. Pooler was rector of Gatton where Mr. Sisson occasionally took duty for him. Hence the close relation between them. Mr. Sisson also acted as curate of Reigate. He was a young man in 1779 and held the mastership continuously until his death in 1800 at the comparatively early age of forty-eight. His successor, the Rev. Joseph Hodgson, entered into a similar undertaking on his appointment. As Mr. Hodgson had independent means and held the perpetual curacy of Leigh near Reigate, the liability for repairs bore less heavily on him than on some of his predecessors, and in 1800 and 1802 the school was repaired by the Overseers at a cost of £136 15s. 9d. provided out of Parker's and Bishop's charities. Nevertheless the school-room floor was reported in 1825 to be in a bad condition. Mr. Hodgson, who lived at the school-house and took both boarders and day boys, served for the unprecedented period of over forty years. The number of free scholars remained at ten, four of them foundationers, four elected by the Bishop trustees and two by the Parker trustees. His total income from the charity properties amounted in 1825 to £22 12s. od. a year, including the rent of the Red Lion which had shortly before lost its licence and ceased to be an inn.

Mr. Hodgson resigned in June, 1842. The Vestry received several applications in response to their advertisement in *The Times* and other papers and proceeded to elect the Rev. G. H. Stoddart of Sheffield " as a fit and proper person to fill the office of master of the Reigate Free school." Mr. Stoddart unfortunately did not take kindly to his new sphere, and disappointed expectations by resigning within six months. The Vestry in disgust promptly resolved to break with tradition by throwing open the vacancy to laymen as well as clerics. The decision was in fact part of a pre-arranged move on behalf of a particular individual who was considered a fitting object for that cheap and easy form of practical sympathy which is exercised at the public expense. The aspirant to this favour was Mr. Timothy Price, a broken-down tradesman of the town, whose principal qualifications were his failure in business and his fervent churchmanship. His appointment, evidently a foregone conclusion, took place at a crowded meeting of the Vestry held at the White Hart, Reigate, 1st February, 1843. Questioned as to his religious belief he solemnly declared himself " a Member of the Established Church and that he was not a dissenter from that establishment." He also undertook to observe the same conditions as to repairs and teaching that had been imposed on his predecessors.

The death of Mr. Price in 1859 marked the end of the old régime and the long period of unregulated control by the Vestry. Of all methods of governing a school that by public meeting is probably the worst. It had certainly been amply discredited at Reigate, and many other endowed schools under similar management were shown to be in a much worse plight when they came to be investigated by the Schools Enquiry Commission during the next decade. The school was not reopened until 1862. Before then the Reigate Charities had been made subject to a scheme of management framed and sanctioned by the Court of Chancery after an enquiry by the Charity Commission. Under this scheme, which before long gave way to another, the appointment of a master was placed in the hands of trustees who formed the new governing body, and the powers of the Vestry were reduced to the election of the representative members of that body.

The modern history of the school can be told more briefly. Between the death of Mr. Price and the reopening in 1862 the old buildings were demolished and new ones erected. The first head master under the new scheme, as a result of which the school became a grammar school in fact as well as in name, was the Rev. John Gooch, M.A. He at first showed promise of being able to build up the school.[6] Later, however, as the numbers declined, he lost the confidence of the governors and was superseded in 1878 by Mr. F. G. Johnson, M.A., who successfully revived its fortunes.[7] In 1865 land for a playground was added by the generosity of the brothers A. J. and W. B. Waterlow. In 1871 a headmaster's house and a school-room were erected and in 1881 a new classroom was added in memory of Mr. Robert Hesketh, a former chairman of the governors. In 1875 the management was transferred from trustees to a board of governors of whom four were co-optative and ten elected by the Borough Council. Under this scheme the various bread and other parochial charities were amalgamated and applied for the benefit of the school. Further, the school was placed on a non-sectarian basis and the object of the old foundation was maintained by provision for ten free scholars. The scheme, though it roused strong local feeling and was bitterly attacked by the Vestry for not providing more free places, remained with some amendments in force until 1909. A new constitution was then framed by the Board of Education placing the management in the hands of a body of governors appointed for the most part by the Borough Council and the Surrey County Council.

The growth in numbers necessitated enlargement of the buildings in 1870 and again in 1907 and 1928, and more recently, and accommodation is now found for 600 boys. With substantial aid from the Board of Education and the County Council, the school in the present century has made phenomenal strides and reached a leading place among the secondary schools of Surrey.

The Education Act of 1944 makes far-reaching changes in the school which becomes what is known as a " voluntary controlled school " conducted under an instrument and articles of government made by the Minister of Education. The Act came into force on 1st April, 1945, from which date all fees were abolished.

NOTES TO CHAPTER X

[1] For a good account of Henry Smith and his benefactions see 22 *Sx AC* 30–49.

[2] Report of Vestry Committee in Bryant's Survey. *Further Report of the Charity Commissioners*, 1825, Vol. 13, pp. 512–3. Cf. 31 *SRS* 101.

[3] Bishop was a yeoman farmer who occupied a farm called Roberts at Hole, now incorporated in the estate of the Philanthropic Society's School at Redhill. His will is dated 14th July, 1698. For these two charities see *Further Report of the Charity Commissioners*, Vol. 13, pp. 514–20.

[4] Williamson's immediate successor as appears from Bishop's will was Joseph Young. Cf. 31 *SRS* 103.

[5] As a member of the Whist Club which met at the White Hart he provoked the following skit, quoted by Ridgeway :

> " Poor Dominie fatigued with daily drubs
> Retires from Ovid to the knave of clubs,
> The pigmy priest full oft is cast a knave
> But thinks his Sunday's work his soul will save."

[6] In 1864 the scholars numbered 36, composed of 28 day boys, 20 of whom were foundationers, and 8 boarders. There was no assistant master. (See *Schools Inquiry Commission : Reports of Commissioners*, 1867–8, Vols. I, VII and XI, which give a full account of the School at that period.)

[7] Mr. Johnson resigned in 1888 to enter the church. The succession of headmasters since then is as follows : Rev. A. C. Fox, M.A., 1888–1895 ; Mr. J. Cordy Keer, who died in 1895, the year of his appointment ; Rev. H. A. Hall, M.A., 1896–1899 ; Mr. R. S. Ragg, B.A., 1899–1910 ; Mr. F. S. Orme, M.A., 1910–1938 ; Mr. C. R. Allison, M.A., 1938–1940, and Mr. A. Clarke, B.Sc., the present headmaster, from 1940.

CHAPTER XI

THE NINETEENTH CENTURY AND AFTER

IN 1801, the year of the first national census, the population of the Old Borough was returned at 923 and of the Foreign at 1,323, a total of 2,246. Houses in the Old Borough numbered 206, including 10 uninhabited, and in the Foreign 228, only 7 of which were uninhabited. The population of the Town had increased some 50 per cent. since the seventeenth century and that of the Foreign had apparently doubled, chiefly no doubt as a result of improved roads and better traffic facilities.

During the early years of the century marriages declined, the annual number for the first decade averaging only 13.4. For this the vicar could find " no better reason than that of Gent^{n.} taking the small Farms into their own Hands, by which they destroy the inferior Yeomanry without improving their own Incomes." The census returns of 1811 lend some colour to his " reason " for they show that the population of the Foreign, in which the farms lay, had remained stationary whereas that of the Old Borough had risen by just over 200.

Ten years later, however, a writer observed that the town " is in a state of great depopulation . . . on account of the large poor rates,"[1] though in the Report of the Boundary Commissioners, 1831, it is described as " a small but remarkably neat Town with a greater no. than usual of gentlemen's houses attached to it " (Plate IX). These divergent accounts are hard to reconcile, and the large expansion of poor rates early in the century was a national, and not a local, phenomenon due to the lavish policy of out-relief.[2]

The workhouse of the united parishes was farmed to a contractor for a lump sum which in 1811 amounted to

CHURCH STREET AND MARKET PLACE, REIGATE, C. 1843.

Showing Ambrose Glover's house (with steps) on right and the Crown Inn and Town Hall beyond.

(From a sketch by Wm. Thornton.)

£1900 per year. A meeting of the Borough Vestry held 21st February, 1803, at the Swan Inn resolved to advertise the next contract for " the house of Industry . . . To carry on the Blankett Manufactory all at, and the Guardians shall have a reserved right to themselves to relieve a Poor Person or Family rather than force them into the House."[3] In 1816 the Guardians advertised in the *Leeds Mercury* for tenders for " the maintenance, clothing and employment of the poor of the said parishes." The advertisement stated that for the last twenty years " a manufacture of blankets and of coarse woollens had been carried on (and which is to be continued) in the Poor House, to which a fulling mill belongs," adding as a further bait, " There is attached to the house 10 acres of very rich and valuable arable and meadow land," a falsehood which could have deceived only those unaware of the intractable soil of Earlswood Common.[4]

In 1826 the Vestry of the Borough considered a report of the Committee of the Foreign appointed " to investigate the internal state and management of the Poor House," and concluded that many abuses existed and that the parish officers of the Borough " be requested to meet the officers of the other Parishes incorporated with them to investigate and make such alteration as they may think necessary." The nature of these abuses and the remedies adopted are not disclosed.

Work for the unemployed was often provided by setting them to dig road metal on the Commons. The Vestry for the Foreign resolved in 1831 that all persons wanting labour " be employed at Digging of Stones on Red Hill, Ray Common, and Reigate Heath to be paid 2s. 6d. per yard for the present and 6d. per yard when the Ground is properly levelled, except single Men to be paid 2s. per yard." The surface of Redhill Common is still heavily scarred with the marks of their handiwork and of similar activity by unauthorised persons who filched soil for their own use.

Another expedient for providing work for the able-bodied poor at this period was that known as the labour-rate which obliged ratepayers to employ pauper labour in accordance with a fixed scale of wages, or in default to pay a special rate

to be assessed on their premises.   The Vestry for the Foreign
resolved in 1833 to make a labour-rate, distinct from the poor
rate, at 3s. in the pound for ten weeks from January, 1834.
Every occupier of land or other property of a rental of
£7 10s. od. or more was liable to pay the rate to the Overseers, or else " to work out " the amount of his rate by
employing men or boys at the wages prescribed.   At the
end of the ten weeks every ratepayer was to make a return
of the labour employed by him during this period.   How
the experiment worked does not appear but in other parishes
where it was tried it had the effect of driving employers
to dismiss their good workmen and replace them with
inefficient paupers.[5]

In 1835 the same Vestry decided to appoint its clerk,
George Doubell, to be Assistant Guardian at a yearly salary
of £30, giving as reasons for this step the inexperience of a
Guardian appointed for one year and his unwillingness to
devote the necessary time to his duties, besides his suscept-
ibility to pressure or intimidation from the paupers who made
a practice of waylaying him at his house.   Doubell was
later appointed to the additional post of Assistant Overseer.

The system of parochial and unregulated poor law
administration had become so costly and inefficient during
the first quarter of the nineteenth century as to call urgently
for reform.   Under the Poor Law Act, 1834, the country
was divided into poor law unions administered by elected
bodies known as Boards of Guardians to control the work
of the relieving officers and workhouse officials.   A central
body known as the Poor Law Commissioners was constituted
to supervise and regulate the local administration.

The Board of Guardians of the Reigate union was created
by an order of the Poor Law Commissioners dated 26th
February, 1836, which combined the whole of the parishes
in the hundred of Reigate, including the Old Borough
and Foreign and three other neighbouring parishes, in one
parochial union.   The Board met for the first time on
13th April following, when Thomas Hart, the younger, was
appointed Clerk at a salary of £105 per annum, and it
was decided to hold weekly meetings at the Workhouse at
Redhill.   Joseph Nash and Thomas Neale, who conducted

a bank in premises at the corner of Bell Street and High Street, Reigate, which came to grief in 1850, were appointed treasurers. It was decided to appoint medical attendants, two relieving officers and, as master and matron, William and Sarah Wade at a joint salary of £50 per annum with quarters and rations.[6]

In the earlier parts of the century a good deal of lawlessness prevailed and the town suffered from outbreaks of hooliganism by the less reputable inhabitants. Sunday afternoons are said to have been seasons of rowdyism and sport with an occasional prize fight in the Market Place.[7] In October, 1807, a special meeting of the Vestry of the Old Borough was held at the Church " for the purpose of suppressing the many daring insults and offences committed against the persons and property of the said Borough." The meeting resolved " that the Guardians, Churchwardens and Overseers of the Borough do . . . bring to justice and prosecute such offenders as have and shall in future be found committing such insults and offences." The root of the trouble was the lack of an efficient police force, and the Vestry dimly perceiving this appointed Thomas Jenkins to act as beadle for the Borough, for which he was to receive one guinea a quarter and be provided with a greatcoat.[8]

Resurrection men or body-snatchers, who plied the grisly yet profitable trade of stealing newly buried corpses and selling them to medical schools, were at work in 1819 and later years. In 1820 men were paid to keep a watch on the churchyard, and in 1821 Mr. Burt, a local attorney, presented his bill to the Vestry " for prosecuting the Resurrection men." The Anatomy Act passed in 1832 put a stop to this gruesome traffic.

Wild disorders marked St. Crispin's day, 25th October, and Guy Fawkes day, 5th November. A letter from Dr. Thomas Martin, the bailiff, to lord Somers in 1837 gives a vivid account of these orgies. " It has been the custom," he wrote, " for many years to hang in effigy some Individual who may have made himself ridiculous or odious in the course of the year on the anniversary of St. Crispin, and this taking place in the middle of the night accompanied by horrid yells and the firing of bombs as they are called alarms very much many of the timid females of the Town and last year was attended with fatal consequences to one most rrspectable and respected Inhabitant. The same figure being taken down in the morning is reserved to make a Guy Fawkes for the 5th November when a monstrous fire is lighted in the Square to the great annoyance of the neighbours as producing imminent danger of fire to the adjoining houses, the Inhabitants being obliged to be provided with pails of water to extinguish the burning flames of fire which fly over the tops of the houses. They take other precautions and are obliged to watch during the whole of the night lest a fire should take place." He goes on to describe the measures which had been taken in that year to prevent the bonfire. These had met with only partial success and he attributes " the depravity of our youth " to the absence of any facilities for their employment or amusement during the winter evenings. He proposes to form a Mechanics' Institute at the Town Hall, a project which he had before atempted without success. The Institute was restarted the same year, this time with better results. It long continued to do useful work by providing a library and reading-room for the working classes with occasional lectures of an educational nature, and developed later into the Reigate Literary Institution.

The first public fire-fighting appliances appear to have been the two fire-engines presented by lord Somers and lord Hardwicke, in 1809, for the use of the parish. The Vestry for the Old Borough directed the Churchwardens to see that the engines were kept in good order and appointed six men to work them for which they were to receive 5s. each, whenever their services were needed, to be defrayed by the Borough and Foreign in equal proportions. In 1854 a parish Vestry called " to consider the propriety of forming an efficient Fire Brigade for the Parish " decided that one fire-engine should be kept in the Borough and one in the Foreign and that the Churchwardens should " appoint 12 competent men to act as a Fire Brigade," six for each engine.

Elementary education for the working-class child depended before the passing of the Education Act of 1902 on the

voluntary efforts of various religious denominations, supplemented in Victorian times by state aid, and through their
agency several schools were provided at both ends of the
parish.[9]   In 1805 a charity school for boys and girls, under
Church of England auspices and supported by voluntary
subscriptions, was opened at Reigate.   From 1816 it was
conducted on the so-called Madras system instituted by
Dr. Andrew Bell.   The school occupied premises in West
Street until the erection of the National Schools in London
Road in 1854.   In 1852 the Nonconformists had erected
the British Schools in High Street, Reigate, to provide
elementary education on the rival Lancastrian system.   In
1855 local church folk erected an infant school at Warwick
Town to cater for the needs of that rising district, and in
1867 the Wesleyans opened a school in Cromwell Road,
Redhill.

To avoid the establishment of a school board under the
Education Act of 1870, an innovation repugnant to local
religious sentiment, fresh schools were opened in 1872
in connection with St. Matthew's Church, and at South
Park in 1873, while some of the existing schools were
enlarged to cope with the need of more accommodation.

In 1831 occurred the first epidemic of Asiatic cholera in
England.   The Government set up a Central Board of
Health to devise means for coping with the disease, and
Orders in Council required local boards of health to be
established throughout the country.   At a meeting of the
Vestries for the Borough and Foreign held at the White
Hart, Reigate, 22nd February, 1832, the vicar and local
surgeons with the Churchwardens, Guardians and Overseers,
were requested " to consider themselves as a Board of
Health . . . to take such measures as they are of opinion
[sic] to ward off, if possible, the pestilential Disease, and
if . . . it should arrive to do all they can to mitigate its
violence."   They were empowered to " provide some
convenient Dwelling out of the Town sufficient solitary to
be rendered available as a temporary Hospital, if required."
The meeting also resolved on measures to discourage " the
passage of mendicants through the Town coming from the
Metropolis," where the disease had already appeared,

and "the resort to the Market of persons from London who sell new and second-hand clothes."

Gas for illumination was first supplied to Reigate in 1838 by a local company formed in that year. The works were erected on land of a quarter of an acre granted by lord Somers on " the southern part of the field called the Pound Field adjoining the back lane leading out of the London Road towards the entrance of Nutley Lane."[10] The company undertook with the Inspector of Lighting and Watching of Reigate town to light twenty-eight public lamps for £60 a year from dusk until 5 a.m. In 1860 operations were transferred to larger works built on Batchelors Field at the northern end of Nutley Lane. The mains did not extend to Redhill, and the growing demand for gas in that part of the Foreign was not met until the formation in 1860 of a private company with works in Brighton Road on the site of part of the existing works. The Redhill Gas Company was incorporated in 1865. In 1921 it acquired the undertaking of the Reigate company and subsequently changed its name to the East Surrey Gas Company.[11]

Reigate first enjoyed the benefit of a public water supply in 1859 on the formation of the Reigate Water Works Company with works at Littleton Lane, a short distance outside the town. In 1867 the mains of the Caterham Spring Water Company were laid to Redhill. This company acquired the undertaking of the Reigate Company in 1896, having previously changed its name to the East Surrey Water Company in keeping with the extension of its services over a wide area in that part of the county.

In 1870 the post offices at Reigate and Redhill were connected by telegraph. The Reigate postmaster at that date was Thos. Nickalls, a watchmaker in High Street. The office opened from 9 a.m. to 9 p.m. and deliveries started at 7 a.m., 10 a.m. and 6 p.m. on weekdays, and at 7 a.m. on Sundays. In 1895, through the efforts of some of the local tradesmen, the present building in Bell Street was erected on ground leased by lady Henry Somerset, the freehold of which has since been acquired by the Crown. Mr. E. H. Cole, whose premises faced St. Matthew's Church, was postmaster at Redhill. The posting box though long bricked up can still be traced in the side wall along the passage by the Sussex Arms. The original office had been opened as a sub-office to Reigate in 1843 at Whitepost House on Redhill Common, where the postmaster, John Comber, also carried on business as a builder.

During the first five decades of the century the population of the parish slowly advanced, but between 1851 and 1861 it doubled, reaching nearly 10,000 in the latter year. This rapid increase was due to the coming of the railway. The main line to Brighton through Redhill, which had been extended from Croydon by the London and Brighton Railway Company formed in 1837, was opened in 1841. That company purchased the line of the Old Surrey Iron Railway from Croydon to Merstham, which was constructed in 1805, and formed a section of the earliest public railway in the world though confined to goods traffic. In 1842 the South Eastern Railway Company constructed a branch line to Ashford, and in 1849 the branch through Reigate to Reading was completed by another company.[12] The earliest local station, known as " Redhill and Reigate Road," had been placed at Hooley, Earlswood, near the present Earlswood Station, but on the formation of the Ashford branch a new station was erected at Redhill and named " Reigate Junction." For some years there was no train service between the two stations, so that passengers coming from Kent, who wished to travel to Brighton, and those going in the opposite direction, had to alight at Redhill or Earlswood and make their own way between the two stations, a distance of nearly a mile. To remedy this inconvenience the Brighton Company arranged with the South Eastern Company for the use of the junction station by its passenger trains.

The east end of the parish thus sprang into prominence as a centre of railway traffic within easy reach of London, while Reigate, which had shown some hostility to the new developments, had to be content with a subordinate station on a branch line with a level-crossing obstructing the main London Road. The site of Redhill town was determined by the position of the junction station and the making of

M

the Station Road with an eastward extension to the top of Redstone Hill. The situation was far from ideal, being low lying and marshy and intersected by meandering streams, the haunt of the snipe and wild duck. The Market Hall, for example, had to be built on piles driven through the bog in a field which bore the significant name of the Rough Moors. Drainage and improved methods of road making have overcome some but not all of these obstacles. In spite of these difficulties builders soon became active, unhampered as yet with any by-laws, and by 1860 a small settlement called Warwick Town had arisen, the earliest development being along Warwick Road and North Street. It was so called after the countess Brooke and of Warwick, widow of the fourth lord Monson, who granted building leases of blocks of land between Linkfield Lane and High Street forming part of the Monson family estate in the Manor of Linkfield.[13] Other estates quickly came into the market and were exploited for building by individuals or companies. In the particulars of property at Hooley offered for sale by auction in 1856 " the railway advantages " are extolled as " highly important, being in direct communication with London on the north, Dover and the Continent on the east, Brighton and other watering-places on the south coast on the south, and Guildford, Reading and the west of England on the west. In these various directions there are upwards of 100 trains arriving and departing daily, of which forty-five are to and from Redhill and London. Annual Season or Return Tickets between these two stations, whether issued by the London and Brighton or by the South Eastern Railway are equally available by the trains of both Companies, as may suit the convenience of the holders." Railway facilities were better then than they became later and helped to establish the locality as an attractive and easily accessible back garden and dormitory for the London business man, a factor on which its prosperity has since so largely rested.

The early stages of this building activity, which included the erection of much of Redhill town, coincided unfortunately with one of the most debased periods of English architecture. One particularly blatant example of the

Victorian "slate and stucco" style then in vogue stands at the corner of Station Road and Linkfield Lane. This building, erected in 1861 as the Globe Temperance Hotel, a purpose which did not answer, supplanted Linkfield Manor House, a fine Jacobean dwelling which in its latter days fell from its high estate and became known as "The Barracks," having it is said been used at one time as a hospital for some of the troops who survived the disastrous Walcheren expedition of 1809.[14]

The new inhabitants included some men of note. John Linnell, R.A., built a house on Redstone Hill in 1851 and lived there till his death in 1882. His son-in-law, Samuel Palmer, greatly distinguished as a painter and etcher, spent his later years at Meadvale, dying there in 1881. Charles Davidson, another artist, who, like Linnell, found many subjects for his brush in local scenery, lived for several years before 1882 in Linkfield Lane and taught drawing at Reigate Grammar School. R. C. Carrington, the astronomer, lived for some years from 1852 at a house known as The Dome on Furze Hill, Redhill, where he built himself an observatory. Harrison Ainsworth, the popular novelist, who knew Reigate intimately and lived there from 1878 till his death in 1882, sounded its praises in his novel *The Old Court*, 1867, going so far as to declare, "We do not know in the whole of merry England a pleasanter or prettier place than the good old town of Reigate, nor one wherein a few summer or autumnal months may be spent more agreeably."

Another writer who early fell a victim to its charms was the Rev. Martin Geldart, minister of Croydon Free Church. He spent part of his boyhood in the town during the 'fifties, and in his whimsical autobiography entitled *A Son of Belial*, which appeared in 1882, recorded the deep impression it made on his youthful imagination. "In Reigate," he wrote, "from the moment that I set foot within our house I felt for the first time thoroughly at home ; and all the years I afterwards spent of youth and manhood in the far North-west were years of perpetual exile. . . . It is the *genius loci* which I adore in Reigate." Prefixed to the chapter containing these remarks are some verses by the author, beginning :

" Dear Reigate, true thou wast and art
    To God, thyself and me ;
  And heart was seldom bound to heart
    As I am bound to thee."

He lived at " The Elms," London Road, a house built by his father.

The rapid growth of population led to demands for new and wider powers of self-government. The agitation for incorportaion of the parish as a municipal borough started in 1859 when a public meeting was called, but three years elapsed before a favourable resolution was carried and a petition presented to the Privy Council. Local tradespeople were on the whole strongly in favour of municipal powers, the chief opponents being the lord of the manor and London business men living in the locality. A public enquiry into the petition was held at the Town Hall, Reigate, in March, 1863. The resulting report disclosed a chaotic state of affairs. The Commissioner found there were no fewer than seventeen different authorities in the parish, some of which functioned to a greater or lesser extent while others neglected their duties. Thus as regards street lighting, some parts of the parish were lighted while others were not ; the evidence revealed one particularly glaring case of this anomaly in which one side of a street just inside the Old Borough had lamps while the other side, which lay in Santon Borough, had none, with the result that the Old Borough paid for the whole lighting of the street. Sanitation was in a deplorable state and it had proved impossible to get the different bodies to agree on a combined drainage system. There existed no proper provision against fire and only one of the petty boroughs had fire-engines. The parish was policed by a detachment of the County Constabulary, consisting of a sergeant and six constables, for which it contributed £642 to the County rate.[15] In view of this report the Privy Council recommended the granting of the petition, and a charter was granted accordingly in September, 1863, and reached Reigate on the 26th of that month. Its effect, briefly stated, was to convert the parish into a municipal borough under the Municipal Corporations Act, 1837, and to constitute the inhabitants a corporation with power to elect a council composed of six aldermen and eighteen councillors presided over by a mayor. The borough thus formed was divided for electoral purposes into two wards—Western and Eastern—the first comprising the old boroughs of Reigate, Santon, Colley and part of Woodhatch ; the latter those of Linkfield and Hooley and the remainder of Woodhatch. The division was far from judicious, since it fostered a spirit of jealousy between the two towns and tended to split the Council into rival camps actuated by sectional interests.

The first election of councillors took place on 2nd December, 1863, and the successful candidates included several well-known local men such as Thomas Dann, Wm. Carruthers, Jas. Searle, Chas. Charman Elgar, Jesse Pym and Dr. Constantine Holman. Mr. Dann, a local lime and coal merchant, who had taken a leading part in the movement for incorporation, became the first mayor.

The election of town clerk produced a close contest between two local solicitors, Mr. C. J. Grece of Redhill, and Mr. Thos. Hart of Reigate, in which Mr. Grece succeeded through the casting vote of the Mayor.[16]

A police force for the Borough consisting of a superintendent, a sergeant and eight constables was formed in 1864. Mr. George Rogers was appointed superintendent at a salary of £90 per annum with quarters and clothing, the sergeant received 21s. per week and the constables 18s. per week in addition to clothing.[17] A commission of the peace constituting a separate bench of magistrates for the Borough was granted in 1869.

One of the first tasks of the newly formed Council was to provide a proper sewerage system. In 1865 it adopted the Local Government Act of 1858 which gave it the necessary powers. The services of Mr. Baldwin Latham of Croydon, a well-known water and sanitary engineer, were engaged and he designed a complete system of main drainage with an outfall at the southern boundary of the Borough on Earlswood Common. The lord of the manor, lord Somers, agreed with the consent of the copyholders to give up the part of the Common required extending to 63 acres on condition that the Council purchased 16 acres forming the top of Redhill Common for use as a public recreation ground, at the price of £3,055. This last piece had been acquired by the War Office in 1862 as a site for a military prison, but mercifully had not been used for that baneful purpose.[18] Its position is still marked on the ground by four dwarf corner pillars. The Council accepted these terms and proceeded with the first part of the scheme—the sewering of Redhill or east end of the Borough, which was completed in 1868 at a cost of £8,500. The sewage was disposed of by the system of broad irrigation which has since been superseded by that of sedimentation and filtration. The sewering of Reigate was commenced a little later and completed in 1876. The main outfall sewer was laid under Bell Street and across the grounds of the Priory into Park Lane. From there it ran in a deep tunnel under Reigate Park and, emerging at South Park, proceeded by Woodhatch to Earlswood Common across the further part of which it continued in a tall embankment skirting the New Pond. The whole scheme was boldly conceived and successfully carried through in spite of many engineering and other difficulties.

The early growth of Redhill was closely associated with the enterprise of the National Freehold Land Society and its auxiliary, the British Land Company. The society was formed in 1849 to enable men of small means to purchase freehold property and qualify for a parliamentary vote under the old 40s. franchise. Its founders included Richard Cobden, John Bright and Samuel Morley. In 1859 the company purchased several acres of surplus land from the London and Brighton Railway Company and laid out Grove Hill Road, Bridge Road and Ridgeway Road. In 1863 it developed the Glovers field estate at Reigate, called after Ambrose Glover who formerly held a lease of the land. It also constructed Woodlands Road and the adjacent roads on Hooley Farm, and played a large part in the development of Mead Vale and South Park.

The United Land Company founded for a similar purpose by the Conservative party bought up the Waterslade Estate and formed Ranelagh, Shrewsbury and Brownlow Roads, named after its promoters, about 1869, and ten

years later developed the Monson Road estate.   The Redhill
and Reigate Cottage Improvement Society Limited was
formed before 1860 to provide working-class dwellings of
which there was a serious deficiency, and erected thirty-one
model cottages in Ladbroke Road.

At Reigate, Wray Park was the first new district to be
laid out. Doods Road was constructed through Doods
Farm by Mr. G. E. Pym about 1864, while lord Somers
and his successors formed Somers Road and other new roads
west of the station.

Between 1861 and 1871, the decade that witnessed much
of this rapid development, the population again leaped
forward and increased by the record number of nearly
6,000. The number of inhabited houses increased by
1000 to over 2,500. Several local institutions and places
of worship took their rise during this and the previous
decade. The Reigate and Redhill Cottage Hospital was
erected in 1866 on the site still occupied by its successor,
the East Surrey Hospital. In 1860 the Redhill Market
House Company Limited, subsequently reconstructed as
the Redhill Market Hall Company Limited, erected a
prominent pile of buildings in the Market Square known
as the Market House and Assembly Rooms, which have
since been greatly altered and enlarged. Reigate, not to
be behind, answered with the erection of the Public Hall
in High Street (1861–2) by a company formed of local
residents, which after an existence of over sixty years went
into liquidation in 1924. St. Matthew's Church, Redhill,
was consecrated by the bishop of Winchester in 1866.
In the same year the Baptist Chapel in London Road,
Redhill, was opened by the Rev. C. H. Spurgeon, and in
the following year the Wesleyans opened a chapel in the
Station Road. St. Mark's Church, Reigate, erected in
1860, was enlarged in 1864. St. Luke's Church, South
Park, was built in 1871, the Congregational Chapel in
Chapel Road, Redhill, in 1862, and St. Joseph's Roman
Catholic Chapel in 1860.

Three " Holmesdale " Societies that originated at this
time and still do valuable work in their different spheres
also deserve mention : the Holmesdale Benefit Building

Society, 1855, the Holmesdale Natural History Club, 1857, and the Holmesdale Fine Arts Club, 1865.

The natural amenities of the Borough owe much to the number and extent of its open spaces (Plate X). In 1794, when the prevailing sentiment strongly favoured enclosure, two inspectors from the Board of Agriculture visited Redhill and Earlswood Commons and reported that " the whole was well calculated to produce all kinds of grain in abundance and its proximity to Reigate would render an enclosure very desirable."[19] Fortunately their advice was disregarded and this beautiful expanse remained open to public enjoyment though considerable portions have in days gone by been lost by illicit encroachment, and through a custom whereby the lord of the manor with the consent of the tenants had power to grant away parts of the waste. In exercise of this custom the sites of the workhouse (1793) and St. John's Church and Schools (1842 and 1843) were carved out of Earlswood Common.[20] Again, in 1817, lord Somers granted a piece of common land at the corner of Mill Street and the new Brighton Road to his relative, James Cocks, as the site of an inn and posting house for the benefit of travellers using that road. The inn was fittingly styled the Somers Arms till the railway cut short its career, following which it became a private residence and was for many years the parsonage house of St. John's parish. Until past the middle of the century squatters were active, particularly around the site of St. John's Church, where a colony of nondescript erections arose and earned the jocular title of " Little London."

A more serious threat to Redhill Common sprang from the power claimed by the lord to dig sand and grant licences to others to do so. Not long after the advent of the railway a sand pit was opened on the east side of the Common and by 1882 the excavations had reached such alarming proportions as to threaten the existence of the hill. At this stage Mr. Samuel Barrow, who had some years previously purchased Lorne House and the adjoining tannery in Linkfield Street, intervened and claimed that his rights of pasture as owner of that property were being seriously curtailed by the sand digging. He accordingly started an action against lord

Plate X.

REDHILL COMMON, 1845.

Looking North-west towards Colley Hill, over Shaw's Corner and Blackborough Mill.

Somers in the High Court for an injunction to stop this depredation. The action was settled on the terms that lord Somers should give up his claim to dig sand and other materials in return for a payment of £3,000, and that a scheme for the future regulation of the Commons should be applied for. This sum was provided by Mr. Barrow, Mr. W. B. Waterlow, another public-spirited landowner, and the Borough Council in equal shares.[21] A scheme was drawn up and a provisional order obtained which received parliamentary sanction under the Commons Regulation (Redhill and Earlswood Commons) Provisional Order Confirmation Act, 1884, to quote the full title. The scheme placed the regulation and maintenance of the Commons in the care of eleven conservators to be appointed trienially of whom six were to be nominated by the Borough Council from its own members. The conservators were to maintain the Commons free from encroachments, and free access and the privilege of using them for games and recreation were reserved for the inhabitants of Reigate, Redhill and neighbourhood. The scheme did not deprive the lord of his ownership but only of certain rights over the Commons, and the freehold remained in him until 1922, when, by the generosity of Mr. Somers Somerset, the commons and wastes of the manor were transferred to the Council in perpetuity. Following their appointment in 1884 the conservators put in hand various improvements under the direction of their surveyor, Mr. T. R. Hooper, of which the most important were the laying out of the sandpits as a pleasure ground and the construction of the upper pond on Earlswood Common.

The local newspaper, *The Surrey Mirror and County Post*, which is published weekly by the Holmesdale Press, Ltd., Redhill, worthily serves the needs of the borough and neighbourhood. It first appeared in 1879 as the *Mid-Surrey Mirror*, and celebrated its jubilee in 1929 after absorbing or outliving all serious rivals.

The division of the Borough into two wards continued for over thirty years though regarded as time went on with growing dissatisfaction by the ratepayers of the eastern or Redhill ward, which had completely outgrown its more conservative rival. On the creation of the Surrey County Council in 1889 the Borough was for county electoral purposes divided into three wards and the Redhill members of the Borough urged the adoption of this division for local municipal elections. At length in 1896, after years of agitation, a majority of the Council carried a resolution in favour of the wards being increased to three. This led to a local enquiry as a result of which the commissioner appointed by the Privy Council recommended an increase to six wards. It then devolved on the Home Office to appoint another commissioner to delimit the wards who, in view of the high feeling betweeh the two towns, decided to create a central or liaison ward as a means of lessening the tension, and to assign three wards to the eastern as against two to the western side of the Borough.[22] This new scheme of division though somewhat complicated had the good effect of reducing much of the old antagonism and fostering the growth of a wider corporate spirit. The first elections for the new wards took place in the same year.

In 1894 another and much older anomaly was abolished by the union of the parishes of the Old Borough and the Foreign, though owing to a strange oversight the areas thus united, which comprised the whole of Reigate parish, were styled the parish of Reigate Foreign, a misnomer that was not corrected till five years later.[22]

In cricketing annals Reigate holds a worthy position. It was the birthplace and early training ground of William Caffyn (b. 1828), and Walter William Read (b. 1855), two masters of the game who played for Surrey and England. The Reigate Priory Cricket Club, of which these players were members, has had a continuous existence since 1852, and in the course of its history has produced several other exponents of the game who have won local renown.[23]

The past record of the Reigate Priory Football Club in the Association game is also a notable one. Between 1882 and 1900 it reached the front rank among Surrey clubs and won the County Challenge Cup for senior clubs on six occasions, its success culminating in 1897, when it won both the cup and the Senior Charity Shield.[24]

The Reigate horse races had a brief existence from 1834

to 1838 and another still briefer on their revival in 1863. The site of the original course on Reigate Heath and its later extension can still be clearly traced. The racing committee consisted of local business men with Mr. Thos. Neale as chairman and Mr. Wm. Thornton as secretary, and their object in starting the races was " to make some return and to give some encouragement to the farmers in the neighbourhood over whom [sic] the Gentry and Sporting Men of the County have been in the habit of Hunting." The meeting during the first period was a two-day one, and in 1834 took place on 7th and 8th May, but in 1835 it was decided to hold them on " Wednesday and Thursday in the week after Epsom Races." The committee also resolved in the latter year " that the course be properly covered with Turf to be laid down under the management and by the direction of Mr. Packer," who acted as treasurer and kept the Swan Inn, and " that a proper temporary Building be erected for weighing the Gentlemen Riders and Jockies." The racing that year took place on 10th and 11th June, the principal of the four events on the first day being the race for the gold cup of 100 guineas presented by Mr. David Robertson, the steward. Of the four events on the second day two called the Farmer's Plate were " for horses not thoroughbred the property of farmers residing within the limits of the Surrey and Union Hunts."

In 1836 the committee desired to enlarge the course, but before commencing work decided to approach lord Somers, lord of the manor to whom the Heath belonged, " to guarantee the free use of the Ground for a certain number of years." They further decided to appeal for contributions towards the cost. The enlargement was apparently carried out later that year.

The races failed to command the backing necessary to make them a financial success and by 1837 the debt stood at over £200 in addition to a sum advanced by Mr. Robertson. Mr. Neale agreed to advance the amount in return for a pledge by the members of the committee to repay him in proportion to their number. The character of the races had been changed by opening them to thoroughbreds

which had damped the interest of farmers. To add to
their troubles the committee discovered that without their
knowledge the stewards had advertised a meeting for next
season in the Racing Calendar. The last races were held
in May, 1838, as advertised and the committee was dissolved
the following year.

Racing was revived in 1863 and a one-day meeting took
place on the Heath in that and the following year, but the
fixture was not a popular one with the townspeople on
account of the undesirable characters which it attracted.[25]

The later volunteer movement which originated in 1859
met with an encouraging response at Reigate, where 71 men
were enrolled before the end of the year to form a company
known as the Reigate Volunteer Rifles. This eventually
became the " A " Company of the second Volunteer Bat-
talion of " The Queen's " Royal West Surrey Regiment.
A second company called the " B " Company was formed
in 1877. The Drill Hall in Chart Lane was built in 1874
and opened in 1875.

Among the many highway improvements executed by
the Council in the present century one of the most important
was the widening of the principal railway bridges in the
Borough, undertaken during the first mayoralty of Mr. F. E.
Barnes, 1897–1902. These crossings which had not been
enlarged since the construction of the lines had, with the
growth of traffic through Redhill, become dangerous bottle-
necks and the tunnel under the station was known as " the
death trap." After lengthy negotiations with the South
Eastern Railway Company agreement was reached in 1901
for the widening and rebuilding of this tunnel and the
Reading arch and the road bridges over the Reading
branch. The work was carried out by the company, but
the major portion of the cost fell on the Council. The
widening of West Street, Reigate, at its upper end in 1905
by the removal of several ancient buildings along its south
side, did away with an awkward bottle-neck entrance to
the town (Plate XI).

The opening of the present century also witnessed other
striking developments in municipal enterprise. The question of new municipal buildings formed one of the burning

Plate XI.

WEST STREET, REIGATE, C. 1890.
Showing Old Buildings at East End, since demolished.
(*From a water colour sketch by Miss M. M. Hooper.*)

questions of the day.[26] It stirred up the old inter-town animosity and led to heated controversy over the rival merits of a central site at Shaws Corner and the one eventually chosen. The buildings in Castlefield Road, now known as the Town Hall, were opened in November, 1901, and provided the Borough with what at that date could claim to be the finest municipal buildings in the administrative county at the very moderate cost of £30,000, which included the construction of the road. The new Isolation Hospital for infectious diseases at White Bushes, Earlswood, was opened in March of the same year and in May of that year the Council's electricity station was completed at a cost including the mains of approximately £30,000. Five years later the public baths in Castlefield Road were erected through the generosity of Mr. J. B. Crosfield.

In 1911 a regular service of motor buses between the two towns was introduced by the newly formed East Surrey Traction Company, Ltd., which soon extended its operations over a wide area of surrounding country. The company was subsequently absorbed by the London Passenger Transport Board without, however, impairing the excellence of the services.[27]

The most important event in the life of Reigate town since the war of 1914–1918 was the sale of the greater portion of it in 1921 by Mr. Somers Somerset. This ended the long régime of single ownership and opened the way to sweeping alterations which have done much to change the face of the town. " Decay in the standards of architectural taste," says a recent writer, " has transformed the High Street from a dignified architectural unity to a medley of mixed and competing styles."[28] Chain shops built to stereotyped plans which pay no regard to the prevailing style have invaded the street and its unity has been further marred by the introduction into old façades of incongruous features such as timber work with the false idea of giving them an enhanced air of antiquity.

The disappearance of the White Hart and Swan Hotels from the Market Place has already been noted. Other old buildings are now threatened by the policy of main-road widening adopted by the local and central authorities regardless of its effects on the amenities. The Barons in Church Street, one of the finest specimens of the Queen Anne style remaining in the country, is marked down by a widening line under the Town Planning Scheme, and a scheme for widening the main road at Woodhatch menaces the existence of the picturesque Angel Inn. Suggestions have also been made for demolishing the Old Town Hall and widening Tunnel Road which, if followed, will rob the town of two of its most characteristic features and hasten the process of uglification and suburbanisation.

In 1932 railway facilities were greatly improved by the electrification of the main line, and the introduction of electric services between Reigate, Redhill and London. The same year saw the execution of much needed alterations to Redhill Station.

In the following year the Borough lost its territorial unity with the parish. By the Surrey Review Order it was from 1st April, 1933, extended to include the adjoining parish of Gatton and parts of the adjoining parishes of Buckland, Horley, Merstham and Nutfield. The enlarged Borough was divided into seven wards in place of six, with the resulting addition of three councillors and one alderman to the Council. The increase in territory amounted to upwards of 4,000 acres with a population of slightly over 3,000 of which Merstham furnished the greater number.

The parish has been favoured with a number of visits from Royalty during this period. On 4th October, 1837, shortly after her accession, queen Victoria left Windsor Castle for Brighton and was greeted on her way by fervent demonstrations of loyalty at Reigate ; she passed through two triumphal arches decked with flowers, one of which erected across Bell Street appears in a contemporary print. On returning a month later she took the road through Crawley, Redhill and Croydon, at which places she changed horses, and reached Buckingham Palace at 3 p.m., having accomplished the journey of 52 miles in just under five hours.[29]

On 30th April, 1849, Albert, Prince Consort, laid the foundation stone of the Philanthropic Farm School under Redstone Hill. On 15th June, 1853, he laid the stone of

the Asylum for Idiots at Earlswood, now the Royal Earlswood Institution for Mental Defectives, and again in July,
1855 attended to open that building.   In 1869 the prince
and princess of Wales, afterwards king Edward, and queen
Alexandra, laid the memorial stone of an addition to the
Asylum.   Fifteen years later on 9th July, 1884, the prince
and princess paid another visit to the Borough when the
prince as Grand Master of Freemasons laid the foundation
stone of the new Chapel of the Royal Asylum of St. Anne's
Society, near Redhill Station, with masonic honours.[30]
During his reign as Edward VII he visited Reigate privately
and stayed at the Priory.

His grandson, Edward VIII, while prince of Wales,
visited Redhill 20th November, 1923, and opened the new
chapel and school buildings of the Southern Provincial
Police Orphanage.

New orthopædic wards at the East Surrey Hospital,
Redhill, were opened 12th June, 1930, by princess Mary,
countess of Harewood, and on 27th October, 1937, princess
Alice, countess of Athlone, opened the new Nurses' Home
in Elms Road.[31]

Reigate during the past one hundred years has completely emerged from its former isolation and has enjoyed
a continuous though at times slow development, broken
only by the two great wars of the present century.   It has
proved to be the natural and convenient centre of the surrounding district for administrative and other purposes.
It was, for example, until 1934 the headquarters of the
Reigate Rural District Council and until 1935 the seat of
the petty sessions for the Reigate division of the county.
During the second great war it was selected to be the headquarters of the newly formed South-Eastern Command.

NOTES TO CHAPTER XI

[1] Aikin, *History of the Environs of London* (1811), 151.
[2] Cunningham, II *Growth of English Industry and Commerce*, 763.
[3] Quotations in this and subsequent paragraphs are from the MS. minutes of the respective vestries.
[4] Webb, *English Poor Law History*, Pt. I, 290 n. 2.
[5] Cunningham, II *op. cit.*, 765.
[6] *Surrey Mirror*, 25th April, 1930.

[7] Hooper, *Guide*, 38.

[8] The earliest beadle on record is John Keasley, appointed in 1727 (Vestry Order Book).

[9] For the history of the Grammar School, see Chapter X.

[10] Now Upper West Street.

[11] Art. by Mr. E. Scears, *Surrey Mirror*, 17th August, 1928.

[12] C. F. D. Marshall, *History of the Southern Railway*, Chapter 1 and pp. 264–268, 379, 381 and 388–90.

[13] Redhill as the name of a community came into use about 1841 and was at first generally applied to Earlswood and other inhabited parts in the neighbourhood outside Warwick Town, St. John's Church, opened in 1843, was called " the Redhill District Church " and served a new parish, comprising the eastern half of Reigate parish.

[14] Hooper, *Guide*, 70 ; Art. by T. R. Hooper in *Surrey Mirror*, 9th March, 1928.

[15] *Accounts and Papers*, 1864, L. 341.

[16] *Surrey Gazette*, 8th January, 1864.

[17] *Surrey Standard*, 20th February, 1864 ; *Surrey Gazette*, 5th April, 1864. The borough police forces of Reigate and Guildford were amalgamated with the Surrey County Constabulary by an order under the Defence Regulations which took effect 1st February, 1943.

[18] *Surrey Gazette*, 1st November, 1867. In the press report of the Town Clerk's statement at the Inquiry into the application to borrow the money the land is said to have been taken for a military prison and not, as commonly supposed, for a fort. See also notice in *Reigate, Redhill, etc. Journal*, 15th September, 1868.

[19] *General View of the Agriculture of the County of Surrey*, by W. James and J. Malcolm.

[20] Art. by T. R. Hooper, *Surrey Mirror*, 6th April, 1928.

[21] Hooper, *Guide*, 76.

[22] Ex information Mr. Alfred Smith.

[23] W. W. Read, *Annals of Cricket* (1896) ; *Seventy-One Not Out : The Reminiscences of William Caffyn* (1899) ; II, *VCH*, 531, 538.

[24] II, *VCH*, 550–54.

[25] The extracts given are from the MS. minutes of the Committee 1835–9. A race card was issued in 1834. See also the *Racing Calendar*, 1835–8, and 1863–4.

[26] Meetings of the Council were usually held at the Town Hall, Reigate, and at the Market Hall, Redhill, alternately.

[27] *Surrey Mirror*, 14th September, 1923.

[28] *Architectural Review*, May 1938, p. 237 in article, " Reigate : A Study of the Town in Transition."

[29] I, *Diary of Royal Movements*, 56 ; Esher, I, *Girlhood of Queen Victoria*, 232.

[30] Hooper, *Guide*, 84–89.

[31] *Annual Reports of Hospital*, 1930 and 1937.

APPENDIX I.

TABLE I.—REIGATE MANOR. FITZALAN, MOWBRAY AND HOWARD DESCENTS.

Edmund Fitzalan, Earl of Arundel, d. 1326 = Alice de Warenne, sister of John de Warenne, d. 1347

Richard Fitzalan, Earl of Arundel, d. 1376

Richard Fitzalan, Earl of Arundel, d. 1397

Elizabeth, d. 1425, = (2) Thomas Mowbray, Duke of Norfolk, d. 1399

= (3) Sir Robert Goushill, d. 1403

Margaret, d. 1422 = Sir Roland Lenthall, d. 1450

Edmund Lenthall, d. 1447 s.p.

Joan, d. 1435 = William Beauchamp, Lord Bergavenny, d. 1411

Richard Beauchamp, d. 1422

Elizabeth, d. 1447 = Sir Edward Nevill, Lord Bergavenny, d. 1476

Thomas Fitzalan, Earl of Arundel, d. 1415 s.p. m. Beatrix of Portugal, d. 1439

John Mowbray, Duke of Norfolk, d. 1432

John Mowbray, Duke of Norfolk, d. 1461

John Mowbray, Duke of Norfolk, d. 1476

Anne Mowbray, d. 1481 = Richard, Duke of York, son of Edward IV, murdered in Tower, 1483

Isabel Mowbray, = (2) James, Lord Berkeley, d. 1463

Maurice Berkeley, d. 1506

William Berkeley, Earl of Nottingham, and Marquis Berkeley, d. 1492 s.p.

Margaret Mowbray, = Sir Robert Howard

John Howard, Duke of Norfolk, d. 1485

Thomas Howard, Earl of Surrey and Duke of Norfolk, d. 1524

Henry Howard, Earl of Surrey, d. 1547

Thomas Howard, Duke of Norfolk, d. 1554

Dukes of Norfolk

Lord Wm. Howard, Baron Howard of Effingham, d. 1573

Charles, Lord Howard, Earl of Nottingham, d. 1624 (The Lord Admiral)

Charles Howard, 2nd Earl of Nottingham, d. 1642 s.p. (1st wife)

Charles Howard, 3rd Earl of Nottingham, died 1681 s.p. (2nd wife)

Elizabeth, d. 1424 = Sir Robert Wingfield, d. 1431

Sir John Wingfield, d. 1481

Sir John Wingfield, d.c. 1512

Joan = Lord Stanley, d. 1459

Sir Thomas Stanley, 1st Earl of Derby, d. 1504

Sir George Stanley, Lord Strange, d. 1497

Thomas Stanley, 2nd Earl of Derby, d. 1521

Edward Stanley, 3rd Earl of Derby, d. 1572

4th to 10th Earls of Derby

TABLE II.—REIGATE MANOR. SOMERS AND COCKS DESCENT.

John Somers' of Worcester, d. 1681

(Sir) Joseph Jekyll d. 1738

Elizabeth. d. 1745

John Cocks, d. 1771

Charles Cocks, d. 1806 created Sir Charles Cocks, Bt., 1772 and Baron Somers, 1784.

Charles Cocks of Worcester, d. 1725

Mary = d. 1718

James Cocks, d. 1750

James Cocks, d. 1758

John, Baron Somers of Evesham, d. 1716, unmarried

Philip Yorke, 1st Earl of Hardwicke, d. 1764

Margaret, d. 1761

John Somers Cocks, d. 1841 2nd Baron Somers, Created Viscount Eastnor & Earl Somers, 1821

Lady Caroline H. Yorke, daughter 3rd Earl of Hardwicke

John Somers Cocks, 2nd Earl Somers, d. 1852

Charles Somers Somers-Cocks, 3rd Earl Somers, d. 1883

Lady Isabel Caroline Cocks (known as Lady Henry Somerset), d. 1921

Lord Henry Richard C. Somerset d. 1932

Henry Charles Somers Augustus Somerset

The name also appears as Sommers

APPENDIX II

BIOGRAPHICAL NOTES OF SOME LOCAL WORTHIES

BARNES, Richard (d. 1812 aged 79). Practised at Reigate as an attorney with his father, Michael Barnes, and from 1758-1786 was clerk to the Reigate Turnpike Trust. He also acted as agent for lord Somers, and supplied William Bray with notes for the *History of Surrey*. In 1808 he carried out excavations on the site of the Roman Villa on Walton Heath (II. *M. and B.* 644-5). His father (d. 1776) is caricatured in the skit on the White Hart Whist Club quoted by Ridgeway :

> " With long gigantic stride and simpering face,
> Young Littleton appears and takes his place."

BRYANT, William (d. 1844 aged 85). Son of William Bryant a tallow-chandler of Reigate. Practised as an attorney in Reigate and London and became political agent for the Hardwicke interest, and a bitter opponent of the Somers family when his father was superseded in the office of bailiff. He was one of the three local attorneys who supplied William Bray with material for the *History of Surrey*. He projected a history of the town and hundred of Reigate which was not carried out, though some of his MSS. have survived, including his Survey of the Old Borough, 1786, and a valuable plan of Reigate Town, 1785 (see page 122 above). In 1810, while living in London, he was made a bankrupt and proved to be owner of, or interested in, a large number of manors and other properties in Surrey and Sussex.

GLOVER, AMBROSE, F. S. A. (b. 1757, d. 1840). Born at Oxted and educated at Reigate he was later articled to R. Barnes (q.v.), whose partner and eventual successor he became. Clerk to the Reigate Turnpike Trust from 1786, and steward of Reigate manor from 1809 till his death. He compiled a MS. history of Reigate Priory, and furnished much information about the hundred and parish of Reigate for Manning and Bray's *History of Surrey*. One of his daughters married Thos. Hart (d. 1876), who succeeded to his practice.

GRECE, CLAIR JAMES, LL.D. (b. 1830 d. 1905). Son of Henry Grece of Chart Lodge, Redhill, a fuller's earth merchant and the last high constable of Reigate hundred. His uncle, William

N

Constable (d. 1861), was for many years surveyor to the Reigate Turnpike Trust.   On the formation of the municipal borough in 1863 he became the first town clerk and held that office till his death besides carrying on an extensive practice as a solicitor. Though a prominent freethinker of outspoken views, this in no way lessened the general esteem in which he was held.

JAMES, SIR ROGER (d. 26 March, 1636) was of Dutch extraction on his father's side.   Knighted by James I, he purchased in 1613 the Rectory manor of Reigate which included the Parsonage (now the Reigate Lodge Estate) with the advowson of Reigate church and the great tithes. He lived at the Parsonage and rented Reigate Castle and grounds adjoining.   He served as one of the members for the Borough in the first parliament of Charles I (1625).   His son, Roger, was member for the Borough 1661–1681, and again in 1688 during the first parliament of William III.   He died 25th July, 1700, in his 81st year, and was buried " late at night privately according to his own appointment."   (Psh. Reg.)

MARTIN, THOMAS, F.R.C.S. (b. 1779, d. 1867).   Born at Pulborough, Sussex, he settled at Reigate in 1800 where he formed an extensive medical practice in which his son, Peter (b. 1812, d. 1863), a man greatly beloved and esteemed, subsequently joined him.   He served as the last bailiff of Reigate manor from 1811 till his death, and took a prominent part in local affairs.   In 1830 he established the Reigate Mechanics' Institute, later changed to the Reigate Literary Institution. Tobacco was one of his pet aversions ; in a letter addressed to medical students he described smoking as " inconsistent with all the characteristics of the medical profession, which are those of elevation and high-mindedness."   After his death striking busts of him and his son executed by Henry Weekes, R.A., were provided by public subscription and are now housed at the Grammar School.

RIDGEWAY, WILLIAM (b. 1741, d. 1830) was the son of Thomas Ridgeway of Reigate, stay-maker, whose shop stood at the corner of High Street and Bell Street.   He compiled a MS. History of Reigate of which at least three versions are extant ; the first dated 1811 is in private hands, the second dated 1814 belongs to the Surrey Archæological Society, while the third and most complete dated 1816 is in the British Museum (Add. MSS. 34,237).   All three versions possess general similarity but the two later contain some additional notes. The work commences with lengthy historical extracts taken, without acknowledgment, from Aubrey, Salmon and other sources, followed by copies of inscriptions in the parish church and churchyard, an itinerary or directory of the town and neighbourhood, and copies of reports on the Parish charities. The MSS. are interspersed with original notes based on personal recollections and it is to these and the itinerary that the work owes its value in spite of the writer's jejune and ungrammatical style.

APPENDIX III

LIST OF THE CUSTOMARY LANDS OF THE MANOR IN THE SEVENTEENTH CENTURY.[1]

Note.—The Yardlands or Virgates nominally contained 60 acres each, the Half-yardlands 30 acres, the Farthinglands 15 acres and the Cotlands apparently $7\frac{1}{2}$ acres. Several bear the names of former tenants.

YARDLANDS

1. Roggers att fforde
2. Dobers
3. Harpours
4. Osbarns
5. Combes
6. Aces

HALF-YARDLANDS

1. Nowardes doth not service[2]
2. Sele
3. Garlands
4. Samptons[3]
5. Salfordys
6. Sketys
7. Lytilcombes
8. Rysebrygge
9. Robards at fford
10. Cecyly at fford
11. Bochyngs
12. Setebyes
13. Trumpours
14. Gybrysebrigge[4]
15. Wattys of Combe
16. Beldys
17. Vygours
18. Chert
19. Stockmans
20. Ffengatys
21. Streters
22. Thowryes

FARTHINGLANDS

1. Cecely at fforde
2. Thom at Wetchyett
3. Robards at Hole
4. Showlands
5. Roger at Waldhatch[5]
6. Yockhurst
7. Kyngeland
8. Cowpars
9. Chertlands
10. Prychetts
11. Hochyns
12. Poteryches
13. Water Ganders
14. Reynold Bawys
15. Reylonds
16. Gybbawys
17. Walders
18. Hopers
19. Heggers

COTLANDS

1. Ganders
2. Tomsyns
3. Banburyes
4. Barfots

[1] See p. 41 above for an account of this list.
[2] i.e., the tenant was no longer liable for reeve service.
[3] A form of Santon, the name of one of the petty boroughs whence the surname Santon.
[4] A contraction of " Gilberts at Ricebridge."
[5] i.e., Woodhatch.

APPENDIX IV

CUSTOMS OF THE MANOR

Extracted from the Manor archives.

HERIOTS. Freeholds held of the manor were, like copyholds, heriotable on the death of the tenant (C.B. 1619, Survey 1700).

" That if any freehold and copyhold tenant die seised of severall freehold and severall copyholds there is due and shall be paid but one heriot for all his freehold lands and but one heriot for all his copyholds." (C.B. 1676 and later Courts.)

The heriot was the tenant's best beast and was due on death or alienation, but not on alienation if the alienor remained tenant of other lands of the manor (Ct. Rs. *passim*).

FELONS. The lords were entitled to waifs, i.e., unclaimed goods, and to the goods found in the manor of convicted felons (Survey 1632).

COMMONS AND WASTES. " The Comons belonging to this Manor are Earlswood the Wray Reigate Heath Redhill and Petteridge Wood which do properly belong to the Lords of this Manor for the soyle and the wood and to the Tenants for the Herbage and therein every tenant hath pasture according to the proportion of his land." (Survey 1623.) In the Survey of 1775 it is stated that every tenant has " a right to stock the wastes in proportion to the value of his estate."

" That the Tenants may dig sand gravel stones and small chalke upon any of the Wastes of this Manor without leave from the Lords." (C.B. 1686). But compare with this the order made by the C.B. in 1675, " that any person digging or carrying away stone clay and gravel, and any forreiner digging or carrying away sand in the Comons or Wastes shall forfeit per load for digging 5s. and per load for carrying away the same 10s."

" That it is the custom of this Manor that any tenant of this Manor may fetch small chalk from Reigate hill to lay upon any land holden with the Manor of Reigate without paying anything for it." (C.B. 1659.)

" That to dig turves on the waste of this Manor is against the custom of the said Manor and to the damage of the Tenants thereof." (C.B. 1695.)

TIMBER.   "Any tenant may fell any timber trees upon his copyhold without a license from the Lord to be employed upon his copyhold about building and repairing." (C.B. 1655 and later Courts.)

BOROUGH ENGLISH.   This custom applied to copyholds but not to freeholds of the manor, so that on the death of a copyhold tenant his holding descended to his youngest son, or failing him the next youngest heir.

REEVE SERVICE.   " By the old Custume of the Mannor every Tenant as well as of the whole yerd land as of the halfe yerd land shalbe Reve as often and when it shall happen hee there-unto shalbe elected.   And that every Tenant of every capitall Messuage or homstall as well of every fferthingeland as of every Cotland shalbe the Bedell when to that office hee shalbe elected." (Note at end of Survey 1623, see p. 31 above, and, for a list of these holdings, see Appendix III).

APPENDIX V

FIELD AND OTHER LOCAL NAMES IN REIGATE MANOR

Note.—The names are taken from the Survey of 1623 save as otherwise indicated.   Other names are dealt with in the text. See also *PN Surrey* 304–307 and 396.

ABSHAM (RAc 1447).   Possibly " Abba's farm " from the personal name *Abba* and OE *ham*.   Perhaps identical with the field called Nethers Apsam in 1623.

ANWORTH GORE or ANNOT GORE.   A field at Dovers Green. *Worth* is OE for " enclosure."   Gore from OE *gara*, " a triangular strip of land."

BAWDEY CROFT (1700).   In Buckland parish.   " Bawdey " was probably used in the disparaging sense of " foul, dirty," " Croft " denoted a small enclosed field.

BAYES INHOLMES.   A piece of demesne land at the south-east corner of Earlswood Common.   " Inholmes " denoted land taken in from the Common.   Peterich Inholmes was part of the demesne south of the Common.

BEASTMORES, the name given to the low-lying marshy ground between Park Lane and Reigate Heath.

BENTLEUGH, BENTLEWE (RAc 1447).   Probably from ME *bent*," coarse grass or rushes," and OE *leah*, " clearing," a very common suffix in field and place names.   The name appears to have died out later.

BERISFELD (RAc 1300).   The first element is probably from *burh* which in field names usually denotes land attached to a manor house (Cf. *PN Hertfordshire* 243, 251).   The second element is " field."

BEVIS and BUTCHINGS.   Two copyhold meadows adjoining the Parsonage, later Reigate Lodge, on the west side of Croydon Road, then called Wray Lane.   " Bevis " was possibly the same as the earlier Bevaynes (RAc 1447). " Butchings " was an ancient local family name which survives as the modern Budgen.

THE BIGINS. At Wiggie. From ME *biggin*, " building."

BLANDERS FIELD. A parcel of arable ground at Wiggie attached to a copyhold farm called Bales held by Richard Ace in 1623. Probably to be associated with the family of Matilda Blandis, 1300, and John Blandis, tenant in 1447.

BONE LAND, BONES LAND, adjoined Hartswood Park, Woodhatch, and is probably to be associated with Thomas Bone, a tenant of the manor in the fifteenth century (RAc 1447).

BONNEYS or BENNEYS (RAc 1300). Probably identical with the later Coxbonny (1700) which consisted of a messuage, barn, garden, orchard and one acre of land in Clifton's Lane near the boundary of Reigate and Buckland parishes. Coxbonny is a compound of two personal names.

BRAGGS MEAD, now absorbed in the site of Redhill town, is probably to be associated with William Bragg who in 1581 is described in the Court Roll as a former tenant of " one toft and one acre of land."

THE BRANDS, BRANDSLAND (Ct R 1619). A field at Woodhatch later divided into Great and Little Brands. Probably called after the family of Simone Brand who appears in the Subsidy Roll 1332.

BRASE LANDS. Meadow land at Wiggie of which the first element may be from *brash* " brushwood," but lack of early forms makes certainty impossible.

THE BREACH. A piece of arable land at Ringley Oak on the west side of the present Reigate Road. From OE *braec*, " land newly cultivated." There was also a field named the Breaches at the south-west corner of Reigate Heath and probably taken in from it.

CABBOTT. The name of three parcels of land at the modern South Park, the etymology of which is unknown.

CASTLE BUTTS, described in 1644 Ct R as a tenement containing one rood of land. It lay on the west side of the castle just outside the fosse. The site is now occupied by a block of cottages known as Providence Terrace. " Butts " here means land next a boundary and had nothing to do with archery butts. (Cf. *PN Surrey* 357.)

CAUSEY, CAWSEY (1565–1584), CAUSEWAY (1822). The Causey was the name applied in the sixteenth century and later to the lane across Earlswood Common from Woodhatch, now called Woodhatch Road. " Causey Land," " Causeway Land," appear in the eighteenth and nineteenth centuries as the names of fields on the Hartswood Estate called after Sand Causeway the lane which led from Price's Lane to Salmons Cross and was subsequently called Sandcross Lane.

CHAPPELL LANDS in the present Reigate Road adjoined the west side of Blackborough land. Possibly they were an endowment of one of the chantry chapels.

CONNEYBERRY MEAD in Woodhatch borough. There was also a meadow " now stored with Connies and called the Connieberrie " attached to Foard, a farm in Nutfield. Coneys or rabbits were plentiful in the wild state and the lord claimed the right to take them under his franchise of free warren. The expense of the lord's " ferets " for the year to Michaelmas 1300 came to 2s. 6d. (RAc).

COOMBE with Flanchford formed one of the sub-manors which had by 1623 merged in Reigate Manor. There were also fields at Flanchford and Hooley called Coombe Field, and a common field of this name (see p. 40 above). From OE *cumb*, " hollow or valley on the flank of a hill." (*Chief Elements in Eng. Place Names* 19–20.)

COPTHALL. The name given in seventeenth and eighteenth century deeds to a house at the east end of Middle Row. From OE *coppede heall*, " hall with a roof rising to a cop, or peak," or surmounted by an ornamental finial (see *PN Middlesex* 36).

COSTY. " One messuage with a garden called Costy." This probably represents OE *cot stow*, " place or site of a cottage " (Cf. *PN Wiltshire* 279).

CRONKS. A meadow at Cronks Hill, probably to be associated with Henry Cranke. RAc 1447.

CROWLYNG (RAc 1447). A lost name of a messuage in Reigate, probably to be associated with Roger Crollyng who in 1361 received a pardon for the death of Robert Laumphrey, the bailiff of Reigate hundred. *Pat. Roll.*

DAMASKE MEAD at Wiggie formed with Lords Mead (q.v.) part of the demesne. Its conjunction with the latter suggests a corruption of " Dames's Mead," or " meadow of the lady of the manor." Possibly identical with Countasmeade which was mown for the lord in 1447 (RAc). Other analogous names are Earlsfeild, a piece of arable land in Wray Lane, and Earlswood.

DAYE HOUSE FARM was part of the demesne of Reigate Priory and lay on the east side of Petridge Wood Common in Horley parish. From ME *daye*, " dairy maid."

DOOBERS *alias* LAKERS (1700). A farm and land in Horley parish on east side of main road between Horley and Redhill. Originally one of the customary virgates.

DOOVERS, the present Dovers Farm. The origin of the name is uncertain but may possibly rest on a yearly payment of 1s. 8d. made to Dover Castle by the Priory. Although Dovers belonged to Reigate Manor, the Priory had land near Dovers Green.

DOODES, GREAT. An estate on the north side of the present Reigate Road. The mansion stood at the corner of Reigate Road and Croydon Road. The name, which is preserved in the modern Doods Road, is possibly from the Anglo-Saxon personal name *Dodda* or *Dudda*.

EDE's COTTAGES AND EDE's FIELDS on the west side of Reigate Park are named after Elizabeth Ede, who owned the cottages in 1860. The spot is also known as " Cabbage Stalk Town."

EVERCOMBE. The name of a field at the upper end of Nutley Lane. Possibly from OE *eofores*, " wild boar," and *cumb*, " valley."

FYGGERS MEAD (CtR 1581) is probably to be associated with the family of Edward Fygge who in 1580 was one of the searchers of leather.

GASSONS, GARSTONS (1700). Land on the south of Redstone Hill formerly demesne land of Redstone Manor ; now part of the estate of the Philanthropic Society. From OE *gaerstun*, " grassy enclosure," a common Surrey field-name.

GOREINGS was the name applied in the eighteenth century to several copyholds of Reigate manor held by George Goreing in right of his wife, Mary, the widow of Thomas Hills of Reigate, whom he married in 1690.

THE HANGER. A piece of demesne land west of Earlswood Common on the Lower Greensand ridge. From OE *hangra*, " a wood on a slope." On this ridge also were two fields named Hanging Brow in reference to their sloping position.

HARNEY CROFTES (see Verney Croftes).

HARPERS or HARPOURS. One of the customary virgates, to be associated with the family of John Harpour who was tenant of half a virgate in the fifteenth century (RAc 1447).

THE HATCH (1700). A house and farm at the present Shaw's Corner, earlier known as Ganders. Nearby were fields named Latchets, Hatchcroft and Hatchfield in reference to a gate across the road at this point. Cf. Woodhatch.

ISBELLS (Ct Rs). At the top of Cockshot Hill, and the site at one time of two windmills, is probably to be associated with Roger Isabell who is mentioned in 1447 as lately holding half a virgate (RAc).

LARKE LANDS. A field on the east side of Earlswood Common forming part of the freehold of Hooley Manor. In 1700 it appears as Lake Lands.

LESBOURNE FIELD, LESBEY FIELD (1700). The name of one of the common fields. It lay between Lesbourne Road and Church Walk and was named from a little stream called the Lesbourne flowing through it from the North.

MOKE. A close of arable ground at Wiggie on south side of Moke Lane which was apparently the forerunner of the present Frenches Road. See, however, Noke Lane below.

MALKIN BROOK was a meadow attached to a farm called Bales at Wiggie occupied by Richard Ace. Possibly applied in a depreciatory sense on account of its liability to flooding by the brook.

NEW DICKETT. The name of a field on the west of Reigate Park. Probably from OE *dic*, " dike or ditch," with addition of *ett*, a very common Surrey suffix which often has a collective meaning. Here the sense may be field " newly marked off by ditches or banks."

NEW POND was the lower of the two existing ponds on Earlswood Common, the upper one being modern. The name has been traced as early as 1363, *PN Surrey* 307. In the Survey of 1700 it is described as " A Larg Pond well stored with ffish."

NUN ERSH. One of the common fields of the manor lying near Trumpets Hill. Ersh is OE *ersc*, " stubble field."

NOKE LANE ran through Wiggie south of Redstone Hill and survives as a footpath, called in 1700 Oke Lane. From *atten oak*, " at the oak tree." It was apparently distinct from Moke Lane (q.v.) but identical with Cumbers Lane, so called from its hollow, sunken condition at the southern end on the slope of the hill.

OSBARNS. The name of one of the customary virgates was probably the home of Henry Osbern who appears in the Subsidy Roll 1332. Two arable fields called Osbornes " lying at the west end of the Wray " are recorded in the Survey of 1623.

PARK MEADE was demesne land on the south side of Earlswood Common. In 1300 it was called Pakkismed and in 1447 Pakkesmede. In the Survey of 1700 it is Pax Meade and in Eve's Map 1861 Pike Mead. The derivation is uncertain.

PENNY PLATT. "A Little pightle called Penny platt." At Wiggie and probably so named from its diminutive size. *Pightle*, " small field, enclosure."

THE PLASHET. A piece of demesne land on the west side of Earlswood Common. The meaning is probably "wet puddly ground" from *plash*, "puddie."

PAPER HILL. An upland meadow in Littleton Lane. Paper is possibly from the personal name *Papa*.

REYNOLDS BOOZE. A homestead at Trumpets Hill, doubtless identical with the farthingland called Reynold Bawys in the seventeenth century, and probably to be associated with the villein family named Baw of the fourteenth and fifteenth centuries.

ROUGHTIE (CtR. 1622). LA ROWETYE (RAc 1300). A field which adjoined Bevis (q.v.), "Rough enclosure." (See *PN Surrey* 366.)

THE ROUNDABOUT is the name applied in modern times to the group of cottages on Earlswood Common near the New Pond, the allusion is evidently to the insular position surrounded by the Common.

THE RUFFETT. Part of the demesne south of Earlswood Common, "the rough place." (See *PN Surrey* 359.)

THE RUSHET. At the south-west corner of Earlswood Common now Rushetts Farm. "Place of rushes." (See *PN Surrey* 359.)

THE RYDONS—LE RUDENE (RAc 1447). Probably from ME *ruden*, "land which has been cleared." See TYLEHURST (below) and cf. Neweruden (RAc 1300) meaning apparently "the newly cleared land," and Longeruden (*Ibid.*).

SALVERS. A small copyhold farm in Horley parish and on the east side of the present main road between Redhill and Horley. The name is a corruption of Salfords.

SEALE LAND. Bray quoting Ambrose Glover mentions a deed of 15 Richard II being a grant of a meadow called "Park Pond Meade lying east upon the lands called Wallensis and upon lands called Seale Hill south," and adds, "Seal Hill here mentioned is Reygate Park, and it was formerly often called by that name. At the foot of it are lands which are called Seal

Lands " (*I M. & B.* 296). In 1300 the reeve accounted for 1 quarter and 2 bushels of coral corn laid out in seed on 5 acres in la Selefeld and for 6 bushels on 3 acres in la Selehull. The word apparently represents OE *sele*, "hall or building." These lands and Selfeild (1700) lay on the west of Reigate Park.

SELSHAMS. A piece of copyhold land on the west side of Nutley Lane. Later the name was rendered Stelsham.

SETBYS. A farm on the south side of Reigate Park at the modern suburb South Park. It was one of the customary half yardlands and was held for many generations by members of the old villein family of Gander. Apparently from OE *sæte*, "dwelling, seat," so "By the dwelling."

SHOOELANDS, SHOVELANDS (1700). Freehold land at Salfords Bridge in Horley Parish held in 1700 by Henry Shove and another. This and the customary farthingland called Shooelands were no doubt named after Shove, an old local family.

SKEITES and LITTLE SKEYTES were fields in Lonesome Lane near Salmons Cross which are to be associated with John Skeete (RAc 1447) and probably formed part of the customary half yardland of that name.

SKOLES, SCOALES (1700). A farm at Wiggie. There were also two small copyhold farms of this name on the east side of Earlswood Common. Probably from ME *scale*, "a hut or temporary building," which is found alone or as one element in numerous place-names.

STREATERS was one of the half yardlands which adjoined the south side of Salvers (q.v.), and amounted in 1623 to 51 acres 2 roods 32 poles.

THAWRIES (1700). Earlier Thowryes, the name of a half yardland near Colley and probably the home of William Thoury mentioned in the Subsidy Roll of 1332.

THOM AT WETCHYETT, one of the farthinglands, lay at Wiggie on the north side of the present Frenches Road. In and after the sixteenth century it was known as Scoles (q.v.). Probably to be associated with the family of William de Wychiett who was one of the manorial officers in 1300.

Tomsyns, the name of one of the cotlands, was probably the home of William Thomasen who held " one small croft " at some time before 1447.

Tothulle (RAc 1300). A lost name meaning " look out hill."

Trumpets Hill. At Santon, later the site of a windmill. Trumpours, the name of a half yardland, and Trumpers Croft were probably called after tenants of that name. Robert Trumpers appears as a tenant of the manor in Elizabethan times.

Tylehurst. " Foure closes of arrable and pasture ground called Tylehurst, Marle Feild and the Rydons," at Earlswood. In 1700 they were attached to Roberts at Hole, a farm the site of which is now incorporated in the premises of the Philanthropic Society. The meaning is possibly " tile oast or kiln." Cf. *PN Surrey* 276.

Waterslade (1700). A farmstead on the northern edge of Redhill Common, the site of which is now absorbed by Ranelagh, Shrewsbury and Brownlow Roads. Slade is OE *slaed*, " low, flat valley." The spring which watered it rises by the East Surrey Hospital.

Watts Popis. The name of a copyhold field of 9 acres the situation of which is uncertain. Probably a corruption of " Walter Pope's," a member of the Pope family, one of the oldest villein families belonging to the manor.

Woodhatch. From wood and hatch OE *hæc*, " gate or wicket," and defined by Aubrey (V *Hist. of Surrey* 402) as " a Gate in the Roads ; and half Hatch is where a Horse may pass but not a Cart." These gates took various forms, their object being to prevent cattle straying from adjoining commons or strips of roadside waste. The name of one type, the slip hatch with a sliding bar or panel, is preserved in Slipshatch Road called after Slipshatch Field which adjoined it. The name Woodhatch was applied to a house and land at the foot of

Cockshot Hill and to one of the petty boroughs. It is now used of a district. The alternative and now obsolete form Waldhatch contains OE *weald*, " forest," in allusion to the vast wooded region known as the Weald which bordered Woodhatch on the south.

WORTH is an OE word meaning " enclosure or homestead." It is common in field and place-names, and applied alone or in combination (see Anworth Gore above) to several holdings in Reigate Manor. A field named la Worth occurs in the Reeve's Account of 1300. In the Survey of 1623 the Worthe appears as the name of a copyhold field in Linkfield Street and Greate Viccars Woorth and Little Viccars Woorth appear as the names of two other copyhold fields on the north side of the present Reigate Road.

INDEX

Ace, Richard, 38, 39, 202
— Robert, account as reeve, 37, 107
Addison, J., 120
Adeney, G. J., 142
Agriculture, local, 95
Ainsworth, Harrison, 179
Ale tasters, 132
Almshouses, 154
Anglo-Saxon cross, 18, 50
Aram, Eugene, 151
Arundel, Archbishop, 45
— earls of, *see* Fitzalan
Ashtead manor, 23
Assizes, 135
Atherfield Clay, 108
Aubrey, J., 56, 61, 76, 95, 100, 104, 110n, 209
Audeley, Major L., 146, 147
Aynscombe, R., 106

Bales, 39
Banstead, 107
Barnes, R., 47, 195
— F. E., 188
Barons, The, 152, 190
Barons' Cave, 47
Barrow, S., 100, 184, 185
Baths, public, 189
Battle Bridge, 18, 19
Bayes Inholmes, 40, 201
Beadle, 173, 192n
Beatty, earl, 73
— countess, 73
— Peter, 73
Beauchamp, William, lord Bergavenny, 27
Becket, St. Thomas, 75
Beer, brewing of, 97–98
Bell Street, 81, 88, 92, 94n
Berkeley, William lord, 28
— Maurice, lord, 29
Bird, John, 61, 75, 149, 164
— Edward, 61
Birkhead, C., 153
Bishop's charity, 163, 165, 166–167
Black Prince, the, 103
Blandis, 202
Blanket making, 171
Blatt, J., 100, 139

— T., 100, 139, 140, 148
Blaundis, S., 113
Blechingley, 74, 116, 117
Bliss, D., 136
Bludder, Sir T., 117
Bondmen, *see* Manor
Bosoyng, A., 35, 48
Borough English, 200
Borough Council, 31, 33, 47, 73, 91, 126n, 180, 185, 190
— — formation of, 180
Bostock, J., 63
Bradley manor, 23
Bray, Rev. T., 64, 66
— W., 75, 76, 195, 207
Brick making, 107, 108–109, 110n
— earth, 109
Brighton, 147, 153, 190
British Land Company, 182
Bromman, S., 34
Bronze Age, 13–16 ; barrows, 15–16
Broughton, A., 84, 159
Browne's Lodge, 153
Bryant, W., 122, 126n, 153, 195
Budgen (Butching, Boching) family, 37, 38, 202
Burgages, 119, 120, 200
Burial in woollen, 150
Bus services, 189
Burney, Fanny, 153
Butler, lady Joan, 36
Bysshe, Sir E., 118

Cage, *see* Prisons
Camden, W., 18, 23, 47
Carieur, Roger le, 106, 112
Carrington, R. C., 179
Castle Butts, 203
Castle, Reigate, 25, 26, 32, 43n, 44ff, 106, 127, 146 ; bailey, 44 ; barbican, 45 ; brattice, 35 ; constable, 48 ; Gate House, 45 ; janitor, 45, 48 ; keep, 46 ; moat, 45, 48 ; motte, 44 ; wall towers, 46 ; wood for, 36
Castleman, N. and W., 102, 136, 148
Catt, M., 102
Causey, The, 107, 203
Cawarden, Sir T., 116